Fighting in the Air

This series is published in association with
The RAF Museum, Hendon, London

Fighting in the Air

The Official Combat Technique Instructions
for British Fighter Pilots, 1916-1945

RAF Museum Series: Volume 7
General Editor: John Tanner, Director,
RAF Museum, Hendon

LONDON: ARMS AND ARMOUR PRESS
NEW YORK: HIPPOCRENE BOOKS, INC.

Published in Great Britain, 1978,
by Arms and Armour Press,
2-6 Hampstead High Street,
London NW3 1QQ

ISBN 0 85368 392 1

Published in the United States, 1978,
by Hippocrene Books, Inc.,
171 Madison Avenue, New York,
N.Y. 10016

ISBN 0-88254-472-1
Library of Congress Catalog Card
Number: 78-60957

The contents of *Fighting in the Air*, as follows, are Crown Copyright © 1978, and published by permission of the Controller of Her Majesty's Stationery Office: *Fighting in the Air*; *Text Book on Aerial Gunnery*; *Fighting the S.E., January, 1918*; *Notes on Aerial Fighting*; *Royal Air Force Flying Training Manual* Part II— Applied Flying; *Forget-Me-Nots for Fighters*; *Bag the Hun!*; Central Gunnery School's *Pilot Gunnery Instructors Course*.

Foreword © RAF Museum, 1978

The quality of both the type and illustrations in the original material used in this volume fall short of the high standard of reproduction normally expected in a modern book; they have, of necessity, been reproduced to complete this facsimile edition.

Printed by Kingprint Limited, Richmond, Surrey.
Bound by Kemp Hall Bindery, Oxford.

Contents

1916	*Fighting in the Air* by Major L. W. B. Rees, R.F.C. & R.A.	7
1917	*Text Book on Aerial Gunnery*	41
1918	*Fighting the S.E., January, 1918*	79
1918	*Notes on Aerial Fighting* 'Bring Down Your Hun!'	83
1933	'Air Fighting' from *Royal Air Force Flying Training Manual* Part II—Applied Flying	103
1940	*Forget-Me-Nots for Fighters* by No. 13 Group, R.A.F.	149
1943	*Notes on Air Gunnery and Air Fighting* by Wing Commander E. M. Donaldson, D.S.O., A.F.C., R.A.F.	191
1943	*Bag the Hun!* (estimation of range & angle off)	283
1943	Central Gunnery School (diagram excerpted from *Pilot Gunnery Instructors Course*)	305

Foreword

by J. M. Bruce
Keeper of Aircraft and Aviation Records,
Royal Air Force Museum, Hendon

The earliest known patent covering the installation of a fixed forward-firing machine-gun in an aeroplane is the German D.R.P. 248.061 applied for by August Euler on 23 July 1910. In subsequent years various schemes for mounting a fixed, or sometimes movable, gun to fire through the airscrew disc of tractor aircraft were proposed and patented by inventors in Germany, France, Italy, Russia and England. All clearly foresaw the use of the aeroplane as a fighting vehicle.

Following the practical pioneering work of Raymond Sauliner, Roland Garros and his mechanic Jules Hue, there appeared on the Western Front in April 1915 the first fixed forward-firing gun in a Morane-Sauliner Type L, and the era of the fighter pilot began. The emergence of the Fokker monoplane with its synchronized gun gave air combat an immense fillip, and within months the military need to destroy and the primitive need to survive quickly compelled pilots to evolve, practise and apply aerial tactics.

Inevitably, there were no textbooks on the subject. Not until the war was fairly well advanced did the R.F.C. ask one of its most experienced and successful fighter pilots, Major L. W. B. Rees, the commanding officer of No. 32 Squadron, to write a document giving guidance on various aspects of air combat as practised in late 1915 and early 1916. As the war progressed, aircraft speeds increased; improved gun sights were introduced; aerial gunnery had to be practised with fixed and movable guns; and more elaborate notes were provided in the *Text Book on Aerial Gunnery*. For those who had to go to war in the SE5a, Captain J. T. B. McCudden wrote a special note on fighting in that aircraft, and this is reproduced here. Later, more comprehensive notes were compiled in F.S. Publication 38 (*Bring Down Your Hun!*).

By 1933 the lessons of 1914-18 had been digested and tactics analysed, yet the weapons of aerial warfare in the R.A.F. remained essentially unchanged from those of the war. There was time for a thoughtful, well-written and substantial chapter to be incorporated in the *Royal Air Force Training Manual, Part II*, and this provides an interesting reflection of the practical thinking of the time.

Enormous progress in aircraft performance was made in the ensuing years, until the outbreak of the Second World War brought new problems of aiming, attack methods and effectiveness of firepower. For the fighter squadrons of the United States Army Air Corps these problems arrived with special suddenness when they found themselves confronted with a whole new standard of air combat that had evolved in the two years before the USA entered the war. The USAAC followed the example of the R.F.C. in 1916 and 1917, by asking Wing Commander E. M. Donaldson, D.S.O., A.F.C., to write a handbook on air gunnery and air fighting. This is an excellent distillation of much hard-won experience.

Bag the Hun! speaks for itself and was a graphic training aid. The Central Gunnery School notes and *Forget-Me-Nots for Fighters* appear as examples of very different instructional documents for R.A.F. pilots of the 1939-45 war, one straight-faced and factual, the other prepared in lighter—but possibly more memorable—vein. Their message and motive were the same as those of the handbooks of 1916 and later, and were similarly designed to further the same military need to destroy and the same primitive need to survive.

1916
Fighting in the Air
by Major L. W. B. Rees, R.F.C. & R.A.

FIGHTING IN THE AIR

These notes are based on experiences of last year, so that it is impossible to lay down any hard and fast rules, as the conditions alter so fast. The deductions are based on the experiences of many R.F.C. Officers to whom I am greatly indebted.

In the shooting problems the results are only close approximations. It has been taken that the bullet moves in a straight line for 200 yards, and that the bullet does not lag, due to relative speed of air and machine.

In the reprint, the notes have been brought up to date, as far as possible to July, 1916.

Comparison of Pilots.

The British Pilot always likes the idea of fighting, and is self-reliant. He is a quick thinker compared with the enemy, so that he has the advantage in manœuvre. He fights for the sport of the affair, if for no other reason. After the first engagement he gains great confidence from the Parthian tactics of the Enemy. Very wisely, he is not hampered by strict rules, and as a rule is allowed to conduct his own affairs.

The Enemy Pilot, on the other hand, is of a gregarious nature from long national training, and often seems to be bound by strict rules, which cramp his style to a great extent. The Enemy Pilots are often uneducated men, being looked on simply as drivers of the machine, while the Gunner or Observer is considered a grade higher than the Pilot.

This last gives a great advantage to us, as, whereas our Pilots act from a sense of "Noblesse Oblige," the Enemy, when in a tight corner, often fail to seize and press an advantage.

We noticed that when there were two Officers in the Enemy machine, they always attacked, but in many other cases the attack was not pressed home. Untrained Enemy Pilots might also account for this.

Comparison of Duties.

Both the Enemy and ourselves divide the machines into two distinct classes. We both have the Reconnaissance and the Fighting machines.

By Reconnaissance machines I mean those that do reconnaissance proper, wireless, photography, and bombing.

The Fighting machines are used for fighting only.

I do not mean to say that the Fighter does not do his best to see what is going on, or that a Reconnaissance machine does not sometimes fight, but their primary uses are as stated.

The chief difference in these types is that the Reconnaissance machine is usually a weight carrier, so that it cannot manœuvre quickly It may be able to "protect" itself very effectively, but is so designed that the view for fighting is bad, or its method of fighting does not lend itself to "offensive" tactics.

The Fighter, on the other hand, is built solely for the purpose of attacking and bringing down the Enemy's machines, and he carries armament of an "offensive" nature.

The Fighting machines are used for Patrol, and for escorting the Wireless, Bombing, and Reconnaissance machines.

The enemy uses his machines differently to ourselves. His Reconnaissance machines come over our side of the Lines only at comparatively long intervals, they seldom come over far, and they travel at great heights. Sometimes fast machines come over singly, and sometimes the slower machines come over in Flights of 6—8.

The fast Reconnaissance machines are so fast that only our fastest machines can catch them. If fired on they immediately dive for the Lines, or for the nearest Anti-Aircraft Battery or Machine Gun. As every village near the Lines has its machine gun, it means that the machines can dive almost anywhere so as to get a covering fire from the ground.

These machines very seldom turn and fight, very rightly going straight back with their information.

The slower machines which come over in flights are as a rule of a single type. They do not seem to have a special fighting escort, but some machines are told off to attack first. They seem to carry an immense amount of ammunition, and start firing— never with any success—at extremely long ranges. This perhaps is likely to maks one's shooting erratic, or make one open fire too soon, till one remembers how bad one's shooting is at long ranges.

It might be remarked here that if machines dive steeply flames, due to excess of petrol, come out of the exhaust. The front cylinders also oil up, so that clouds of smoke come out of the exhaust as well. If the dive continues for any length of time the machine must land on account of oily or sooted plugs, and not on account of any aid which it may have obtained from the Lewis gun.

Many of the Enemy Pilots are heavy handed, so that the machine turns over on landing, if the ground is at all rough.

Our Reconnaissance machines, on the other hand, are continually over the enemy lines, and they go so far afield that they have to turn and fight when attacked.

The Enemy Fighters never come our side of the Lines, so that our Fighters have to go for miles to get a fight. This affects the tactics in so much as the Enemy can risk getting hit on the engine or through the tank, knowing that he will suffer no more than an ordinary forced landing. Our Fighters have to be more careful, as hits on the engine usually mean that the crew of the machine must be taken prisoners.

For this reason we must make better shooting than the Enemy. We must fight to the very best advantage, and having decided to open fire we must aim to disable the Enemy during the first few rounds, or at any rate during the first drum. There should be no long range shooting, and if we can manage to disable the Enemy quickly, there will be no need to go out of action in the middle of an engagement while the drum is being changed.

One will not be able to effect this without great training and much thought.

Types of Machines.

The Enemy slow Reconnaissance machines are as a rule tractors, travelling at a speed of from 80 to 90 m.p.h. I do not think that they climb very fast, as one seldom finds them travelling very low. The Pilot sits in front of the Observer, and the Observer sits in a little barbette. This barbette permits of an all-round arc of fire, except where it is masked by the fusilage or planes. The top of the barbette is armoured, which may deflect a few bullets, but is of such shape that it woud seem to be little more than useless weight.

As these machines never attack, they do not usually fire ahead. They can fire at an angle of 45 degrees with the line of flight ahead. They can fire over the whole semi-circle astern. They can fire straight up, and fairly well straight down.

These machines use both lead, tracer and armour-piercing bullets, fire belts of perhaps 200 rounds, and when the belt is finished they pause quite a long time, apparently to re-load.

When attacking these machines on the **Enemy** side of the Lines, when one is creeping up apparently unobserved, the Enemy A.A. Batteries fire ahead of their own machine, and so call his attention to the danger.

The Enemy fast Reconnaissance machines travel at perhaps 100 m.p.h., so that unless one has a large amount of height in hand one cannot catch them.

The Enemy Fighting machines are of four types.

The first type is the small, very quick monoplane, the small Fokker type. Apparently they are very hard to fly, as the Enemy do not seem to possess more than two or three. One can tell them at once at a distance on account of their apparent speed compared with the other machines in the sky. The Americans say that they are so fast that they cannot make a forced landing across country. This may not be so, but this is the only allowable case in which a few long shots might be fired, on the chance of verifying this statement.

They have a stream line in front of the propeller, which makes them appear ——O—— instead of the usual monoplane ——◯—— For this reason they are very hard to see against the haze which always hangs over one's horizon.

The Pilot sits up very high in his nacelle, so that he gets a splendid view. He has a fixed gun, and can apparently fire only straight ahead.

The machines try to creep up behind their targets unseen. If seen or fired on they dive immediately and come up again after a short while. They do not as a rule accept a set battle.

The second type is the machine a little larger than the one above. It also is a monoplane, and carries either a Pilot alone or Pilot with a Gunner. They fly in flights of four or six, and travel at a great altitude. When they attack a machine they dive at it firing the whole time, one after the other. They do not stop to re-load, but go straight down, even if they are not fired on. They do not usually return to the attack. They fire straight ahead and straight up, but do not usually fire astern.

The third type is the large unwieldy machine, not meant to manœuvre, but which carries an armament heavier than can be carried in a small single-seater. The twin-engine twin-fusilage machines are of this type. These machines have everything duplicated and a practically all-round arc of fire. They are fairly fast and are fairly good climbers. They are not as useful as would appear at first sight, because machines attacking from a flank are extremely hard to hit.

The fourth type is the slow, very heavily armoured machine, which cannot climb much. It carries a comparatively heavy gun—a 2-pounder, 1½-inch machine gun, or something after that style. This type is not developed, as no machine can carry armour heavy enough to be really effective.

Bullets penetrating armour carry with them fragments of the armour, so that more damage is done on soft material (spars, tubes, etc.) by bullets which have pierced armour than by bullets which make a good clean hole.

The Use of a Fighter.

As I have mentioned above, the duty of a Fighter is to put the enemy's machines out of action. Most of the fighting takes place on the Enemy's side of the Lines, so that it is not sufficient to make a machine land, as machines are comparatively easy to obtain. Every effort should be made to disable the Enemy Pilot, as this nearly always ensures the destruction of the machine as well, even if dual control is fitted. In any case, it prevents the Enemy using his armament effectively and stops the machine manœuvering.

If the Pilot be taken as the target, the shots which miss the target will hit the Observer and engine, or may cause damage to the rigging.

To be of real use the Pilot of a Fighter must be extremely keen sighted. I believe one can intimidate the average Enemy Pilot more by showing that he has been seen than by doing anything else. It is very hard to see machines at any distance at all, yet there must always be machines in the air within attacking distance. One can often pick up the Enemy machines by finding out what the Anti-Aircraft Batteries are attacking. Machines have a habit of appearing from apparently nowhere, so that if a Pilot is not alert he is taken at a disadvantage. If an unobserved machine opens fire it takes at least 2 seconds to pick him up and to come into action. By that time the enemy has fired 12 rounds, which are quite enough to do serious damage.

This question of seeing things cannot be impressed too strongly on Pilots of Fighting Scouts. From a height of 12,000 feet one appears to be vertically over a circle of about 20 miles diameter. One can apparently see the smallest speck on the ground. Most machines are invisible in the air when four miles away, unless one is lucky and sees a quick movement.

The Target.

When one sees a machine one is apt to think that hits anywhere will be effective. One is trained to imagine that a small thing, such as a frayed cable, is certain to cause a wreck. Yet machines go up every day and return absolutely under control, but having dozens or even hundreds of holes in different places. It should be remembered that after being over the Enemy's Lines, machines should be brought back with the greatest care. Machines are sometimes wrecked over their own aerodromes because a thoughtless Pilot does a steep spiral, perhaps not knowing that his main spars have been pierced.

The only useful target to really attack is the Pilot himself. This target is very small, being of a size about 2' by 1' 6" by 1' 6", and even then shots which hit this target are not certain of putting the Pilot immediately out of action. Therefore, one must concentrate one's attention and one's shooting on this small target, the Pilot, till one has attained one's object.

If we attack a machine from directly in front or in rear the engine may cover the Pilot's body, or vice versa. This is the minimum target which the machine can present, and any shots hitting the target do damage, but there is a lot of room round the target in which shots which do not actually strike do no damage.

Now, if we imagine a machine being attacked from the side, or straight from above or below. The target which we must aim for still remains the same small one, but now the rounds, which before were non-effective, will hit the engine and Observer, and will become effective.

This leads one to suggest that the way to attack is straight at an Enemy from above, below or from the side, keeping one's own machine end on to him.

It is very hard, when looking at a machine in the air, to know where the Pilot is sitting. This may sound incorrect, but if approaching from below one sees only the bottom of the Enemy's fusilage, and as the machine is unfamiliar the exact spot we want to hit is hidden. Even if we could hit a small practice target every time, the service target of a similar size, hidden behind fabric, is quite a different proposition to tackle.

With a small Fighter we should close as soon as possible, keeping end on to the Enemy, so that he will have no chance of setting any sights he may have. We are then never at a disadvantage, and we have the advantage of being the attacker. A machine coming at one quickly always makes one a little nervous, especially if one does not know the Pilot.

With a heavy machine it is different, as a heavy Fighter can carry elaborate sighting devices. By using his very unwieldiness to make the machine a stable gun platform, he has more chance of concentrating his fire on the target than the little machine which is trusting to manœuvre. Once a machine starts to manœuvre the shooting is upset till the changes in speed and direction become again constant.

If we get a small Fighter against a large Fighter, if each is equipped with suitable armament, both machines should fall together. But one must remember that the small Fighter has the advantage of the initiative, that the large Fighter has a bigger area on which hits will take effect, and that it should always be possible to make the large Fighter manœuvre by getting into a blind spot. Once the large machine manœuvres it is at the mercy of the small one, because good shooting cannot take place from a variable motion platform.

Estimating Relative Speeds.

When two machines meet and both manœuvre it is very hard for either to estimate the relative speed. Take the case of two machines of equal speed revolving round a fixed point.

The relative motion is apparently nil, but the actual relative motion at the moment of firing is practically the same as though each machine were flying straight.

Enemy ↑
└──────○──────┐ Our
              └ machine

(plan)

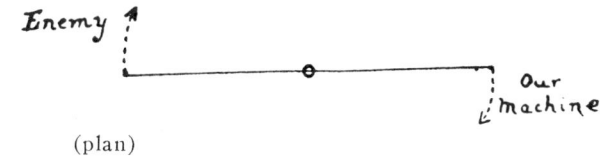

The Enemy apparently sits on the gun sights without motion, but the maximum allowance for speed must be made.

Then, again, as both machines are banking over, it will be very hard to estimate if there should be an allowance, because the gun is apparently elevated.

If one machine steers a straight course at a known speed he has something to go on, and can use the sights and range or speed-finders, which he has prepared beforehand.

Armament.

The armament depends on the type of machine, and it should be borne in mind that a little extra weight in machines, light machines especially, makes great alteration in the climb. (It does not so much affect the speed.)

Carry a primary and a secondary armament, i.e., a Lewis gun and a stripped rifle or pistol. If the machine will take the weight, carry at least two guns for each Pilot and Gunner. Guns used in pairs do not seem to jamb so frequently as guns used singly. The rifle can be used for taking long shots, as it does not use ammunition at the same rate as the gun, and is just as unlikely to hit.

Take up at least five drums of ammunition per gun, as this should account for a Flight of machines, with a drum to spare.

If rifle grenades are used, the range must be very short, as the grenade is a very low velocity projectile.

One 10 ℔. bomb or a few hand grenades can be dropped on the Enemy machines from above, and may save one losing height. Anyhow, the Enemy will see the bomb falling, and not knowing how many are carried, will keep clear from below. The extra weight can always be dropped when quick climb is necessary.

Keep any gadgets inside the machine, so as not to affect the streamline. Make certain that the use of the gadget will repay the loss of power due to extra weight or head resistance.

When night flying carry dark glasses, so that the gun sights may be used, even if one is within the Enemy's searchlight.

Ranges.

The ranges at which fighting takes place may vary from 400 yards to 4 yards. It is very hard to approach a machine to within 100 yards without being seen. Hundreds of rounds are fired every day at machines at ranges estimated at 50 yards or less without doing any damage. At 200 yards one may expect to get hits, and I have taken that as the normal fighting range. I do not think that there has been a single instance in which machines have been brought down at ranges over 400 yards.

Thus we see that it is useless waste of ammunition to fire at long ranges, and that one should try and close to within 50 yards in order to do any damage.

Do not fire 'just to show him you are there": fire always for effect.

Tracer Bullets.

When tracer bullets came in it was thought that they would make close fighting impossible. They have not made the difference that one would expect. One reason is, that it is very hard to estimate the range in the air, just as it is at sea. The tracers burn for a comparatively short time, so that they go out before hitting the target. This means that the bullet apparently hits, but really falls away from the target.

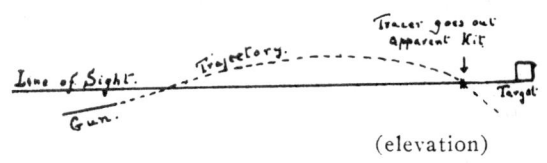

(elevation)

When firing to a flank the tracers appear to travel in a curved path, due to the speed of the machine.

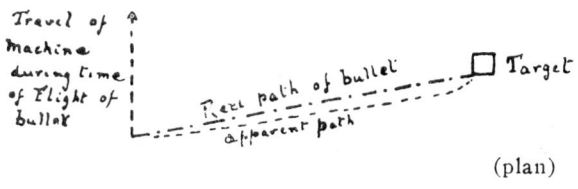

(plan)

If you in your younger days have ever tried to concentrate the curved trajectory of the garden hose on the nurse or gardener, you will know how hard it is to obtain effective shooting if the target dodges.

Even if we can see the hits of the bullets it is very hard to keep the proper point of impact during quick manœuvre.

If tracer bullets are fired in the centre line of one's own machine the observation would be much easier than if they are fired to a flank.

Before Ascent.

All Gunners and Pilots, if they use guns, should make certain themselves that the guns have been properly cleaned, oiled, and adjusted. It is sometimes not realized by the mechanic in charge of guns that although on a warm day, on the ground, the gun will work perfectly, having been cleaned with "Vacuum" oil, yet, when the gun is taken and kept at a great height, the oil freezes and the gun jambs.

I do not intend to go into the care and adjustment of the Lewis gun, but I must mention that any deviation from the methods laid down nearly always means a jamb.

See that the implements for freeing a jamb are carried in the machine.

Care in gauging and selecting cartridges makes for certainty of action.

The adjustment of the sights with regard to the gun barrel must be frequently checked, both when the gun is out, and also in the machine. Fire the gun from the machine at ranges at which it is intended to get hits, and see that the sights are aligned on the point of impact of the shots. Do not take it for granted, even, that the sight is made properly, till you have tried it on the range.

It is also useful to fire one or two shots at a target on the ground when leaving the aerodrome, as this checks the sighting, and ensures the gun being cocked. If this is not done one will perhaps forget to cock the gun before coming into action. (Yes, it has been done.)

You can also check any adjustment you have made for allowing for your own speed.

Think out all possible plans of attack before leaving the ground, so that no situation may be sprung on you.

Always attack, as then you need not worry about means of defence.

Identification of Machines.

Take great care in identifying machines. Do not take it for granted that any machine which approaches is necessarily an Enemy. The Fokker and Morane, the "Two Tail" and the Caudron, the Albatross and the Curtiss have very much the same silhouette, especially if seen from the front. All machines are becoming more and more alike, and new types are being flown every day.

If one keeps between the sun and the machine under observation, then his marks become visible before he can see ours. You have seen the halo which surrounds one's shadow when it is cast on haze or clouds. The phenomenon takes place when one is on a tower, a hill or in the air. If you keep the Enemy within the black patch in the centre of the circle he will probably not see you till you are quite close.

To prevent being caught like this there is a service issue of tinted glasses for the goggles for use in sunny weather. This glass prevents glare, and enables one to see fairly well towards the sun.

The Enemy rounded cross in a white field is something similar to the Allied marks.

If glasses are used for identifying machines they should not magnify more than six diametres the vibration of the machine interferes with the view from glasses of greater magnification. Glasses of x6 magnification are a service issue.

On Sighting the Enemy.

Make certain that the gun is loaded and cocked, so that one can turn one's whole attention to the Enemy.

If you are flying a small Fighting Scout you can fly in any direction, including straight up for short distances, so that you can attack from anywhere you wish.

When practising manœuvre in a small machine it should be done at heights over 10,000 feet. Near the ground the small machines have a great reserve of power, and they can be made to sit right upon their tails for an appreciable time. At great heights the machine is near its limit of climb, and consequently, when one puts the controls hard over, the machine "stalls," and will not obey. I do not mean to say that this is dangerous, because there is no danger in "stalling" any modern machine at a height from the ground, but the machine does not answer as quickly as one expects, and one loses an opportunity.

A Scout should be able to get within 1000 yards (or less) of the Enemy without being seen, if it keeps between the Enemy and the haze over the horizon, climbing to the attack as the Fokkers do.

When you have seen the Enemy, do not bank the machine more than is absolutely necessary. At long ranges the sun shining on the planes makes the machine very visible, and at short ranges banking makes one's marks more visible.

Keep end on to the Enemy as long as possible, because that position is the most invisible, and the end on target is the smallest.

If the character of a machine is doubtful, the marking on the tail usually shows up before anything else.

Scouts approaching from 2000 feet above are very often not observed.

When within 800 yards of the Enemy do not fly straight unless you have reason to think that you are unobserved, because it is not known what range and speed-finders the Enemy uses.

If there is reason to think that the Enemy has seen one, open fire **before** the Enemy, as one always runs the risk of being hit by stray bullets at 400 yards range. Always so long as you do not open fire at a longer range than that at which you know you can obtain hits.

Close to within 100 yards if you can.

Having decided to open fire, go **all out.** This gives the best chance of hitting, and intimidates the Enemy.

The above statements are in places contradictory; it depends on one's temperament what one should do.

Having taken every possible precaution, trust to one's luck as far as possible. It is well known that Napoleon considered unlucky men of no use as fighters.

Usual Enemy Tactics.

The single-seater Fokker tries to approach from behind. If seen or fired on he dives, to come up again a short time after. They attack in this fashion time after time.

The slightly larger Fokkers dive at their target from any angle. Having fired they go straight down.

Sometimes now they dive under one, and then climb quickly, so that when next seen they are above and behind one's machine. To prevent this, hustle the Enemy to prevent him coming up again.

Reconnaissance machines dive for the nearest A.A. Battery and fire over their tails.

The heavy Fighters aim at bringing all their guns to bear.

Machines seldom fly straight and make a proper attack.

The Engagement.

Open fire before the Enemy.

Open fire at the shortest possible range.

Open fire under the most favourable conditions.

Try to disable the Enemy at once.

Close as soon as you can, so as to prevent the Enemy setting his sights and taking aim.

It is useless expecting to hit successfully at ranges over 400 yards.

Reserve your fire till within 100 yards of the Enemy, but if discovered open fire before the Enemy.

At ranges of 50 yards and under, if attacking from the flank, aim at the Enemy's leading edge as you see it (one or other wing tip). This statement is only a guide.

If one must collide go straight up, as the Enemy nearly always goes straight down. Then if one hits the Enemy one hits him with one's undercarriage.

Do not collide unless by accident. If the Enemy Pilot is disabled the Enemy machine may travel quite normally for a long time, so that one runs the risk of wrecking one's machine uselessly.

If it is necessary to change drums, dive under a tractor, as that upsets his aim.

As a rule it does not pay to follow a machine below 3000 feet. At that height the machine guns from the ground become dangerous, and if the Enemy machine is not disabled before that it will probably not be disabled at all.

It is dangerous to cross the trenches at heights below 2000 feet.

If no Enemy is in sight never fly straight, even on our side of the Lines. This prevents the Enemy getting the size of the machine accurately. If the size is known it is very easy to get the range at short distances, as used in fighting in the air.

Do not take anything for granted. Work out all your own deflections, etc., for your own machine. No two machines fly normally at the same speeds.

Do not get put out when you find that your pet theory does not work.

Machines Meeting.

Machines can move at the present time in any direction the Pilot wishes. The speeds of a Fighting Scout may vary from 40 m.p.h. when climbing to 100 m.p.h. on the level, and to nearly 150 m.p.h. when diving.

These machines can change from one speed and direction to any other very quickly indeed.

Tractor v. Tractor (meeting).

Suppose that two tractors fly towards one another, each flying at a speed of 100 m.p.h. (= 150 feet per sec. = 50 yards per sec.). Suppose that they fly at the same level and that they do not fire through the propellor.

Each machine hopes that the other will turn, but at 200 yards the Pilots think that something must be done, so they both swing outwards so as to bring the guns to bear.

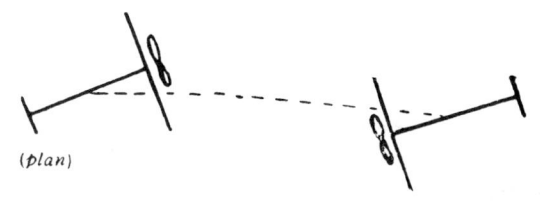

(plan)

If both Pilots go straight on the machines will be out of range in 6–8 seconds, the time it takes to fire one drum of ammunition.

During that time the deflection error alters from about 50 feet ahead (2 lengths) to about half that when the machines are closest, and back again to 50 feet as the last rounds are fired.

This means that one has to sweep 50 feet with 50 rounds; therefore, as the target is small, each round must be moved almost exactly one foot from the last, so as to keep all shots on to the target.

As the gun fires the rounds form quite a large cone, so that the shots which would have been in for line are possibly out for elevation, so that only very few hits are likely to be obtained.

The deflection for the normal travel of one's own machine can be altered automatically very easily, but if devices for this are used the machine must travel on a level keel in a straight line at the pre-arranged speed.

As a rule, when fighting, machines are going up or down, so that the speed may be nowhere near the prearranged speed.

Thus we see that machines firing from a flank cannot expect to obtain good shooting.

The following is the diagram for the above:—

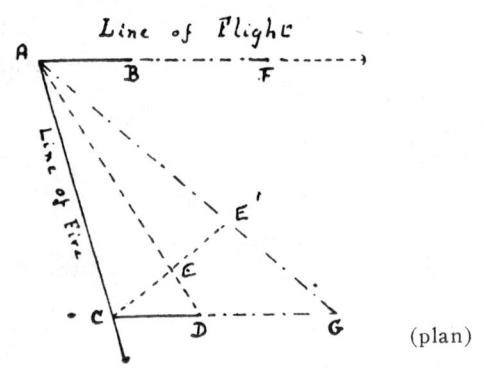

(plan)

ABF is the line of flight of our machine.

AB is the distance travelled during the time of flight of the bullet (.25 secs.) at the range (200 yards), when the machine is climbing at 50 m.p.h. (= 75 f.p.s.).

The distance is about 20 feet.

AF is the distance as above when travelling at 120 m.p.h. when diving (= 180 f.p.s.).

The distance is about 45 feet.

C is the target (stationary at present).

Draw CDG parallel to ABF and make CD and CG equal to AB and AF.

Then, if no deflection is used, the bullet travels along the lines AD and AG in the two cases.

Therefore, we miss the target by CE or CE'.

If we decide to always climb or always dive when fighting, it would be very easy to allow for the errors CD = 20 feet or CG = 45 feet, but there would always be the unknown error DG = 25 feet, which is very hard to estimate and allow for.

If the sights are set for normal speed the error is about halved.

Now the target may be travelling with or away from our line of flight, so that the relative speed error may be halved or doubled, and as I have said before, it is very hard to estimate the Enemy's speed and direction.

Besides firing in the hardest direction we present the largest possible target to the Enemy.

Tractor v. Tractor (going same way).

If two tractors are going the same way in straight lines, if the Pilot steers so as to collide at some point ahead, the gun should be fired with zero deflection, so as to obtain hits, no matter what the speeds of the two machines may be.

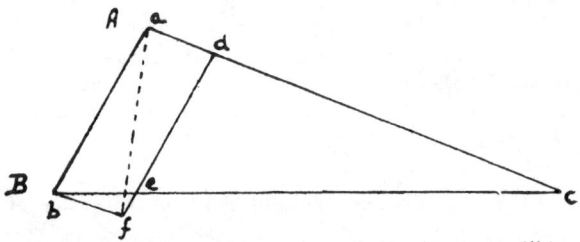

Suppose that machines A and B aim to collide at c.

A fires at B with no deflection.

A travels from a to d and B from b to e during the time of flight of the bullet over range a b.

As the machines will collide at c, triangles cde and cae are proportional, so that de is parallel to ab.

Therefore, bullet travels along af, where df equals ab.

Now de is long compared with be, so that e and f are practically at the same point; that is, the machine B has arrived at e just in time to catch the bullet.

Tractor v. Pusher.

Suppose that a tractor meets a pusher.

If the tractor does not turn before it reaches 200 yards from the pusher, it may be disabled before it can fire a single shot.

Sooner or later it must turn.

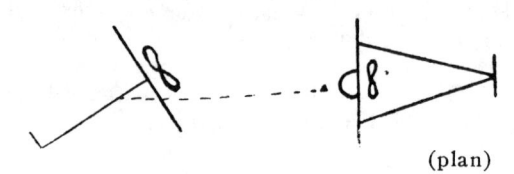

(plan)

The first thing the tractor has done is to increase his target without making the pusher increase his.

The tractor has the same hard problem to tackle, as shown above. The pusher can disregard his speed altogether, and has only to guess the Enemy's speed.

The pusher, if firing in the line of flight, makes the same errors as the tractor, but this time the errors are in range instead of direction. The only practical effect is to make the bullets hit the target harder.

As before, suppose A fires at the target C at 200 yards.

The errors due to climbing or diving are as before CD = 20 feet and CG = 45 feet.

The errors on the target are CE and CE', due to the curve in the trajectory.

Now the highest point of the trajectory in 200 yards is about 4 inches above the horizontal, so that the greatest error is (very approximately) 4 inches by

$$\frac{45 \text{ feet}}{100 \text{ yards}} = 1.2 \text{ inches.}$$

This error is negligable.

Pusher swinging with a Tractor (an approximation).

The tractor still has his difficult problem, while the pusher must estimate the Enemy's speed, and swing well in front of him.

We will hope that the tractor will lose his nerve and start to dive as soon as he hears the shots come anywhere near, when the chances of having our machine hit are very small.

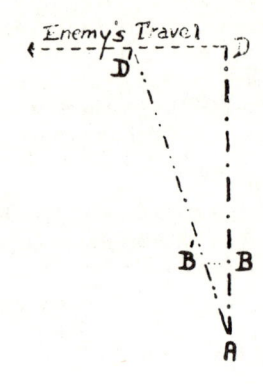

(plan)

Our machine at A is going for the Enemy, who is travelling from D to D'. The machine swings with the Enemy.

Now the time that the bullet takes to travel down the gun barrel is very short, so that we may consider that the machine is for all practical purposes simply rotating about its CG.

The gun muzzle is about 10 feet from the CG of the machine, so that while the Enemy travels from D to D' the gun muzzle travels from B to B'.

AB is 10 feet and AD 100 yards.

Suppose that DD' corresponds to 100 m.p.h. ($=$ 150 f.p.s.), then BB' corresponds to 5 f.p.s.

Now the Enemy travels during the time of flight of the bullet ($=.12$ secs.) a distance of 18 feet and the bullet in the direction DD' goes only **·7 feet.**

Therefore, at 100 yards we must make a correction for the Enemy's travel across our front of about 17 feet.

If the Enemy is below, and turning, allowance must be made for the turn as well as the speed, because shots aimed in a straight line ahead of the Enemy will only hit him on the wings, and do no damage.

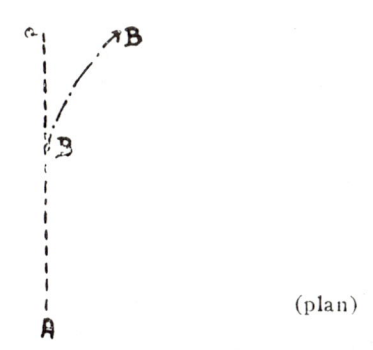

(plan)

A is our machine firing straight ahead of B, who is swinging as shown.

The shot strikes "a" when the Enemy has got as far as B', and so misses.

Tractor with Gun mounted on top plane.

To enable tractors to fire ahead guns are sometimes mounted on the top plane. This method of mounting is more efficient than fitting deflector propellors.

In some machines the top plane is at least 2 feet from the sights on the fusilage of the machine. The line of sight and of fire are made to converge at any range, say 200 yards. If fire is opened at any other range the shots miss as shown. As the target is very small, only about 2 feet by 1 foot 6 inches at the most, this error is inadmissable.

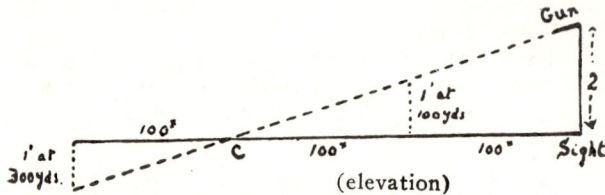

(elevation)

A the gun fires at the target C on which the sights are laid, at a range of 200 yards.

If the range alters to 100 or 300 yards the shots will miss the 2 foot target as shown.

It is very hard to judge ranges of 200 yards and over.

Tractors Firing straight ahead.

Some small tractor scouts are having the gun mounted on the fusilage of the machine, and the firing mechanism is connected with the engine by means of a gear.

This enables the gun to be fired through the propellor without touching it, and does away with the deflectors on the propellor.

Machine Diving.

If a machine is diving after another and does not follow its path it may miss its target as shown in the following diagram:—

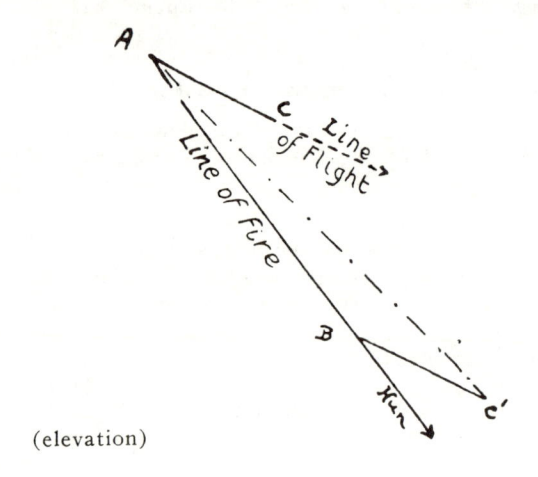

(elevation)

A is a machine diving at B.

During the time of flight of the bullet the machine A travels from A to C.

If BC be drawn parallel to AC the bullet will travel along the line AC', and will miss the target, unless a prediction is made.

Setting of Sights.

If one has a gun set at an angle to the line of flight of the machine, and fixed, it is easy to make allowance for the normal speed of one's own machine. If a suitable backsight is then used, one can make a fair estimation of the Enemy's speed, and one will obtain hits.

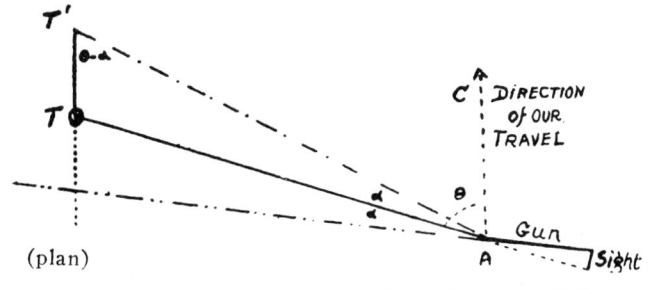

(plan)

To find the distance that the backsight should be set from the line of sight.

Suppose that our machine A is travelling in the direction AC, and that it is shooting at the target T.

If no deflection is used the shots will hit at T', where TT' is the distance our machine moves during the time of flight of the bullet at the range.

Suppose that the range is R (= 200 yards), so that the time of flight of the bullet is t (= .25 secs.), and that the speed of our machine is x feet per second.

Then TT′ is xt feet, and we must alter the line of sight an angle "a," equal to TAT′, in order to hit the target.

Suppose that the gun is set at an angle of ⊙ degrees with the centre line of the machine.

Then $\dfrac{TT'}{\sin a} = \dfrac{3R}{\sin ⊙ - a}$

$\sin a = \dfrac{xt}{3R} \sin(⊙ - a)$

$\sin a = \dfrac{xt}{3R} (\sin ⊙ \cos a - \cos ⊙ \sin a)$

$3R = xt \left(\dfrac{\sin ⊙}{\tan a} - \cos ⊙ \right)$

$\tan a = \dfrac{xt \sin ⊙}{3R + xt \cos ⊙}$

And if "l" inches is the distance between the fore and back sight, then s inches, the distance to set off the back sight, is given by:—

$s'' = \dfrac{l xt \sin ⊙}{3R + xt \cos ⊙}$

The actual figures can now be substituted for the signs in the above.

Sights which depend on the rotation of a fixed arm.

There are a number of sights that depend on the rotation of a fixed arm. The length of the arm bears the same relation to the distance between the sights that the distance moved by the machine (during the time of flight of the bullet) bears to the range.

The arm rotates as the gun is moved, so that it is always parallel to the centre line of the machine.

These are only approximations, and become more and more inaccurate as the speed of the machines increase.

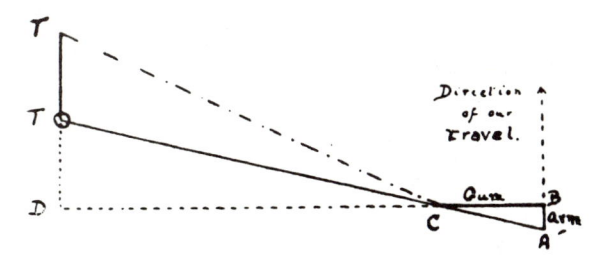

```
T
 ┌
 │  ╲  ─ ─
 │      ╲ ─ ─                    Direction ↑
T│          ╲ ─ ─                  of our
 o───────────────╲──────────────   travel.
 │                   ╲ ─ ─
 │                        ╲ ─ ─ Gun  •B
D·- - - - - - - - - - - - - - - - - ╲arm
                                   C   A
```

Let AB be a rotating arm at the rear of the gun, and let C be the foresight. The machine is moving in the line AB.

The machine moves forward a distance equal to TT' from the target T during the time of flight of the bullet.

Therefore, the bullets aimed at T with no deflection would hit at T'.

Make TD equal to TT'.

Now TT' (=DT) : Range DC : arm AB : gun CB.

ACT is the line of sight and BCD the line of fire, so we aim at T, and the shots get carried from D to T, a distance equal to TT'.

This is only an approximation, as we take the range DC equal to the range to target CT, and this is not quite so.

The actual error with a 100 m.p.h. machine when firing almost at right angles to the line of flight is about 1' 6" at 200 yards.

A type of rotating arm sight.

If the gun is to be used over a large arc, if the distance between sights bears the same relation to the length of the revolving arm as the range does to the distance moved by the machine during the time of flight, then the shots will very nearly hit the target.

Some device must be employed so that the arm always remains parallel with the centre line of the machine while the gun carrying the foresight follows the target.

One way of doing this is with a gear.

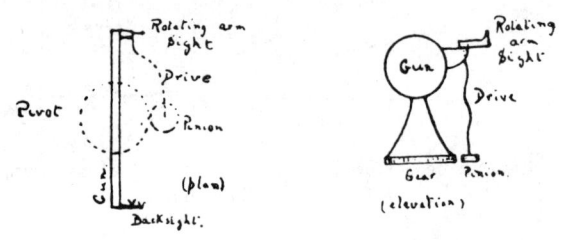

The arm is so geared that it revolves once while the gun revolves once, so that it is always parallel to the centre line of the machine.

The drawing shows the arm set when the gun is traversed right out to the left of the machine.

Another way of effecting this is to fix an independent sight to the machine while the foresight is fixed to the gun. The distance of the sights from the pivot gives the required relation of the sights to a fixed point.

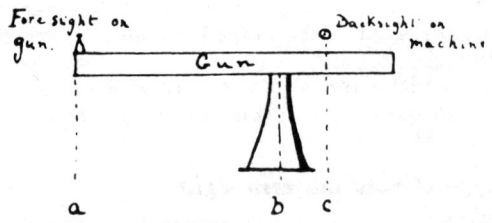

ab : bc : Range : Distance machine travels in time of flight.

This sight is better than the above, as it gives some correction when the gun is fired up or down.

Telescopes.

In order to do away with the trouble of aligning the two sights of the gun on to the target, and also the difficulty of placing one's eye in line with the sights, it is convenient to use a sighting telescope.

These telescopes have the pointer mounted in the focus of the object glass or erector.

The object appears:—

It is as easy to put the pointer on the target as it is to put the point of a pencil on any part of a picture, but suffers from the same drawbacks.

The arrangement of glasses is:—

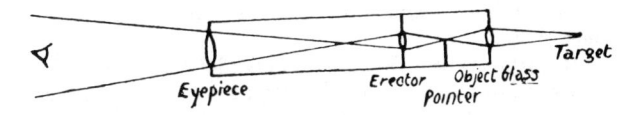

The telescope must not magnify more than two or three times or the vibration of the machine interferes with it. The field should be large, 10 degrees or larger, and the eye piece is so arranged that the full field is obtained when the eye is held about a foot from the telescope. This enables one to use goggles or a wind screen.

The gun used with this telescope is mounted in the centre line of the machine, and the telescope is adjustable to allow for crossing shots.

So long as the eye is within the angle shown it need not be in the centre line of the telescope in order to obtain the full field.

An iris diaphragm over the object glass would enable one to shoot towards the sun.

Flight Flying.

When machines fly in flights they can fly in line, diamond formation or echelon.

I rather prefer the echelon formation, with the Flight Commander well out to the front.

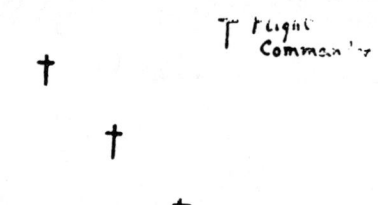

†　Flight Commander

†

†

†

If this formation is used any disabled machine can easily turn out of the formation without interfering with the others.

The Flight Commander can be seen by every machine.

In attack the Flight Commander can use his distance to the front in order to gain height, so that, if a single Enemy machine is attacked, the Flight can bring a cross fire to bear from the sides and from the top.

If the Enemy are also flying in formation, because the shooting is at present so bad, I do not think that there would be much extra danger if Enemy machines are singled out and attacked one after the other.

When attacking as a Flight, do not attack singly, or the machines may be defeated in detail before the others can help.

Single out one machine of the Enemy, and let say, four attack it all together from four directions, so that the Enemy cannot turn. This gives each machine a single standing target, while the Enemy will have four to take up his attention.

When attacking a large number of machines, cut off a number according to the "n^2 law." This law is explained in Lanchester's book on Flying.

The law is—if perhaps 5 machines meet 7 machines, they should divide the 7 into two bodies—4 and 3, and attack first one and then the other party.

Since $5^2 = 4^2 + 3^2$, the 5 machines have every prospect of success, whereas if they attack 7 all together they should be beaten.

When flying as a Flight keep close together, so that the formation cannot be broken.

Escorts.

Sometimes small Fighters are sent out to escort other machines, and fly above them.

In a case like this one should be careful when diving to the attack not to overshoot the target. Remember that a very small angle of glide helps to put up the speed enormously.

When protecting a machine do not let the Enemy come too close to it, or it may be damaged before the escort can help.

1917
Text Book on Aerial Gunnery

MACHINE GUN SHOOTING IN THE AIR, USING RING SIGHTS.

Part I.—INTRODUCTION.

1. In all the following it is assumed that a machine gun is used with Mark VII ammunition or tracer.

Difficulty of taking a Steady Aim in the Air.

2. Experience has shown that a gunner firing from an aeroplane cannot hold his gun very steadily upon a mark which is passing him, but that, even after considerable practice, he will as a rule scatter his bullets over a fairly wide area around that mark. This is principally due to two distinct causes—the difficulty of traversing a gun steadily so as to follow a moving object, and to small angular movements of the aeroplane, due to unsteadiness of the air.

3. The scattering, due to want of rigidity in the mounting, is small compared with that due to the above two causes; for it is easy, when firing from an aeroplane on the ground at a fixed mark, to obtain groups much more concentrated than can be obtained in the air under average conditions.

Size of Group under various Conditions.

4. If the air is at all " bumpy," as it nearly always is within 1,000 feet of the ground, the scattering due to bumps is greater than that due to any other causes. The group of shots round an object aimed at under these conditions has seldom been less than 50 feet across at 250 yards range; and this size of group has often been greatly exceeded, even by an experienced gunner.

5. In perfectly steady air, however, such as rarely exists near the ground, but is often found at high altitudes, it is quite possible to concentrate nearly all the shots fired into a 20-foot circle at 250 yards range, provided that the gun has not to be traversed (when, for instance, two aeroplanes are flying side by side at the same speed). If, on the other hand, the gun has to be traversed at all rapidly, the shots, even under the steadiest conditions, will not be contained in less than about a 30-foot circle, except when fired by a very good gunner.

6. In general it will be assumed in what follows that, under the conditions usually met at high altitudes, a practised gunner will spread the majority of his shots over a circle of about 30 feet diameter, or 15 feet radius around his point of aim, when the range is 250 yards. The size of this circle will vary roughly in proportion with the range, except when it is necessary to traverse the gun very rapidly, as is often the case at short ranges.

Allowance for Speed of Gunner's Aeroplane.

7. When a gun carried in an aeroplane is pointing across the line of flight, the motion of the aeroplane carries the bullet ahead of the spot at which the barrel is pointing. Thus, to hit an object fixed in the air, when flying past it, the gun must be pointed behind the object, and therefore the sights must be tilted so as to point ahead of the gun.

8. In a machine flying through the air at 100 m.p.h., the allowance for this effect—called the gunner's speed allowance—amounts to 46 feet at 250 yards' range, and at other ranges is in proportion to the range.

Gunner's Speed Allowance Automatic.

9. In the sights now issued the gunner's speed allowance is made automatically, either by carrying the foresight on a wind-vane so that it is offset by a certain amount when the gun is pointing across the aeroplane, or, in the case of the telescopic sight, by mechanism which tilts the telescope in relation to the gun.

10. In most existing designs the sight is adjusted for one particular speed, and the allowance is correct for that speed only. This is chosen so as to be near the average speed of the aeroplane on which the sight is used.

11. When the aeroplane is not flying at this speed the allowance will be incorrect, but the error will usually be such that it is covered by the scattering of the individual shots. For instance, if the sight is correct for 80 m.p.h. and the aeroplane dives at 100 m.p.h., the error in aiming at 250 yards will be about 10 feet. Hence with a group 30 feet in diameter, the target will still be within the group if the gun be otherwise correctly aimed.

12. For the present, therefore, the gunner will be taught to neglect the changes in his own speed, for he has quite as much as he can manage to allow for the enemy's speed in the time usually at his disposal. It is possible that future sights may be devised to allow automatically for changes in the gunner's speed, but these, if they come, will only increase the accuracy of shooting without in any way altering the training required.

13. The gunner, therefore, when using these automatic sights, takes no account of his own speed, but aims exactly as he would were he firing from the ground.

Sights for Fixed Gun.

14. In fixed guns firing straight ahead, no allowance for own speed is necessary, since the speed of the aeroplane is merely added to that of the bullet and gives it no sideway drift.

15. On fixed guns firing at a small angle with the aeroplane a fixed allowance for gunner's speed only is required. With any fixed gun, therefore, only fixed sights are provided, and all wind-vanes and other moving mechanism are dispensed with.

Allowance for Speed of Enemy Aeroplane.

16. The automatic allowance for the gunner's own speed enables him to hit a target stationary in the air. When aiming at a target which is itself moving through the air it is necessary to make an additional allowance by pointing the gun ahead of the target, because the target will move through the air during the time that the bullet takes to reach it. This is called the enemy's speed allowance, and is rather greater than the gunner's speed allowance for the same range, owing to the fact that the bullet slows down during its flight.

17. If the machines are flying in opposite directions the allowance for gunner's and enemy's speed add up, so that if each aeroplane is flying at, say, 100 m.p.h., the total allowance that would be necessary, if no automatic sights were used, would be nearly 100 feet at 250 yards' range.

Method of Allowing for Enemy's Speed.

18. With either the ring and wind-vane sight, or the Aldis optical sight, the correct sighting line to allow for the gunner's own speed is arranged to pass through the centre of a ring of such a radius that an aeroplane, flying directly across the line of sight at 100 m.p.h. air speed, would pass from the edge of the ring to the centre in the time taken for the bullet to reach the aeroplane. This is true with sufficient accuracy for all ranges at which air shooting can be profitably carried out.

19 If, therefore, the gunner should see a target aeroplane flying at 100 m.p.h. directly across his line of sight—*i.e.*, if the body does not appear foreshortened—he must lay the gun so that the vital parts are on the edge of the ring and the *body pointing towards the centre.*

20. Should he see the aeroplane flying partly towards or away from him—*i.e.*, if the body does appear foreshortened—he must place the vital spot somewhere within the ring, at a distance from the centre that depends on the amount by which the body is foreshortened.

21. Should the body be pointing straight towards or **away** from him, he will place it in the centre of his ring and aim **point** blank.

22. In any case it is absolutely essential that the body should point towards the centre of the ring.

Allowance independent of Range.

23. The gunner should be taught that the correct position of the aeroplane in the ring for a given speed depends upon the foreshortening of the body only and *not upon the range*, for although theoretically there is some difference in allowance at different ranges, this difference is insignificant.

Early Training to Assume a Fixed Enemy's Speed.

24. For the sake of simplicity, all the early training should be done on the assumption that the enemy aeroplane is moving at the correct speed for which the ring is intended, *i.e.*, 100 m.p.h. with the sight issued. The training should not be complicated with additional allowances for probable variation of speed due to diving, climbing, etc., until the gunner has become thoroughly accustomed to making his allowance correctly on the simpler assumption of a fixed speed.

Necessity for continual Training in making the Allowance.

25. The estimation of the amount the body is foreshortened, and the operation of laying the gun so that the target aeroplane appears at the corresponding distance from the edge of the ring and with its body pointing to the centre must, therefore, form the fundamental part of the training for all gunners intending to use these sights in the air. In most aerial fighting the target is altering its appearance with bewildering rapidity during the entire fight, so that it is essential that the gunner should have developed by constant practice, the habit of laying his gun correctly for the momentary appearance of the aeroplane and of following the target's movements whilst he is firing, so that it continually occupies the correct position in the ring. Not until this can be done almost as easily and well as the gunner can lay a sight directly on a target, will he be of much use in an actual fight. If he has to think much before laying the gun he will fail to get in his shots in time.

26. The gunner, therefore, must practise continually, both during training and in the intervals between fights, at estimating this allowance as rapidly as possible, and as it is usually impossible to get sufficient flying to give him the amount of practice required, he must work continually on the ground, either at the aiming model or at the picture target, or by any other means which may from time to time be devised to give him a realistic view of a target aeroplane and an indication as to whether he has made his allowance accurately.

Necessity for generality in the Training.

27. During the whole of the training great care should be taken never to let the gunner practise for long at any one range, or at any one aspect of the aeroplane. If he is allowed to do either of these things he invariably forms habits of making the allowance by some means which is peculiar to the range or aspect at which he is working; since both range and aspect are always rapidly altering in a real fight, this is the very worst thing he can do.

28. For instance, if, when using the aiming model, the range is not altered, the gunner rapidly finds out that he can score a hit by aiming so many body lengths ahead, and instinctively forms the habit of doing this, to the complete ruin of his shooting in the air.

29. Again, if the picture target on the range is not altered the gunner will soon find that by laying his ring on some part of the machine—say, the tail—he can score a hit.

30. In actual fighting the target may be seen from any point of view whatever, and on account of the gunner's own speed may appear to be moving in any direction, regardless of the direction in which its body is pointing. For instance, if the enemy aeroplane is approaching from one side, it will appear to be moving rapidly sideways in the direction of the tail of the gunner's machine, even although its body may be pointing directly at the gunner. Or, again, should it be flying alongside and in the same direction as the gunner, it will appear to be travelling backwards if it is a slower machine. The gunner, on the other hand, has to learn to make his part of the allowance depend only upon the direction in which the body is pointing, so that any practices he may use should teach him to do this from whatever point of view he sees the target and wherever it may appear to be moving. For these reasons, in practices at moving models, the models should be constantly varied and be made to move so that the aeroplane does not appear to be moving along its own body.

Also, in practices at picture targets (*see* Part VII), not only should the pictures be constantly changed, but care should be taken that the direction of the body of the aeroplane on the picture is varied. Moreover, the gunner's cockpit should be rotated sometimes one way, sometimes the other, or the rotation may even be stopped and reversed while the firing is proceeding.

Range at which to Open Fire.

31. The maximum range at which fire may be profitably opened must depend very largely on individual skill, and on such circumstances as the relative speed and aspect of the two aeroplanes. It is impossible at present to lay down anything very definite on this point, nor will it be possible until experience has been gained of the actual results obtained with the new pattern

sights by men thoroughly trained in their use. Sufficient information has been obtained, however, to show that under some circumstances fire may be opened with advantage at 300 yards, but that that range should rarely, if ever, be exceeded. On the other hand, at ranges of 100 yards or less the relative position of the aeroplane may be changing so rapidly that the average man cannot use his sights with any effect, but must rely on manœuvre and tracer bullets. Thus it would appear probable that very fast and handy scout machines will try to close with the large two-seaters, so as to get full advantage from their power of manœuvre, while the large machine must rely on accurate gunnery at long range to keep off the attacking scout. If the latter can get within 100 yards he will usually have the big machine at his mercy. On the other hand, the big machine having more guns and field of fire has the advantage at longer ranges between 100 and 300 yards.

32. For the present, therefore, observer pupils should be taught to reserve all fire to within 300 yards and to try to get in as much as possible at about 200 yards. The range can be judged by the apparent size of the target within the ring. Considerable practice is required, however, before this can be done accurately, because the size of an aeroplane at a fixed range will appear to vary considerably when it is viewed from different aspects. The best training for this purpose is to carry out aiming practice at the picture target and at the aiming model, at all ranges up to the equivalent of 300 yards, but never beyond so that the target will look unfamiliarly small at ranges above this distance. Particular attention should be paid to this point when using the gun camera.

33. The above considerations do not, of course, apply when attempting to affect a surprise attack, or when from any other cause it is possible to get in shooting at close range with the two machines moving practically in the same direction, so that the relative velocity is small. In this case the shorter the range the better from the gunner's point of view.

Use of Tracers.

34. Tracer bullets give but little indication of the allowance necessary for relative velocity, and should therefore be disregarded when the sight can conveniently be used. At close range, however, under 100 yards, they form a good substitute for a point blank sight, and can often be used with effect when it is impracticable to use the sight, owing to want of time, or to the difficulty of getting the head into position behind the sight.

Fig. 1.

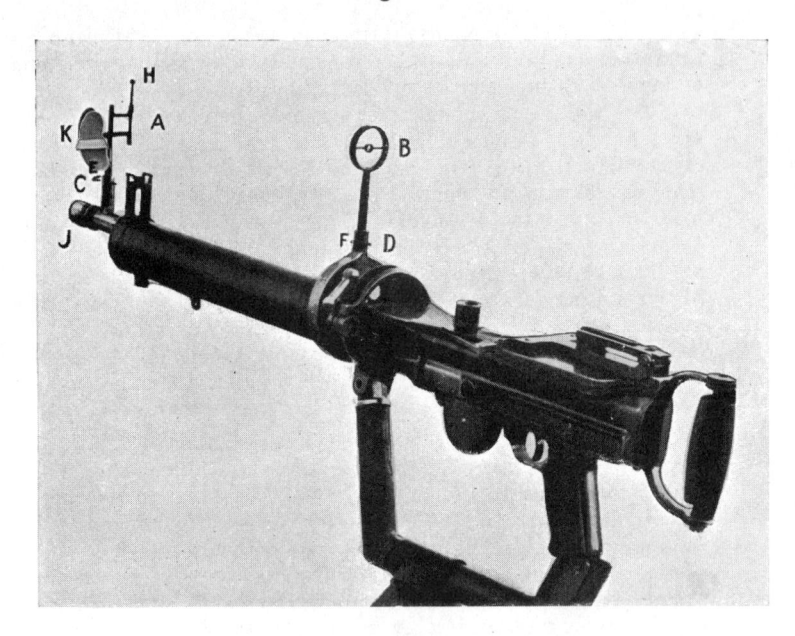

PHOTOGRAPHS ILLUSTRATING RING BACK-SIGHT AND WIND-VANE FORESIGHT (NORMAN PATTERN).

Part II.—INSTRUCTIONS FOR USING RING BACK-SIGHT AND WIND-VANE FORESIGHT (NORMAN PATTERN).

Description of Sight.

1. The illustrating photographs (Fig. 1) show the sight in place on the gun.

2. The foresight A consists of a bead H, which is moved by the wind-vane K so as to allow for the speed of the gunner's aeroplane, no matter in what direction the gun is pointed.

3. B is the ring backsight, by means of which the necessary allowance is made for the enemy's speed.

4. The sights are carried on the gun by means of the adapters C and D, from which they can be easily removed and replaced without disturbing the accuracy of setting.

5. The adapter C is jammed on to the taper part of the barrel by means of the nut J, and, as there is no key to prevent the adapter from turning upon the barrel, this nut must be very firmly screwed home. Special nuts for this purpose will be provided; until these can be issued the barrel mouthpiece from a land gun may be used.

6. The adapter D grips the front band of the small radiator casing as shown in the photograph, the yoke being clamped on the rear band.

7. A fixed bead foresight may be put in place of A to check the setting of the adapters, and for use either with the Hythe camera gun or the aiming model.

Adjustment of Sight.

8. Lateral adjustment only is needed with these sights, as the positions of the holes for the pins E and F are such that the sights, when aligned laterally and upright on the gun, are also correct for elevation.

9. Lateral adjustment can be affected by loosening the adapters and tapping them round until both sides are upright on the gun, with their stems parallel. It should be possible to do this with sufficient accuracy by eye, but if a check is required, replace the foresight A by the fixed bead and adjust by looking through the barrel of the gun at a distant object in the ordinary way. The centre of the ring backsight and the fixed bead should then line up on the same distant object as the barrel of the gun.

Method of Using the Sights.

10. Two wind-vane sights are issued marked respectively "80 m.p.h. at 18 inches" and "100 m.p.h. at 18 inches."

11. When the sights are correctly adjusted the centre of the ring backsight B and the bead H give the correct sighting line for the bullet to hit an object stationary in the air, when fired from an aeroplane moving at the marked speed (80 or 100 m.p.h.) through the air. This is true, no matter in what direction the gun is pointing out of the moving aeroplane, because the wind-vane sight A automatically applies the necessary correction for the aeroplane's speed. The gunner therefore has no allowance to make for his own speed and need not consider it at all when firing.

12. When firing at an aeroplane which is itself moving through the air, however, the gunner must make a further allowance so as to aim at the spot in which the target will be when the bullet arrives there. For this purpose the ring backsight is provided; this is marked " 100 m.p.h. at 19 inches," and is correct for use against a target moving at 100 m.p.h. through the air when the eye is placed at 19 inches behind it.

13. When aiming, first align the eye so that the bead H appears to be in the centre of the ring of the backsight B. The head must be held in this position throughout the firing, and must be kept approximately over the handle of the spade grip so that eye is about 19 inches behind the backsight. An error of 1 inch either way in this distance does not matter, and with practice it is not difficult to acquire the habit of placing the eye within these limits. This is best done by resting the chin or cheek upon the hand holding the spade grip, or upon the pad above the handle, if one is provided (*see* Fig. 1).

14. If a butt stock is used it should be cut down until the eye comes at the correct distance behind the sight, otherwise the eye will be too far behind the ring and the allowance will be suitable for some speed lower than 100 m.p.h.

15. With the head held in position as above, the target aeroplane must be placed within the ring of the backsight, in a position which depends upon the aeroplane's appearance, and which is described in detail below.

Correct Position of Enemy Aeroplane n Ring (*see* Fig. 2).

16. The position of the enemy aeroplane within the ring at the moment of firing must be such that it will fly into the centre of the ring by the time that the bullet reaches it. For this reason the first essential is that the body of the aeroplane must be pointing directly towards the centre of the ring.

17. The distance that the vital part of the aeroplane must be placed from the centre of the ring depends upon the angle at which it is approaching or moving away.

18. If it is flying directly towards, or away from, the gun, it must be placed exactly in the centre of the ring (A in Fig. 2).

Fig. 2.

PHOTOGRAPHS ILLUSTRATING USE OF RING BACK-SIGHT WITH WIND-VANE FORESIGHT (NORMAN PATTERN).
B.E. 2c on 100 m.p.h. Ring Sight.

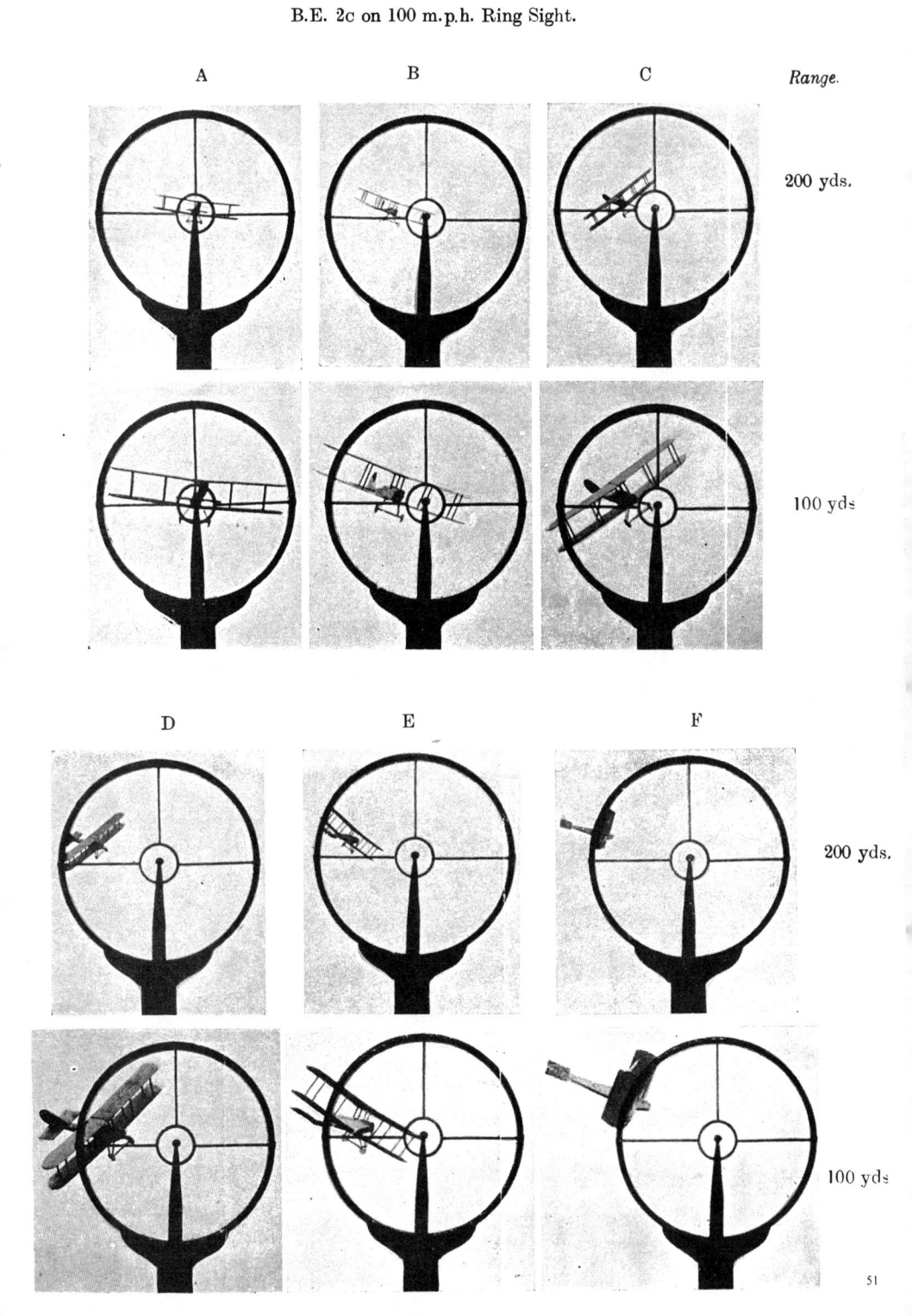

19. If it is flying directly across the l'ne of sight it must be placed on the outer ring (F in Fig. 2).

20. If it is flying obliquely towards or away from the gun it must be placed between the centre and the outer ring, at a distance from the centre which depends on the angle of approach. This distance can, with practice, be judged with sufficient accuracy from the appearance of the aeroplane (B, C, D and E in Fig. 2).

21. The distance of the vital part of the aeroplane from the centre of the ring should depend only on the angle at which the target aeroplane is approaching or moving away from the gun and not upon the range, or apparent size of the target in the ring.

22. Care should be taken to avoid estimating the necessary allowances in body lengths of the aeroplane, since any system based on this method is correct at one range only and will be wrong at other ranges.

23. The correct use of a ring sight requires considerable practice to enable the gunner instantly to associate each aspect from which he may see the target with its correct position in the ring and to accustom him to making his allowance independent of the target's apparent size. Useful forms of practice are described in parts 5, 6 and 7 of these notes.

24. With some people the operation of laying the gun to allow for the enemy's speed, is most easily performed by making the enemy aeroplane touch an imaginary sphere, which just fits the ring in such a way that he is flying towards the centre of the ring.

This method of making the allowance is quite correct.

Part III.—RING SIGHT FOR FIXED MACHINE-GUN ON AN AEROPLANE.

Description of Sight.

1. This sight consists of two concentric rings 5 in. and 1 in in diameter respectively, and four radial lines joining the inner and outer rings.

2. It can be used either as a foresight with a fixed bead backsight or a peep-hole, or as a backsight with a fixed bead foresight. In either case the radius of the outer ring is correct for use against an enemy aeroplane travelling at 100 m.p.h. when the *ring is* 38 inches from the eye. If placed further from the eye the speed allowance is reduced in proportion, thus at 42 inches it corresponds to 90 m.p.h. and at 34 inches to 110 m.p.h.

Use of the Sight.

3. The sight is used exactly the same way as the ring and wind-vane sight described in Part II The head must be placed so that the bead appears in the middle of the inner ring, and the aeroplane manœuvred until the enemy aeroplane appears in the correct position in the ring to allow for its own speed. This position is found exactly as described previously.

4. The only differences between this sight and the ring and wind-vane sight are that the movable bead on the wind-vane is replaced by a fixed bead (this is because no allowance is necessary for the gunner's own speed) and that the ring is twice as large and twice as far from the eye (this is to allow the gunner twice the margin for error in the position of his eye).

Use of Sight with Fixed gun not Parallel to axis of Flight.

5. If the fixed gun is pointing at an angle to the direction of flight, the sight can be set up as follows :—

6. Fix the ring at the correct distance from the eye.

7. Erect a temporary bead so that the line joining it to the centre of the ring is parallel to the barrel of the gun.

8. Set up the permanent bead so that the line joining it to the temporary bead is parallel to the direction of flight and so that the distance between the two beads is equal to $\frac{1}{18}$th the distance between the temporary bead and the centre of the ring.

9. If the bead is a backsight the permanent bead must be behind the temporary bead, but if a foresight it must be in front.

10. Remove the temporary bead ; the permanent bead is now correct for a speed of 100 m.p.h in the gunner's aeroplane.

Part IV.—THE ALDIS OPTICAL SIGHT.

Description of Sight.

1. The Aldis sight is virtually a telescope which does not magnify or diminish, and which, unlike an ordinary telescope, can be used with the eye several inches from the end of the tube.

2. When looking through this tube at a distant object, the effect is exactly as though one were looking through a napkin ring : the object appears the same whether it is seen through the tube or outside it.

3. Within the tube is a glass screen carrying the sighting circle, which is so placed between the lenses that on looking through the tube at a distant object the ring is seen with its centre on the

spot at which the tube is pointing, no matter where the eye is placed If the eye is moved sideways the ring appears to move with it through the telescope, so that the direction in which the tube points is always towards the centre of the ring

4. The tube, when fixed rigidly to a gun, therefore, constitutes a sight which offers practically no obstruction to the view, and which shows instantly the spot at which the gun is pointing, without the necessity of aligning the eye upon a front and back-sight.

5. The sight can with advantage be used with both eyes open, one eye sees the object and the circle through the tube, and one eye sees the object direct. The effect after a little practice is that the object is seen as clearly as though there were no sight at all, but that a circle appears in the sky, the centre of which is the point where the tube is aiming.

6. These tubes are supplied in two sizes—1-inch diameter and 2-inch diameter. The former is intended for use with a moving gun and the latter with a fixed gun. The special advantage of the large size is that the eye can be held further from the end of the tube, and has more freedom of movement, whilst still keeping the target within the field of the telescope.

Use of the Sight.

7. For use with fixed guns firing directly forward from the aeroplane, the sight must be fixed parallel to the axis of the gun. The centre of the circle will then always fall on the point that the gun will hit if that point is not moving through the air ; in this case no allowance for the speed of the gunner's aeroplane is necessary.

8. If, however, the sight is used on a movable gun, means must be provided for tilting it to a small angle in relation to the gun, so as to allow for the speed of the aeroplane, which slightly deflects the bullet in relation to the gun, when the gun is not firing straight ahead. This corresponds to the correction given by the windvane foresight when open sights are used. The telescopic sight has to be tilted mechanically and requires a special mounting and gear for this purpose. These mountings and gears are not yet issued for service use ; until they are, these telescopic sights should be used for fixed guns only.

9. The ring seen in the sight forms a guide as to how much to aim off for the speed of the target aeroplane, the target aeroplane being placed in the ring in such a way that it will fly into the centre of the ring by the time the bullet reaches it. This is done exactly as though using a bead and ring sight. The telescope in fact, when fixed, exactly replaces the bead and ring sight used with fixed guns, and when carried on a compensating mount, replaces the ring and windvane sight for movable guns. The only difference is that the gunner is released from the

necessity of holding his eye aligned on two sights or of keeping his head at a fixed distance from the ring. So long as he can see the ring at all it is in the correct position for aiming.

10. The training, therefore, with the ring sights is exactly applicable to the Aldis, except that those parts of the training relating to the aligning of the eye and fixing of the head, are no longer necessary.

Fixing of the Sight.

11. For fixed guns, firing straight ahead, the telescope is held in a pair of brackets which are adjustable for line. So far as possible the fixing of the telescope is so arranged that, once adjusted, it remains correct. But it is necessary to check it from time to time. This can be done in the usual way by looking through the barrel of the gun at a distant mark with the aid of a mirror, and seeing that the mark falls in the centre of the ring.

12. The sight should be removed when not in use, by loosening the wing nuts on the clips attaching it to the brackets.

Part V.—INSTRUCTIONS FOR USING MODEL AIMING AEROPLANE.

(See Fig. 3.)

Description of Model.

1. This consists of a model of an aeroplane to 1-20th or 1-10th scale, and is intended for practice in aiming off to allow for the enemy's speed, and for judging range to determine the correct moment for opening fire.

2. The model is mounted upon a universal joint and carries a rod, sliding in its body.

3. On the end of this rod is a ball, which forms, when properly adjusted, the correct point of aim when allowing for the aeroplane's speed, no matter from what point of view the aeroplane is observed.

To set up the Model.

4. Set up the model and arrange practice guns and sights around it at the required range, so that the model appears against the sky or some uniform light background.

5. The actual range should be 1-20 or 1-10 the real range, *i.e.*, if working at 200 yards, the gun, when using a 1-20 model, should be 10 yards from the model; other ranges in proportion.

6 Set up the guns on some form of mount such that they can be moved easily on their pivots but remain wherever put, (*i.e.*,

the pivots should be very slightly stiff and the guns balanced upon them).

7. It may be found convenient to use dummy wooden guns for this purpose.

8. If the training is for a ring and windvane sight, the windvane must be replaced by a fixed bead before beginning practice; if for an Aldis optical sight, the sight must be fixed rigidly to the gun.

9. If the training is to be on the assumption that the speed allowed for corresponds to the ring on the sight provided, it is now necessary to draw out the stick from the body until, with the model flying directly across the line of sight and the centre of the ring on the bead, the vital part of the model is on the edge of the ring. This can be done either by trial on the spot—*i.e.*, by drawing out the rod until, when using the sight correctly, the above is true—or by having the rod marked to correspond with various ranges at the given speed.

10. If an advanced training including estimation of increased speed due to diving, etc., is required, the rod must be marked and adjusted accordingly, using the fact that at any range the distance between the ball and the vital spot in inches should be $0.024\ V \times R$. Where V is the velocity in miles per hour and R the actual range in yards.

11. In any case it is of course necessary to readjust the position of the sliding rod whenever the range is altered.

To Use the Model.

12. The first training consists in turning the aeroplane to various positions and making pupils aim at the ball and note the appearance and position of the aeroplane in the ring. After some practice at this, remove the rod altogether and allow pupils to guess the correct position of the aeroplane in the ring, corresponding to its appearance; then check their aim by replacing the rod and observing how nearly the ball falls upon the centre of the ring.

13. The rod should always be removed entirely and not merely pushed right into the model, as if this is done the tail of the rod, protruding behind the tail of the body, unfairly assists the gunner in aiming so that the body points towards the centre of the ring.

14. The photo herewith shows the appearance of a 1-20 scale model at 10 yards corresponding to 200 yards on the full scale The distance between the ball and the centre of the ring gives the error in setting the sight.

15. This practice should be carried out at several different ranges, less than the equivalent of 300 yards on the full scale, and should be continued until the pupils can get the ball within the

Fig. 3.

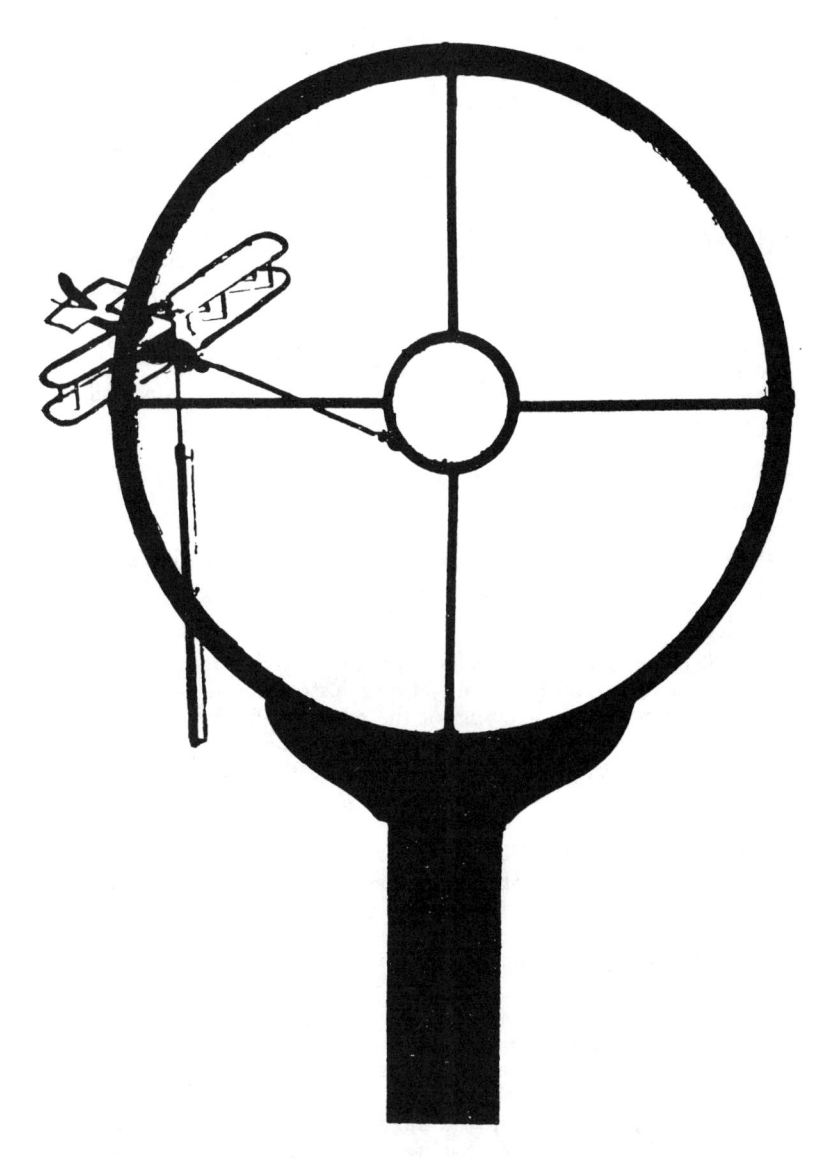

DIAGRAM SHOWING USE OF AIMING MODEL.

inner ring practically every time, whatever the position of the aeroplane and whatever the range.

16. In this way the laying of the aeroplane on the ring in the correct position, having regard to its appearance and not to range, should become instinctive; in addition the pupil should have become familiarised with its apparent size in the ring at the correct range for opening fire.

17. The training should not, at least in the first place, be complicated by any allowance for speed differing from those for which the rings are intended; attention should be concentrated solely on the two points; opening fire at the correct range and placing the aeroplane correctly in the ring.

18. In the early trials plenty of time should be allowed to lay the gun, but later this should be cut down to two and even one second.

19. It is very important to vary the range from time to time to prevent the pupil forming the habit of estimating his allowance in body lengths, a thing which he is very apt to do, and which is incorrect.

Part VI.—INSTRUCTIONS FOR USING THE HYTHE GUN CAMERA: Mk. II.

General.

1. The gun camera has been designed with a view to improving aerial gunnery. With the aid of this instrument it is possible to check the aiming or laying of the gun and to obtain graphic records of results: in other words photographs are produced showing where the bullets would have gone had the gun actually been used.

Instructions for Setting Up.

2. Care must be taken before practice to ascertain that the setting of the screen in the camera coincides with the sight on the gun.

3. The method of doing so is as follows:—The gun is mounted on a tripod with the camera (focal plane type Mk. II) clamped on the right hand side of the barrel casing. Take out the back of the camera and the metal film holder, and open the lens by turning the film changing handle slowly clockwise until it nearly reaches the lock, when the capping shutter will be heard to fly back. At this point stop the handle and release the shutter; then turn the handle slowly backwards until a certain resistance is felt, when it will be found that the screen is exposed enough for sighting.

4. Align the gunsights correctly on a sharply defined target some 100 to 200 yards distant; then set the camera so that the centre of the image of the target coincides with the centre mark on the screen. Lateral movement is obtained by moving the screen itself; vertical movement by adjusting the screw on the top of the screen-holder. When the target is correctly centred on both gun and camera, continue turning the handle in a clockwise direction, moving the lock in order to allow the handle to pass.

Use of the Gun Camera.

5. The gun camera is used in practice aerial duels, and it determines whether the gunner has succeeded in laying his gun correctly upon the enemy aeroplane. In actual shooting it is necessary, when laying the gun, to make allowance for the speed of the enemy aeroplane, and the gun camera shows whether this allowance has been correctly made. It cannot, however, be used to check the allowance, necessary in real shooting, for the speed of the gunner's aeroplane; therefore, as this speed is allowed for in all modern sights, it is necessary to remove whatever automatic allowance is provided on the sights in use on the gunner's aeroplane. With a ring and windvane sight this is done by replacing the wind vane sight by a fixed bead, and with the Aldis compensating sight the alteration is made by removing the compensating gear and fixing the telescope parallel to the axis of the camera.

6. To use the gun camera the gunner lays the sights on the target aeroplane, and presses the trigger of the gun at the moment when he considers that he would hit his opponent if he were actually firing. The effect of pressing the trigger is to expose the film in the gun-camera, and the resulting photograph when developed and measured shows how far he was right or wrong in his aim.

7. The handle on the right hand side of the camera must be turned once between each exposure. About 11 exposures can be taken on each roll of film.

Instructions for Working Out Results.

8. The film when developed shows a photograph of the target aeroplane and, either a series of ruled lines dividing the film into squares, or a series of concentric circles, this depending on which type of screen is used. In either case the true centre is clearly shown. (The screen should have been previously aligned with the gun sights.) (*See* para. 4.)

9. It is possible from this photograph to determine where a bullet, fired when the trigger was pressed, would have hit or passed the aeroplane had it been flying at any given speed and had an accurate automatic sight to allow for the gunner's own

speed been used. In other words it is possible to tell whether the gunner has carried out his part of the shooting correctly.

10. To do this proceed as follows :—

11. Scratch a line on the film through the body of the aeroplane parallel to the direction of motion (in a B.E. this line passes through the propeller boss and the front edge of the fixed tail plane where it meets the body).

12. From the centre mark on the film scratch another line parallel to the above line, and measure along this second line from the centre mark, in a direction opposed to that of the flight of the aeroplane, a distance corresponding to the allowance for the target speed. This distance can be found approximately by methods to be described later.

13. The point so found, called hereinafter the point A, is the spot where a single bullet, fired when the trigger was pressed, would have passed the target; the distance between this point and the spot aimed at on the picture of the aeroplane represents the gunner's error in laying the gun.

14. If a series of real shots had been fired they would have been spread over a fairly wide area around this point.

15. A circle of 0.22 inches radius drawn about A as centre will represent the spread of a drum of bullets fired by an average gunner under average conditions. If the vital parts of the aeroplane do not lie within this circle it is very improbable that they would have been hit; if, however, they do lie within it the chance of a hit depends on the number of shots fired and the range. Half a drum grouped within this circle at 200 yards range would represent an even chance of a hit. This applies when the target aeroplane is flying more or less across the line of flight. Where the target is flying straight towards the gunner, the chance is reduced because the vulnerable parts are in line and cover one another. On the other hand the shooting under these conditions is usually easier.

Method of Finding the Correct Allowance.

16. The distance of the point "A" from the centre of the film depends upon the assumed speed of the target aeroplane and the angle at which it is crossing the line of sight.

17. The target may or this purpose be assumed to have any pre-arranged speed, which need not necessarily be that at which it was actually moving. This assumed speed will generally be that for which the ring sight, used by the gunner, was designed (*i.e.* 100 m.p.h. with the sights now issued).

18. If the assumed speed is 100 m.p.h., and if the target is flying directly across the sight line, the distance of "A" from the centre of the film is 0.73 nches, or the radius of the largest circle, when using a camera which marks circles on the films.

19. If the target is flying towards or away from the camera

this distance must be reduced in proportion to the foreshortening of the body, and should a rough estimate only be required, can be guessed from the appearance of the aeroplane (*e.g.*, if the body appears to be foreshortened to half its natural length the distance of " A " from the centre is reduced by one half or to 0.37 inches at 100 m.p.h.

20. If a more accurate estimate of the allowance is required it can be obtained by reference to the 56 pictures (reproduced in Fig. 4) of a B.E. aeroplane taken from different aspects. These pictures are arranged in such a way that all in one column require the same allowance, so that it is only necessary to determine in which column the picture that most resembles the photo on the film lies, and then to note the allowance corresponding to this column.

21. To pick out this picture in the series it is necessary to consider from what point of view the actual photo was taken, and hence into which of the two groups of pictures it falls (*e.g.*, if it was taken from behind and below or in front and above it will fall in one group, and if from behind and above or in front and below, in the other). The comparison is then easiest made by rotating the film until the body of the aeroplane is parallel to the bodies of the key aeroplanes, and then noting the angle of the wings and position of the tail etc. In some cases it is necessary to reverse the film and look at it from the back to simplify the comparison.

22. When once the column containing the picture most nearly resembling the photo has been decided, the distance of the point " A " from the centre of the film can either be read off in inches at the top or the bottom of the column, or measured by dividers from the lengths given at the bottom of the columns, or if the films are marked with concentric circles the required distance can be marked off without any measurement at all, since the numbers 20, 40, 60, 80, 100 beneath the column represent the radius of the five circles on the film ; thus if the chosen picture is in the column above the number 60 the allowance is equal to the radius of the 60 or third circle and so on.

23. Another way of looking at this matter is to consider the numbers beneath each column as representing the speed at which any aeroplane in the column is crossing the line of sight, assuming that it is travelling through the air at 100 m.p.h. The radii of the five circles on the film represent the allowance which it is necessary to make, when using Mark VII ammunition, in order to hit any object crossing the line of sight at 20, 40, 60, 80 or 100 m.p.h. respectively.

24. The above operations, though lengthy to describe, can be performed very quickly ; with practice a few seconds only are required to spot the key picture which most nearly resembles the photograph, and hence to determine the proper allowance.

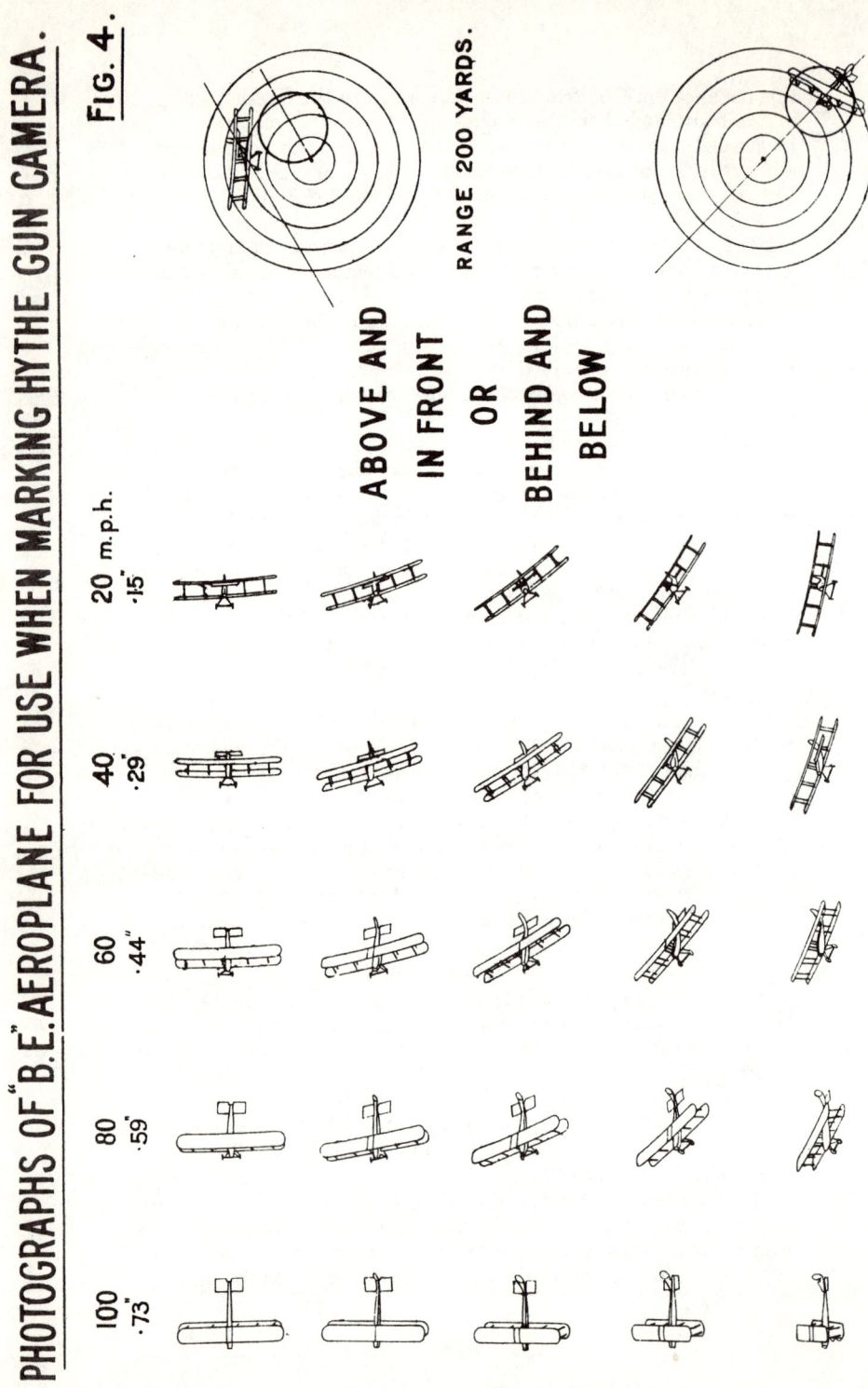

PHOTOGRAPHS OF "B.E." AEROPLANE FOR USE WHEN MARKING HYTHE GUN CAMERA.

FIG. 4.

RANGE 200 YARDS.

ABOVE AND
IN FRONT
OR
BEHIND AND
BELOW

| 100" .73" | 80" .59" | 60" .44" | 40" .29" | 20 m.p.h. .15" |

RANGE 130 YARDS.

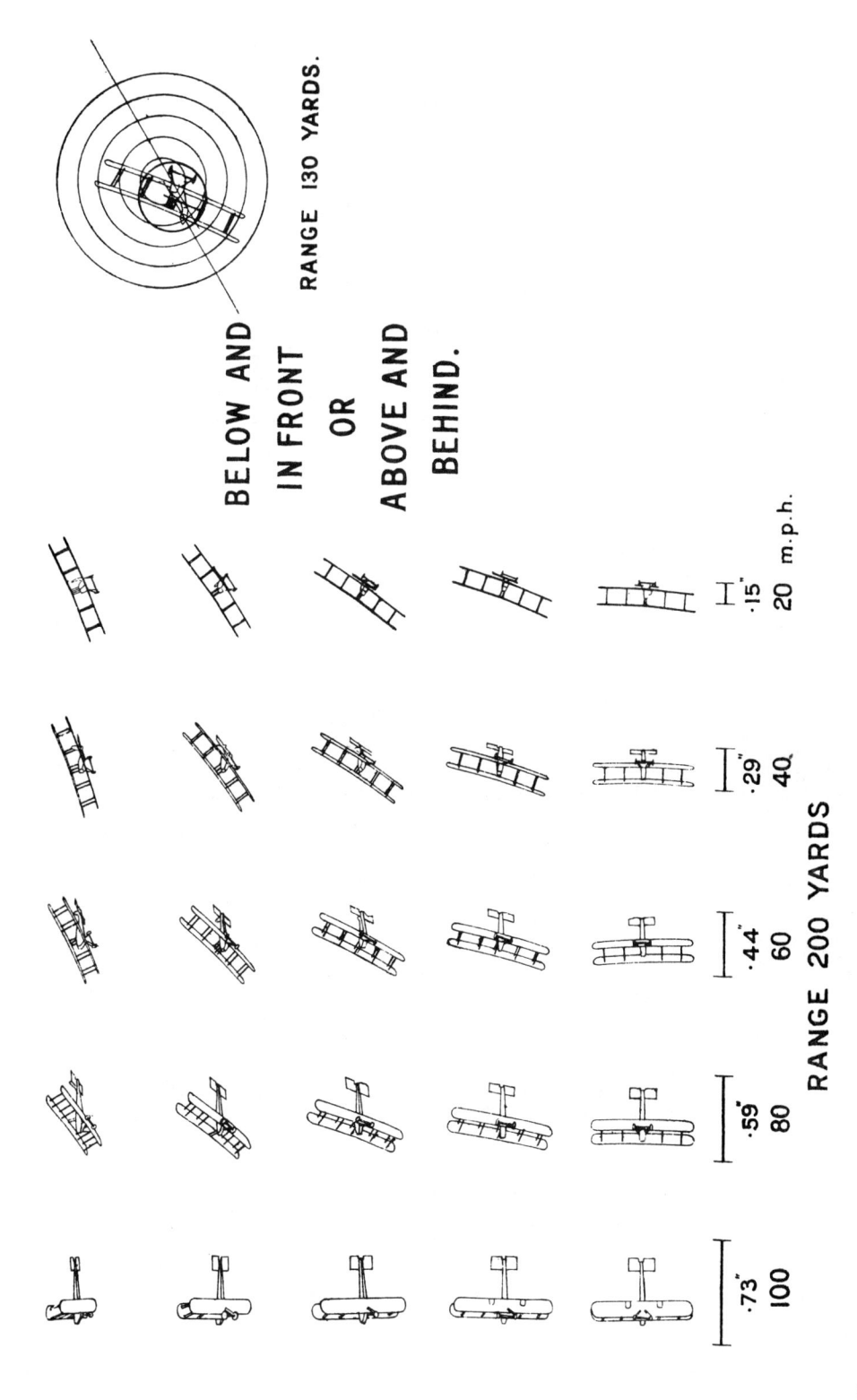

BELOW AND
IN FRONT
OR
ABOVE AND
BEHIND.

					.15"	20 m.p.h.
					.29"	40
					.44"	60
					.59"	80
					.73"	100

RANGE 200 YARDS

25. Should other speeds than 100 m.p.h. be assumed when using the camera, the allowances worked out must all be increased or decreased in proportion to the speed.

26. Distance of "A" from the centre of the film is independent of the range. If it is desired to find the range proceed as follows :—

27. Measure any well defined length of the photograph of the target aeroplane, *e.g.*, the apparent span, as foreshortened, and then measure the corresponding length in the chosen key photograph. The range in yards is then obtained by dividing the first of these lengths (photograph of target) into the second, and multiplying the result by 200.

28. If the target aeroplane is not a B.E., fairly accurate results can still be obtained from the key pictures if it is of the same type as a B.E., *i.e.*, tractor biplane, but if the span and body length are much different from those of a B.E. (*e.g.*, in a Bristol Scout) the range must be altered in proportion.

Note.

29. The actual key pictures were all taken from in ront, no pictures taken from behind are shown because these would, so far as outline and allowance is concerned, exactly produce the series taken from in front, except for the effect of perspective, which at these ranges is negligible.

30. An example of a graded series of practices with the gun camera is appended. These practices are in use at Hythe in the instruction course for aerial gunners.

(a) **On the ground, gun on ordinary Lewis tripod.**

Practice 1.—Pupil to be seated on the tripod with the gun camera in usual position on the gun. A stationary aeroplane is 200 yards away—front view.

The holder is taken out of the camera and the shutter opened. Each pupil is then told to aim directly at the centre of the machine, *i.e.*, (propeller boss) getting the circle and bead of ring sight in correct alignment with machine as though firing at it. The instructor checks his aim by ooking through the screen of camera. After pup ls have had a certain amount of practice a film is placed in camera and each pupil takes one aim at machine, presses the trigger and turns the handle one revolution.

In this practice the pupil's power of correct y aiming, correct use of sight, and also his ability to manipulate the camera, is observed.

Practice 2.—As for 1, except that the machine is placed at right angles to the firer. The holder is again removed and each pupil practises aiming at the machine as if it were flying at the speed represented by the ring on the gun, *i.e.*, he places the pilot of target machine on the edge of the ring, his aim being checked as in 1; the pupil then takes one photograph as in 1.

Practice 3.—As for 2, from the ground, but in this case the machine is flying across the front at about 500 feet. Pupil takes three consecutive aims at the machine allowing for deflection by means of the ring sight, placing the pilot of target machine on the edge of ring as in practice 2. In order to carry this practice out correctly it is essential that the target aeroplane maintains a straight course, flying at right angles to firer.

(b) Aerial practices.

Practice 4.—As for 1, but carried out in an aeroplane in the air. One machine is sent up as target, another machine (B.E. 2c.) is sent up containing a pupil armed with gun camera mounted on the Strange mounting. The target machine will manœuvre to follow directly behind machine with camera. The pupil then takes six consecutive aims, turning handle one revolution between each aim. In this practice the pupil must not open fire until he is within the limit range, *i.e.*, 100 to 300 yards. Marks will be allotted for correct aiming and ranging.

Practice 5.—As for 4, but the machines approach each other at various angles, and the gun is mounted on the side mounting. Each pupil takes six consecutive aims, placing the target machine within the ring sight according to its angle of approach.

Marks will be allotted as in Practice 4.

Practice 6.—Two pupils are sent up in separate machines and are armed with gun cameras. They are told to engage in combat, allowing for the movement, etc., of each other's machine exactly in the same manner as though actually fighting. Each pupil takes six aims as before and the results are checked by:—

- (*a*) The range at which fire was opened.
- (*b*) Position of machine in ring.
- (*c*) The angle at which the opposing machine was engaged so as to obtain a blind spot.

Part VII.—SHOOTING PRACTICE AT A PICTURE TARGET.

Object of Practice.

1. When shooting in the air with any ring sight, whether it be of the ring and wind vane type, or of the Aldis optical type, it is generally necessary to aim off the target aeroplane so that it appears in the ring in some particular position depending upon its aspect. The ability to estimate the correct position corre-

sponding to any aspect can best be acquired by constant practice at the aiming model, as described in Part V. Even when this knowledge has been attained, considerably more practice is required before a man can hold a firing gun on to a moving target and maintain continuously the correct allowance.

2. For this reason it is important that some form of practice on the ground shall be available which allows a gunner, already trained upon the aiming model, to put this experience into practice with an actual Lewis gun firing at a picture of an aeroplane. This practice must be so arranged that the concentration of his group and the correctness of his allowance can be easily checked, and so that the gunner does not remain fixed on his stand while shooting, but has to swing his gun in the same way as he would have to do in the air in order to follow the moving aeroplane.

3. Since the movement of gunner and target in the air is only relative, it is immaterial whether in the ground practice the target or the gunner is moved. For instance, if two machines are flying parallel and at the same speed, each will appear stationary to the other. This is represented on the ground by having a fixed picture of an aeroplane on a reduced scale broadside on, the gunner firing from a fixed point at a range reduced in proportion to the scale of the target so that the aeroplane has the same apparent size as on full scale. He is provided either with a fixed bead foresight and with ring backsight, or with an Aldis telescope fixed parallel to the axis of the gun. In either case he aims ahead of the picture in the direction of its apparent flight, making the correct allowance, and his bullets make a group somewhere ahead of the picture.

4. Again, the case of the target aeroplane flying directly at the gunner, but at right angles to his line of flight, so that he is shooting over the port side of his machine, the target will appear to move from right to left, that is, it will appear first well ahead of the gunner's machine on the port bow and as he flies on will gradually move astern. To follow it the gun must be swung from right to left while firing.

5. Any relative movement of gunner and target may be represented on the ground by fixing the target and putting the gunner on a turntable and slowly turning him round. The effect of this is to make the target pass across his field of fire, and in shooting at it he has to swing his gun so as to keep it bearing on the target, exactly as he would do in the air. Practice under these conditions will enable him while swinging the gun to keep his sights on the target, always with the correct allowance.

6. In order to correspond with conditions in the air it is important that both the range and aspect of the target should be constantly varied. This may be done by having a large number of pictures of aeroplanes in different aspects, ranging from flying

straight towards the gunner to flying straight across him, and by making him fire at these targets at different ranges.

7. A range with which this practice can be carried out can be very simply made as follows.

Construction of a Suitable Target and Range (*see* Figs. 5, 6 and 7).

8. The target, which is fixed, consists of a wooden frame about 15 by 12 feet, covered with light canvas (Fig. 5). In front of this screen, and touching it, is hung a light batten frame A, covered front and back with stout millboard or three-ply wood or other similar material, the frame being supported by cords D D attached to two corners and slung over the top edge of the screen ; these cords carrying balance weights at the other ends.

9. Other cords may be attached to the lower corners of the frame and fastened to hooks at the foot of the screen ; these prevent the frame from blowing about with the wind.

10. Several sheets of paper showing pictures of aeroplanes in various aspects to 1/10th scale are required. These pictures show the aeroplane from different points of view, and the more realistic they can be made the better, because the gunner should have every legitimate aid possible to enable him to estimate rapidly the aspect at which the picture aeroplane is presented to him.

11. These pictures are pasted on the millboard of the target frame, and should be so placed that, if the gunner shoots with the correct allowance, the bullets will strike on the canvas part of the screen. Care should be taken not to place the picture so that the body of the aeroplane is parallel to the edges of the frame, as this unfairly assists the gunner in estimating the direction in which the body is pointing. If a number of target frames are prepared each carrying two pictures, one on either side, they can be very quickly changed, and thus the aspect and direction of flight of the target can easily be varied for each shoot.

12. The bullets fired will then show upon the canvas screen, and the accuracy with which the allowance has been made can be rapidly checked by a method explained later. If the screen be whitewashed from time, to time, all old bullet marks will be obliterated, and new ones can be easily distinguished.

13. The gunner fires from a gun mounting, preferably a Scarff mounting, fixed in a mock-up of part of a nacelle which is carried on a turntable (A in Fig. 6). An ordinary contractor's 2 ft. gauge railway turntable does very well, but the surface on which it runs should be good so that the gunner can be turned round smoothly and without shake. It is best to mount the turntable 3 or 4 feet from the ground, so that the gunner fires slightly downwards, as by this means the size of the butt behind the target may

Fig. 5.

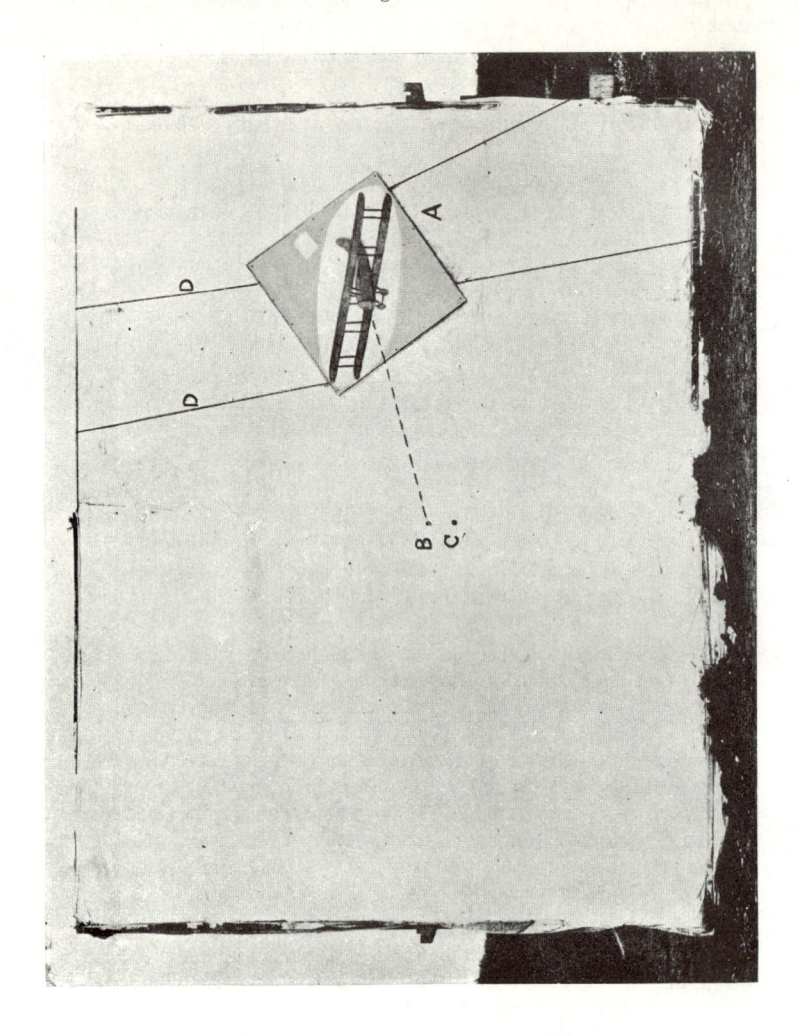

Following Fig. 5.

Fig. 6.

be reduced. Attached to the turntable is a lever by means of which a man can turn the gunner round, as shown in Fig. 6.

SKETCH OF ARRANGEMENT OF TURNTABLE NACELLE FOR TARGET SHOOTING PRACTICE.

Fig. 7.

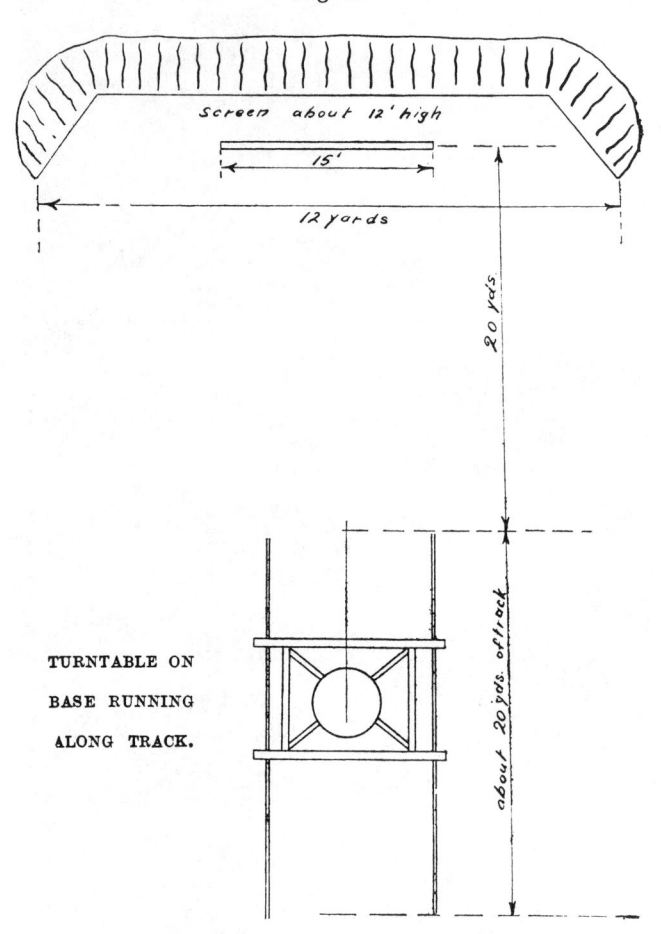

Screen about 12' high

15'

12 yards

20 yds

TURNTABLE ON BASE RUNNING ALONG TRACK.

about 20 yds. of track

14. It is a good plan to mount the turntable and its stand on wheels, running on rails or otherwise, so that it can be easily moved a few yards towards the target. These should have a sufficiently wide base for the platform to be quite steady when the nacelle is being turned. By this means the distance of the gunner from the target, which it is important to vary constantly

in order to correspond to the varying ranges which occur in actual practice, may conveniently be changed between the shoots, from say 10 to 30 yards. By turning the gunner and at the same time moving him along the track during the shoot, the conditions are made still more realistic; if this is done, however, the marking becomes more difficult, as the correct grouping centre varies during the shoot. This system of mounting the turntable on a truck is not shown in Fig. 6, but it is shown in Fig. 7, which is a dimensioned plan of a range constructed according to this system. The butt behind the target will be of such a height as is necessary for safety.

15. In using this range the gunner is first turned away from the target so that he cannot see which silhouette is being put on the target. One of the silhouettes is then hung up in such a position that the bullets, if correctly aimed, will fall on the canvas screen. The turntable is then slowly turned round, until the target comes into the view of the gunner, who begins to shoot as soon as he can bring his gun to bear, putting on the correct allowance by means of the ring sight in accordance with the aspect of machine shown on the silhouette. His rotation may be continued right round during his shoot, or may be stopped and reversed, and then possibly again reversed and moved ahead. The rotation of the turntable at any moment may be in any direction and at any speed up to the rate of two revolutions per minute, corresponding to the maximum rate at which he is ever likely to have to traverse his gun in practice.

16. In this way the gunner can be suddenly presented with a target of unknown aspect at an unexpected range, and he will thus have to decide the necessary allowance and fire his shots correctly, in the time taken by the target to cross the field of fire.

17. The silhouettes provided for this practice are all of 1/10th scale. Consequently a distance of 20 yards on this range corresponds to 200 yards in actual practice. Also, the allowance on the target is 1/10th of the allowance for the movement of the target aeroplane at the corresponding range on a full scale. If the gunner has fired correctly at the picture his bullets will not have struck the picture itself, but will have hit the canvas screen at a point ahead of it equal to this distance.

Method of Checking the Accuracy of the Allowance.

18. To find the spot which should have been hit, proceed as follows :—

19. Lay a straight edge, or a stretched string, along the axis of the body of the picture, and on this line mark off a point " B " at a distance in front of the vital part of the picture corresponding to the correct allowance (*see* Fig. 5). This is the point on which the centre of the ring should have been laid if the gun were aimed correctly.

20. The actual bullets would, if correctly fired, strike about 6 inches below the point " B " because the barrel of the gun is about 6 inches below the sight line. Mark off, therefore, a point " C " 6 inches below " B." This is the point where the bullets would have struck had the gun been correctly aimed.

21. The photograph of the target, Fig. 5, shows a silhouette in place, and the points " B " and " C " marked on the canvas. These points should not, of course, be visible to the gunner in actual practice.

22. The distance of the point " B " in front of the vital spot depends upon the ring sight used, the range, and the apparent angle of approach of the picture target. With a 100 m.p.h. ring sight, and a picture of an aeroplane flying directly across the screen, the distance is almost exactly one-fifteenth of the range, *i.e.*, at 20 yards this distance is equal to 4 feet and at 30 yards it is 6 feet. For a foreshortened photograph the distance is reduced in proportion to the foreshortening of the body, *i.e.*, if the aeroplane is shown flying at 30 degrees to the line of sight, the distance is halved.

23. A series of poster pictures of aeroplanes seen from different aspects will be issued for this practice. These pictures will carry two marks to give the correct line of flight, and a mark in the centre of the vital region. Each picture will also carry a table showing the appropriate allowance at different ranges. Until these can be provided, however, silhouettes can easily be made locally.

24. A perfect shoot at the target should show a small group with its centre at C. If it is desired to ascertain whether a vital hit would have been scored, prick off the shots and also the point C on a piece of thin paper and then transfer the paper, keeping it parallel to itself, so that the point C on it lies over the pilot's seat. The pricked shots will then show where the aeroplane would have been hit in real shooting.

Or :—Prepare beforehand outline drawings on tracing paper, one for each of the poster pictures. After the shoot has been made, and the point C found, place the tracing drawing corresponding to the picture target, with its centre of the vital region on the point C and its body pointing in the same direction as the body of the aeroplane on the picture. This affords a quick check upon the gunner's shooting.

Part VIII.—NOTES ON THE USE OF VARIOUS PRACTICES.

Necessity for Ground Practices.

1. In most air fighting the gunner, before actually firing, has to get his gun to bear upon the enemy aeroplane, decide whether the opportunity is worth the expenditure of ammunition, and estimate and make the necessary allowance for the enemy's speed. In a close fight all these things have to be done with the greatest rapidity if any effective shooting is to be got in at all, and the gunner is generally working under very considerable difficulties owing to the diving, banking, &c., of his own aeroplane.

2. For this reason no operation which cannot be performed almost without conscious thought will be of much value in a close fight. The gunner requires all his thinking powers to attend to the general features of the fight and has practically none to spare for the details of aiming.

3. It is generally found very difficult to get anything like sufficient actual flying to develop the required instincts to the high pitch necessary for accurate air shooting, under actual fighting conditions, and it is therefore essential that every air practice should have its counter-part upon the ground, where an almost unlimited time may be spent in practice. These ground practices should, as far as possible, teach exactly the same operations as are required in the air, so that the gunner, when he gets his necessarily limited air practice, may not have to learn anything new, but may give his whole attention to applying the skill he has obtained on the ground to the more difficult and uncomfortable conditions necessarily met in the air, and may have his mind free to consider such questions as the extra allowance necessary for possible variation in the enemy's speed due to diving, climbing, &c.

Distinction between Aiming and Grouping.

4. For a man to become a good air gunner he must acquire skill of two kinds :—

   (1) Skill in estimating the necessary allowance for the enemy's speed.
   (2) Skill in holding the gun steadily in relation to a moving target despite the recoil of the gun and the oscillations of the aeroplane that carries it.

These can be taught separately at first and eventually combined when the pupil has become familiar with the methods of allowing for enemy speed and is able to hold his gun fairly steadily on a target when rapidly traversing his gun.

5. The following is a possible scheme of practices to achieve this end. The apparatus necessary for all these exists and is in constant use either at Hythe, Orfordness or elsewhere.

6. The reason that so many different practices are included in the scheme is that it is impossible to devise any single practice that will combine all the requirements necessary for good shooting under actual fighting conditions. This can only be obtained in a real fight where both combatants stand a great chance of being killed. The essential parts of the operations necessary are all contained in the following practices, but each individual practice necessarily leaves out some essential to real fighting. The notes on each practice, which follow the table, are intended to indicate roughly the reason for the practice and the deficiencies in it which make the other practices necessary.

7. **Table of Practices for Training with Ring Sights.**

For teaching aiming off without shooting.

On ground	... ...	Aiming Model. See Part 5.
In air	... ...	Gun camera. See Part 6.

For teaching shooting without aiming off.

On ground	... ...	Practice aiming direct at fixed targets, from a revolving mounting.
In air	... ...	Shooting from aeroplane at large fixed targets using compensated sights.

For teaching shooting and aiming off combined.

On ground	... ...	Picture target. See Part 7.
In air	... ...	Shooting at flag targets from an aeroplane.

Aiming Model.

8. This shows quickly and simply the reason for the allowance in shooting, and allows a very great amount of practice at judging the allowance to be obtained in a short time. Several pupils can work at once with one model and instructor, and all their shots can be rapidly checked.

9. The deficiency in this practice is that it does not give the idea of judging a constantly changing allowance on a moving object. It should therefore be considered as giving only the ground work for training in aiming off. It does not at all follow that a man who can aim off correctly at the model will be able to do the same in the air, without considerably further practice.

Gun Camera.

10. This provides a means of checking aiming in the air under fighting conditions. Practice under these conditions is essential as the difficulties, both physical and mental, of bringing the gun to bear on the enemy with the correct allowance are very great, even to a man who knows at a glance what allowance should be made under all conditions. It is also essential that a man's performance under these conditions should be checked, as it is difficult even after considerable experience to tell whether one has judged one's allowances and ranges correctly, and the results on the films are often very surprising, especially those taken in a vigorous fight.

11. The elements lacking in this practice are the necessity of holding the allowance correctly on a moving target, and the recoil of the gun. It is very much easier to pick an opportune moment when the allowance is correct and expose one film, than to hold the gun steadily and correctly on a moving target. It is hoped to produce a cinematograph camera for this purpose, but this is not yet available.

Direct Ground Shooting.

12. This is no doubt necessary for early training and is comparatively easy to provide. It should be remembered, however, that shooting from a fixed mount at a fixed target is very unlike shooting in the air, as the gunner can in this case steady himself and set his muscles in a way which he cannot do in air fighting, where the enemy is always moving relatively to himself. Quite a slow rate of revolution of the mounting is sufficient to make the gunner keep his muscles on the move and makes a very great difference to the size of group obtainable.

Air Shooting at a Fixed Target.

13. This should always be done at a large target using compensated sights. The object is to teach the gunner to get a good concentrated group aiming directly at an object from the air, and to give him confidence that his compensating sight really does allow approximately for his air speed. The target must therefore be large or the concentration of the group cannot be observed, the number of hits on a small target in any one shoot being largely a matter of luck, even if the shooting is good.

14. Quite useful work can be done with a large target lying on the ground, but if a large flag target suspended from a kite balloon can be obtained, the shooting can be made much more realistic, the aeroplane passing below and on a level with the target, as well above it.

15. The defect of this practice is that the relative movements of the target and the aeroplane are very different from those of

two aeroplanes in a fight. The gunner therefore does not get any useful experience of shooting in a fight, but merely checks the accuracy of his aim and of his own compensated sight when in flight.

Picture Target Practice.

16. The object of this practice is to combine aiming with allowances, and firing while traversing the gun. Even although a gunner may know exactly what allowance to make for any given appearance of an aeroplane, and may be able to make a good group with his gun, a certain amount of practice is necessary before he can combine the two. If a ring and bead sight is used the practice is also of value in training the gunner to hold the bead in the centre of the ring whilst at the same time observing that the aeroplane is correctly placed in the ring.

17. This practice has the merit that the gunner has to estimate his allowance from the appearance of the picture, and has to put his estimation to immediate effect by actually firing the gun, exactly as he would in the air; the accuracy with which he has done this can then be checked very easily and quickly.

18. The defect of the practice is that a certain amount of imagination is required to see the silhouettes or pictures as though they were approaching or receding from the observer, and it is for this reason that it is important to have good pictures where possible. The practice of course gives no experience of actual fighting conditions but it is intended merely for training the gunner in the actual operations of aiming and firing. Fighting experience to supplement this practice is obtainable with the gun camera. A gunner who can do well both at the picture target and with the camera in a sham fight should certainly prove to be a good shot when he comes to a real fight.

Air Shooting at a Towed Flag.

19. This practice is valuable in that it provides the only chance the gunner gets of firing at a rapidly moving target from an aeroplane, and thus gives him confidence that his previous training, hitherto rather unreal, has in fact enabled him to hit a rapidly moving target in the air from a rapidly moving aeroplane.

20. One defect of this target, however, is that it does not look like an aeroplane, and gives very little indication of its angle of approach, so that the gunner's previous training in estimating the angle of approach of an aeroplane is of little use to him. Another defect is that the area presented to the gunner becomes very small when the target is flying towards or away from him.

21. For the above reasons it is only practicable to fire at the flag when it is moving across the field of view, so that the gunner

gets little or no practice at judging allowances and very little experience of actual fighting conditions.

Notes on other Forms of Practice.

22. Other practices such as aiming at clay pigeons, shooting at disappearing aeroplanes, &c., may be valuable to train the gunner's general powers of quick decision, but bear no other definite relation to the problem of shooting in the air. Although these may be useful to keep up the gunner's interest in his work, they should not replace practices, such as those outlined above, which teach a necessary part of air fighting.

23. Shooting directly at a small travelling aeroplane, unless the aeroplane always points directly at the gunner, is apt to be misleading, because this is the one thing that never should be done by a gunner using compensating sights.

1918
Fighting the S.E.

FIGHTING THE S.E., JANUARY, 1918.

Having been requested to write some notes under the above heading, I must ask pilots to consider them as the method of an individual (myself) and not as an effort to lay down anything like hard and fast rules when fighting the S.E.

Scouts.—Enemy scouts are not often seen above 15,000 feet during the winter months, the reason being, I suggest, that the Albatross Scout, which constitutes the bulk of enemy scouts, is a very cold machine in comparison with the S.E. 5, so that enemy pilots do not go up high during the cold weather unless for some good reason; therefore, I usually take my patrol over the lines at anything over 14,000 feet.

Nine times out of ten I am above enemy scouts during the whole of my patrol.

In attacking enemy scouts, surprise is usually aimed at, but the sun and wind direction are a great help when intelligently used.

If you think the E.A. have not seen you, try to attack from the east, and when going down give the rear machines of your own formation plenty of time to close up, so that each member can attack one E.A simultaneously.

Whilst attacking E.A. scouts, one should keep plenty of engine, so as to keep zooming above the formation of E.A. the whole time. I find that if S.E.'s attack E.A. from above, that they can remain above the whole time, but now I find that as soon as we attack scouts, one of them, more likely than not their leader, flies off out of the fight and climbs his utmost until he is above the top S.E., and then he comes back, and it is just the thought that there is one Hun above you that divides your attention and nullifies your advantage in height, so as soon as I see the one Hun going off I climb as well and this usually frustrates his intentions.

I consider it a patrol leader's work to pay more attention to the main points affecting a fight than to do all the fighting himself. The main points are—(1) arrival of more E.A. who have tactical advantage, *i.e.*, height; (2) Patrol drifting too far east; (3) Patrol getting below bulk of enemy formation. As soon as any of these circumstances occur, it is time to take advantage of the S.E.'s superior speed over E.A. scouts and break off the fight, rally behind leader and climb west of E.A. until you are above them before attacking them again.

When any of the above circumstances occur I fire a red light, which is a signal to my patrol to break off the fight and follow me, and we find that this is very effective.

Two-seaters.—I have had many more combats with 2-seater E.A. than scouts, so hope I am able to give a few tips.

I think a lot of pilots over-estimate the death-dealing qualities of the 2-seater's rear gun ; at the same time, however, one should not become careless, because enemy observers are usually highly trained and can shoot very accurately, especially at quite long range. Therefore, when attacking a 2-seater, it should be a pilot's main object, after surprise, to get to close range (100 yards) without letting E.A. gunner shoot at you. This is quite possible, because, in December, I shot down six 2-seaters in succession without any E.A. gunner getting a single shot at me, although in each case the E.A. had seen me approaching and had good time to make up his mind what to do. The six E.A. were not shot down in one fight but were successive combats on different days.

Two-seaters keep a very good look-out above but pay very little attention under their level. Therefore try to surprise them from underneath and climb up under their fuselage and tail plane. The position from which a pilot can do most damage to a 2-seater at the least risk to himself and machine, is 100 yards behind it and 50 feet below. If, however, you are in this position and E.A. turns, you will at once come under his fire, and your object is to keep out of his field of fire as much as possible, so, therefore, keep in a direct line behind his fuselage, so that, if he turns to the right, you turn to the left and *vice-versâ*. To do this manœuvre successfully, one must have superior speed to do the outside circle, which is the inevitable position if one is to use E.A.'s tail and fuselage as cover to the best advantage whilst E.A. is turning. As soon as E.A. gunner sees he cannot fire at you from this position he will try the other direction.

Now whilst changing from one bank to the other, E.A. will be in a good position to fire at if you are quick enough. Try a short burst to confuse the pilot. His tendency when alarmed is usually to dive, which is just what you want him to do. No gunner can stand upright in a machine that is doing over 130 miles per hour and do accurate shooting, because the wind pressure against him at this speed is enormous. In several cases I have seen a 2-seater dive so steeply and fast that the gunner has been blown flat on the fuselage. When this happens you need not worry about E.A.'s rear gun. I find that when diving on the tail of a 2-seater, one usually does not need to allow a deflection, but just shoot straight into him. The chances of a decision when fighting a 2-seater are greater west of the line than east, because when a 2-seater is attacked west of the line, nine times out of ten he will push his nose down and do " S " turns, shooting at you as opportunity offers, but after you have had some practice you will be able to sit under his tail as safe as anywhere provided that you do not become careless. On the contrary a 2-seater attacked east of the line only needs to keep going round in one direction for any length of time and he can then do all the shooting whilst you can do practically none. Whilst turning like this, help for the E.A. is practically certain to arrive in the form of E.A. Scouts. In fighting 2-seaters west of the line, pilots should think before attacking what the E.A.'s work is, so as to let E.A. get as far west as he wishes to, so that you will then have ample time to shoot him down before he gets east of the line. Most 2-seaters will stand a lot of shooting about before giving any evidence of damage.

The above method of attacking a 2-seater is what I advise, but a good deal of practice is necessary before you are able to keep up with a 2-seater at close range without being shot at.

I find that it is very difficult to shoot the pilot from directly behind because you probably hit the gunner first, who collapsed in a heap in his cock-pit, and you go on shooting and are simply filling the gunner with lead, and also a hugh petrol tank which is usually situated between pilot and gunner, and the pilot gets off without a scratch, so once you have shot the gunner you can afford to close right up and shoot the pilot at your leisure.

I have had a lot of combats with 2-seaters and have been hit by their fire very seldom indeed, and then only a few bullet holes.

The advantages and possibilities of this form of attack should be obvious to anyone who gives the subject thought. Even at 50 feet below an E.A. at 100 yards, one has to zoom ever so slightly to get one's sights on E.A., and it is to be remembered that the S.E.'s guns fire at an upward angle to the line of flight.

In conclusion, I wish to point out that, although I have achieved good results with this method of attack, I think the Huns will take measures to repel it in one way or another, and I also contend that a 2-seater in which the pilot and observer co-operate well, is more than a match for a Scout, no matter how well handled.

As a final tip, one should be very alert when firing at an E.A. at close range, so that, when E.A. falls to pieces, as they very often do, after being fired at a lot, that one does not fly through the wreckage. I narrowly missed flying through a pair of E.A.'s wings recently.

1918
Notes on Aerial Fighting
'Bring Down Your Hun!'

BRING DOWN YOUR HUN!

Object of a Fighting School.

Pilots and observers are taught, during their training, to fly and to shoot, and the object of the fighting school is to combine the two so that the pilot automatically puts his machine in such a position that he can use his guns accurately, without the enemy being able to use his. The school also teaches co-operation between pilot and observer, and between a number of machines working together. At the school the pilot gets used to manœuvring his machine in close proximity to a number of others.

Divisions of the Course of Training.

Pilots and observers are tested to see that they can correct jambs immediately, and to see that they can use their sights. Pilots are further tested to see that they can fly their machines without thinking about it.

Then the instruction in the air commences. The instructor takes up a pupil in a two-seater machine and fights another machine, both on a pre-arranged scheme. The instructor should talk to the pupil the whole time while this is being done, telling him what the attacker is doing, and what is being done to defeat the attack. This period finishes with a short fight between the two machines.

The instructor then fights the pupil on a service type machine till the pupil can make a good fight.

Pupils are next sent up to fight each other.

At some period of this fighting the instructor leads a formation of pupils. The formation is taught to fly low, to dive at ground targets, to break up and reform, and to look for machines in the air.

Pupils are now sent up in service type machines, fully armed, and are taught to fire at stationary targets, moving targets, and towed targets.

The pupil is thus shewn everything which is necessary for him to know in order to bring down enemy machines. The only thing the school cannot teach is the little extra amount of determination which makes the successful fighter. This determination shews the difference between the useful and the useless fighter, but as every pupil belongs to the English speaking people, only a very few pupils fail.

All pupils should know how to attack both two and single seaters, and how to defend themselves on their service type machine.

The principles for attacking large machines with more than one engine, and which are usually employed for night work are the same as those for attacking heavy two seaters.

While at the school pupils should be given as free a hand as possible to practise the things in which they are weak; but as time is limited there should be no straight flying done merely to put up the flying hours.

When practising low flying, care should be taken to choose those places where no damage will be done to stock, where the low

"BRING DOWN YOUR HUN!"

machines will not annoy other people, and where they will not interfere with the tilling of the ground by frightening the horses. On no account should low flying take place near remount and racing stables. Machines which fly low near the hangars delay instruction and become a perfect nuisance, so that this should not be done.

Discipline.

A pilot, in order to become a good fighter, must be well disciplined, in the best condition physically, and, above all, determined to bring down every enemy machine he sees. This latter remark does not mean that every pilot should barge into any number of the enemy he sees, but that he should use his head in the approach, and, once fire has been opened, he should not leave his Hun till the latter is downed.

Just as an infantry man does his foot drill with precision, so also must a fighting pilot be able to keep a good formation and perform all manœuvres correctly and automatically. The leader of a formation relies altogether on his pilots for the successful carrying out of his ideas; and the safety of each unit in the formation depends almost entirely on the support given by the others. It is no longer the rule for pilots to play a "lone" hand, and the success of an attack is ensured by the close co-operation of all pilots.

The word "Discipline" does not mean a mere passive obedience to signals or commands; neither does it mean that pilots should huddle together. One often hears the remark applied to the Huns after they have made one of their mass attacks—"What splendid discipline!" .As a matter of fact it is usually far from being so. Men are often driven forward at the muzzle of a pistol, and the Huns attack in mass merely to prevent the indisciplined rank and file from running away.

The discipline required of a fighter is much more than this. He must always be in his place, and should be so used to his leader's methods that he can anticipate the next command. If the pilot is not in his place, he will not bring down the enemy aircraft which the leader has put in his way; and there is nothing worse than missing a good chance. The enemy seldom stand and fight so that a chance missed hardly ever recurs.

A fighting pilot should learn all he can on the ground and when flying near his aerodrome. He should be familiar with his machine, and make certain that he can perform all manœuvres correctly both near the ground and also at a height. This latter is important as machines can be stunted much better near the ground than they can be at a height; if one is not ready for this chances will be missed.

Pilots with a little experience find that all machines are the same to fly. New types are always unhandy to the touch. Therefore it is necessary for every pilot to practise on the type of machine he will use at the front. All pilots get to like the type of machine to which they are accustomed, and the expert on any modern type is just as good as the expert on any other modern type. No pilot in a squadron can know when any type becomes obsolescent because he has not the data to go on to which Headquarters have access.

One type of machine in 1916, admittedly out of date, brought down 11 Huns in a week without a single casualty in the squadron.

"BRING DOWN YOUR HUN!"

When coming into action all pilots must follow their leader closely, and the leader should manœuvre his formation into the best position for the attack. It is taken for granted that all pilots know how to shoot, and how to correct stoppages.

A certain machine was attacked by four Huns, all much faster. The Huns dived to the attack. The first was brought down, and the gun jammed. The next two Huns did not dare approach, they fired from a long range and went down. The fourth Hun came to see why our machine was not shooting, and arrived exactly at the moment the gun again came into action, with fatal results for the Hun.

Directly a pilot has decided to attack, he must attack ALL OUT. Nothing else matters compared with this. If one is really determined, and has made up one's mind that the enemy is coming down, the enemy *is* coming down for an absolute certainty. When one fails it is absolutely one's own fault—call it luck, want of judgment, or what you like. A few Huns can equal us, none are better, most are very much worse.

For the fighter there should be no question of defending one's-self alone. Every manœuvre that one does should be made with the idea of getting into a favourable position for the attack. The only safe method of defending one's-self is to attack the enemy. Fights should only be broken off with the intention of enticing the enemy to break up his formation and render himself more vulnerable, or in order to gain height, the better to attack.

A moderately good pilot who is really determined is better than, and will bring down every time, the undecided pilot, no matter how good the undecided pilot may be.

It is a curious thing, but there is hardly a case in which a first-class enemy pilot has been brought down on our side of the lines. With us it is different, and our best pilots take the same chance as our last joined.

Does this mean that the enemy dare not attack us when the odds are even?

To illustrate this the following are some instances:—

One of our pilots, early in the war when machines were unarmed, met an enemy machine on the enemy side of the line. Our pilot dived and zummed at the enemy till the latter lost his nerve and landed, completely wrecking his machine. I believe this machine was the first one brought down by one of our pilots. The pilot of our machine has since been taken prisoner, being forced to land, owing to lack of petrol, during a long reconnaissance.

Immelmann, although one of Germany's pilots, was advertised by them as though his mere name could frighten us, shewing that they did not have many men who could fly well. He was shot down by quite a young pilot on the enemy side of the lines.

Boelcke, another fine pilot, was run into by one of his own formation, consisting of 12 machines, on the enemy side of the lines, when attacking two English machines.

It is believed that neither of these pilots came our side of the lines or that when they did come they lost all their "dash," because little really first-class piloting by the enemy has been seen behind our trenches.

"BRING DOWN YOUR HUN!"

When talking about the enemy pilots, one should recall the fight put up by Voss when he single handed attacked 11 of our machines, all faster than his own. He went for the nearest of our machines each in turn, and his power of manœuvre was so great that he was able to catch each at a disadvantage for a long time. At any moment he could have broken off the fight and gone home, but quite contrary to the usual enemy tactics, he elected to stay and fight it out to a finish. It was unfortunately necessary to bring Voss down. He was far and away the finest fighter the Huns have ever had or are likely to have; and he stands out all the more because the Huns as a rule are heavy handed and hate close-in fighting.

Let us go back a long time. At the Battle of Hastings (1066) we formed up in a line of triangular formations, almost the same as the formation we now use in flying, *i.e.*, the best man in front and the others supporting him in the shape of a wedge. This formation could not be broken by the enemy till they pretended to run away; when our formations broke up, and were defeated in detail.

This is usually the fault of the present-day formations. The enemy nearly always run away, and we break up and chase them and thus lose touch. The national characteristics are much the same now as then, so that this battle should be a warning to us. Remember that by breaking our formation on that one day we lost the whole of England to the enemy.

At the battle of Auray (1365) our very mobile archers were up against the very heavily armoured knights, and they found that the arrows glanced off the armour. The archers threw down their bows, seized the battle axes out of the enemy's hands, and proceeded to hit the knights on the head with their own weapons. Here we get the lesson of close in-fighting which should not be forgotten.

The Analogy of Cavalry and Aeroplanes, showing their similar development.

When one reads the accounts of Cavalry actions, it will be noticed that there have been very distinct periods.

At first the horse was used to carry the rider from place to place, and the rider never thought of coming into action on his horse. The machines early in 1914 never fought, and were used merely to carry the crew to different places from which the enemy could be seen, *i.e.*, somewhere above them.

Then came the period when horsemen were heavily armoured. They came together slowly and could not be brought down by the firearms of the day. This period corresponds to the time when the Germans sent "Copper-bottom," a heavily armoured, slow machine, to fly low over the trenches. Our similar machine was the "Tin Vicker's," amongst others.

Then came the period when cavalry were armed with pistols. They cantered up to the enemy, fired from the saddle (a very unstable position), and cantered on to the attack. This corresponds to the tractor machine period, when machines had to turn before they could fire, so that they could never really press home the attack. The cavalry were always beaten off by musket fire.

"BRING DOWN YOUR HUN!"

The last period was when the Duke of Marlborough definitely committed the cavalry to shock action. They were not now allowed to fire from the saddle before the charge. They charged straight in on the enemy. Note how well they did in the campaign of 1702–13 in Flanders.

This is the period we have now reached in flying. We must hold our fire till we are right in on the enemy, and although we do not actually collide, we should beat the enemy by weight of fire and the prestige which a quick attack gives.

As guns improved it was possible for horsed artillery to work with the cavalry. This stage we are approaching, as we can already use large guns on machines.

Fire Discipline.

Fire discipline means that fire must be opened only and exactly at the moment that the leader intends it should be. Indiscriminate and long range fire must be stopped altogether. Machines working in teams should open fire together, or when it helps both machines, otherwise the enemy will be driven off in an undecided action. Care should be taken, when more than one machine attacks a Hun, that all machines have enough air space in which to manœuvre, so that pilots need not spend all their time avoiding each other. Every Hun who is engaged and not brought down gets a little more experience, so that next time he is attacked it is harder to down him.

Fire discipline was considered so important by the Duke of Marlborough, that he used to put the whole army through the platoon fire exercise by signal of flag or drum (1707).

The English speaking peoples have always been famous for their cool head and accurate aim, and this is still borne out by the large numbers of Hun machines brought down with such little loss to the Service.

STUNT FLYING.

The Loop.

First of all tie yourself into the machine, making certain that your belt fits. This will prevent your being anxious in case you miss doing what you intend.

In order to loop, the controls should be worked just as gently as they are for any other manœuvre. If the elevator is pulled too hard the machine stalls before it gets over the top of the loop, and falls sideways or tail first. This does not matter, except that you have not done what you intended.

It is not necessary in a fast machine to push the nose down before looping, and in some machines a better loop is made if the engine is throttled down a little as one gets to the top.

It might be thought that one would lose less height if one flew the

"BRING DOWN YOUR HUN!"

machine right round with the engine full on, but this is not the case. If the engine is kept on, the machine is pulled downwards a long way before recovering, and although the time of the loop may be less, the distance flown will be greater.

To come out of a loop quickly, directly the machine is upside-down, push the control forward as though one were trying to push the nose of the machine up. The machine will stall at once, the nose swinging down very quickly, giving one control in a very short distance.

In a small machine if the controls are worked roughly, because they have such a large surface compared with the machine's wings, the machine will not obey quickly, but will stall owing to the drag of these surfaces.

In any modern machine there is never any danger, but the machine will obey quicker if the controls are worked gently.

Stalling to One Side.

In order to do a quick turn without losing height, a useful manœuvre is to pull the control back till the machine is flying vertically upwards. Put on rudder to one side or other and the nose of the machine will fall to that side. The rudder must be put on before the machine loses flying speed, otherwise one gets no control, and the machine will hang in the air. As soon as the nose is pointing downwards the control may be pulled back, and the machine will fly on a course parallel to the original course, about one machine's length away, and in the opposite direction.

Half Roll.

In order to "half roll" pull the control back and to one side, at the same time put on rudder in the same direction. These movements should be done quickly and firmly, but not violently. The nose of the machine rises a little, and the machine turns over on its back. Put the controls central and then pull back the elevators. The machine will then come back and will fly along a course parallel to the original one, and below it. Less height is lost if the control is pushed forward when the machine is upside-down so that the machine stalls as in the case of the loop. A combination of these two manœuvres enables the machine to be turned very quickly and in a small radius, without losing height.

The Roll.

With the engine on, pull back the control, and pull it to one side as far as it will go. At the same time put on full rudder on the same side. The machine will turn completely round and go on flying in the original direction. In some machines the control must be put central before the machine has completed the roll or it will go on rolling more than is intended. Compared with a machine flying normally the roll causes a machine to lose about 60 yards, so that it may be useful to roll when a machine is close behind, thus making him overshoot his target.

"BRING DOWN YOUR HUN!"

The Spin.

In order to get into a spin the control must be pulled back till the machine is stalled, and then full rudder must be put on one way or the other.

To get into a good spin one should put on full rudder and warp the same way as well as pulling back the control. To stop a spin put all the controls central, and then the elevator may be pushed slightly forward so as to help the machine to get into a nose dive. Pilots should have no hesitation in putting the nose of the machine vertically down in a case like this. The machine in this position soon gathers speed and the controls can be used in the ordinary manner. Remember to put the controls central or the machine will go into a spin the opposite way owing to lack of flying speed.

This is one way of getting an enemy off one's tail. It is not recommended as one loses such a lot of height; it is very hard to come out at exactly the angle one intends, and after all, one finds the enemy waiting for the machine to steady down, when he gets a practically sitting shot at it.

Side Slipping.

If one is flying on a level keel, and if one puts on rudder the machine will travel crab-wise, and not in the direction in which the nose is pointing. This may be useful as it gives the enemy no indication of the way the machine is travelling, and the manœuvre may be useful in misleading the enemy who may be firing from the ground.

The Tail Slide.

If the machine is flown vertically upwards, and if the engine is cut off, the machine will start to fall tail first. This fall can easily be converted into a nose dive by putting on rudder or elevator. It should be remembered that the controls work the opposite way to the normal. Thus pulling back the elevator makes the machine fall forward. This manœuvre is not recommended because one is liable to let the machine fall too far. One then uses more control than one intends, and the control surfaces become strained.

The practically vertical stall has been used with good effect in fighting. When attacking a machine vertically below, the nose of our machine may be made to point vertically down by stalling the machine. (This is a slow method and is not recommended. The better way is to bank the machine vertically, putting on bottom rudder to bring the nose down.) The machine is thus pointed downwards before it has gathered speed, and one gets a longer burst of fire than if the machine had been merely flown vertically downwards off the even keel.

Flying Upside-down.

Machines with rotary engines, if they are not too stable, can easily be flown upside-down. In machines with fixed cylinder engines the propeller will probably stop, necessitating a long ver-

"BRING DOWN YOUR HUN!"

tical dive in order to regain it. The machine can easily be turned over on its back by making a slow half roll, or by going straight on after the top of a loop. This manœuvre has not been used practically in any fight.

The Engine.

If the engine is not used properly many chances will be missed.

When you have crept up under the enemy's tail, throttle back to the enemy's speed, so that you will get in a good long burst of fire, no matter what the enemy does.

When diving after the enemy the engine may or may not be flown at full throttle. Full throttle is not good for the engine and it does not increase the machine's speed, owing to the inefficiency of the propeller at great revolutions.

With rotary engines a common fault is to choke on the dive. This takes a few moments to rectify, and chances are missed.

FORMATION FLYING.

The basis of all formation flying is the triangle, *i.e.*, the formation leader in front, and a pilot on each side, both slightly above and behind. This formation is adopted because in the attack, when the machines dive on to the enemy, the two rear machines will travel slightly faster than the leader. The three machines thus arrive practically together and afford each other very strong support. If this formation is attacked, and if one of the enemy manages to sit on the tail of one of the rear machines, the other rear machine can bring down the enemy by simply turning. It is essential in all formation flying to keep as close as possible so that the enemy machines cannot dive through the formation and isolate single machines. (Leave a little distance for manœuvre.)

A useful formation for an offensive patrol consists of the double V formation. The leader flies ahead with his two machines slightly above and behind. A little above this flies the deputy leader with his two machines, flying in like manner. Slightly above and behind again come two single machines.

The duty in this formation is divided thus. The leader and his two machines dive right into the enemy, and break them up. The two top machines immediately dive, and bring down any stragglers. The deputy leader and his two machines stay up above, and prevent any high Huns from diving into the mêlée unperceived. They do not take part in the general battle, but can be used as a cover under which the leader can reform the patrol.

As has been stated before, the battle generally resolves itself into a series of single combats, but it should be practicable, in well trained formations, to bring at least two machines against one at any

"BRING DOWN YOUR HUN!"

one moment. This is true no matter how large the enemy formation may be. Formations are seldom perfect, and one or more stragglers can be cut off before the main formation can give help. Sometimes if the last man is attacked, he dives under the main formation, when it is at once broken.

In the case of **engine failure** the machine should try and keep up with the main formation by losing height, and should fly vertically below the formation. Any machines which try and attack it are in turn dived on by the main formation.

Machines when flying in formation should keep in the formation by opening and closing the throttle. When flying straight, machines should not gain nor lose height, because then the leader will never know exactly where his machines are; and his time will be taken up in looking after his own machines when he should be looking for the Huns. Formation flying should be absolutely automatic.

The only time when machines should lose or gain height is on the turn, when the inner machines should very nearly stall, while the outer ones should dive slightly in order to keep the relative position. When the turn is completed the outer machines can open the throttle, and come up into their proper places.

Every machine in a formation must keep a look out for the enemy. In the double V formation the leader and his machines are responsible for in front and below. The deputy leader for in front and above, while the two rear machines are responsible for the rear. This does not mean that machines should not look all round. Every machine should keep a general look out, and specialise in these places.

In case a machine other than the leader sees one of the enemy, and if he thinks the leader has missed him, the machine dives in front of the leader and rocks the machine from side to side, and then points it in the direction of the Hun.

Every machine in a formation should carry a Very's Pistol and coloured lights. It is convenient to clip the pistol in the machine so that it will fire through the bottom of the machine by merely pulling the trigger. It should be so fixed that it can be reloaded with one hand.

The colours used are:—

Red.—Meaning " Follow me " and in the larger sense " I am going to attack, follow me."
When used by a machine other than the leader it means " I want help."
This is the colour used when the leader wants his machines to pull out of the Dog-Fight in order to reform.

Green.—Meaning " I have engine trouble."

White.—" The duty is washed out, we are going home."

*N.B.—In France these signals vary. This code is for use at Schools only.

All other signals are given by the leader by rocking the machine from side to side. Thus a turn to the right is signalled by rocking the machine to the right, then left, then to the right and turning. And so on.

"BRING DOWN YOUR HUN!"

Rocking the machine fore and aft means that the leader is going to climb or dive steeply at some object underneath.

The usual mistake in formation flying is that machines open out, so that machines can be attacked by the enemy before help can arrive from the main formation. The other mistake is that they do not form up quickly enough after the Dog Fight, when the leader fires the reform signal.

The duty of the leader is not so much the fighting as to lead the patrol to the attack. Once fighting has commenced he should see that none of his machines are getting a bad time. If they are he goes to the machine's help. His real duty is to watch the weather condition, and to watch for other Huns. A new pilot can never see Huns as an old hand can, so that he should trust to his leader implicitly, and not go on fighting after the recall signal has been fired.

The formation can be picked up without any signal from the ground. The leader goes off quickly followed by the others. He then does a circuit in order to give the machines time to close up. This circuit is usually done at the height of a few thousand feet. An extra machine always leaves the ground with the formation, and comes back to the aerodrome as soon as he sees that all the machines are flying correctly. If any machine has to fall out, the spare machine takes its place.

On most patrols it does not pay to send out less than a certain number of machines. If the number falls below this it is usually better for the whole formation to come home together.

Low flying is becoming increasingly important and all machines should be able to open fire at targets on the ground at the same time as the leader.

The total number of hits obtained by the anti-aircraft guns on a formation is very much less than the total hits which would be obtained if the machines flew singly. This is due to the difficulties of range finding, and to the tendency the guns have of " browning " the formation. Range finding observers find great difficulty in both laying on the same machine at the same time, so that large errors are made.

When flying low, artillery cannot be used against the formation, and bullets go far behind, because it is very hard to estimate the rate machines are travelling, when they fly close overhead.

Observers in a formation usually fly with their backs to the pilot, and look outwards and astern. They thus halve the pilot's duties.

Although the words " keep close formation " have been used, this means that the machines must keep a suitable distance, and this varies with the different types of machines. It does not mean that machines shall jamb up the leader, and prevent him manoeuvring.

Precautions before leaving the Ground.

In order to ensure the success of a patrol, it is necessary to do a lot of work on the ground. This, one is apt to forget. The machine must be properly rigged, and the gun must be in perfect working order. If the machine is nose or tail heavy, or if there is any kind of drag on it, one will not be able to outclimb the Hun and

"BRING DOWN YOUR HUN!"

out-manoeuvre him. This entails constant checking and supervision. It is the habit of some pilots to hand their machine over to any mechanics who happen to be on the aerodrome as soon as they land. The very first thing the pilot must do is to tell his own mechanics what the machine has done on the patrol and how she has flown. This takes a few seconds, and can be done as one gets out of the machine. If the pilot does this his mechanics will work all they know, and he will find that his machine is always ready for him. The pilot should see every adjustment made himself, and should look over his own engine after every flight. When there has been a lot of flying the mechanics are very hard worked. As there are only two men to each machine, if the pilot also gives a hand in the actual cleaning of the machine, he just about halves the work for everybody. Incidentally, he learns a lot about his own machine.

With regard to the gun, any deviation from the instructions means loss of efficiency, *i.e.*, not using the proper oil, not testing and cleaning ammunition, &c. Another most important point is to check the alignment of the gun and sights. If the machine has been stunted, or if the landing has been heavy, it is quite likely that the relative positions of the gun and sights have altered slightly. This is often enough to make you miss the Hun. It should not be necessary to lay stress on this point, but it often is so. Here, also, the pilot should see his gun assembled after it has been cleaned, and should consider himself responsible that his gun is going to work in a fight.

Any alteration to the machine should be kept inside the streamline, because head resistance affects the machine much more than does a little extra weight.

Machines at the present time are all standard, and it pays one better to learn how to use the standard fittings rather than change these for a fitting which may or may not be better. When changes are made, the pilot sooner or later gets caught by some unfamiliar gadget, and chances are missed.

Constantly check the shooting of the gun and the alignment of the sight, both on the ground and also in the air.

Pilots and observers have been known in the past to have left the ground without their guns. It is unnecessary to point out that, at this stage of the war, this is absolutely fatal. In action, a man's best friend is his gun; this is as true now as ever it was. The Hun is out to bring you down, and the safest way to prevent this is to bring him down first.

The crew of a machine should be on the aerodrome at least half-an-hour before the time to start for any duty. The engine should be run and the machine checked to see that it is all right.

Flying clothes should then be put on, and the crew should be in their places 10 minutes before the time to start. The engine should then be run and warmed up, and the pilot will be ready for the leader's signals.

Flights should be commenced with dry socks, gloves, and underclothing. It is a great mistake to look for Huns when you are cold and miserable. When you are warm and comfortable you do not mind how many machines you bring down.

"BRING DOWN YOUR HUN!"

One ought not to be in a hurry just before starting on patrol. This means that one gets hot and perspires. This is a cause of frost-bite at high altitudes and should, therefore, be avoided.

This last remark applies also to alcohol. By taking alcohol just before a flight the body temperature is lowered, and this causes great suffering from cold at the higher altitudes. No alcohol should be taken till flying is over for the day; and it is better to do without alcohol altogether while engaged on flying duties.

No young pilot realises how long it takes to get machines ready to leave the ground. This is one of the ways of telling the difference between a good and a bad squadron.

The Rendezvous.

Machines rendezvous before patrol &c. when the units do not come from the same squadron. It is usual to do so at a given time, height, and above a certain place. The leaders are always named These instructions should be followed out very carefully.

Sometimes machines can exactly perform their duties, and no more, *i.e.*, Scouts with small tanks. If a wind springs up these machines have only a small margin of petrol, so that it is criminal to delay a formation by being late at the start merely through slackness. Formations of different types of machine often work together, so one should think of these various types besides the type one happens to be flying.

When formations split up in a fight, it is necessary to reform as soon as possible. When the leader wants to break off a fight for any reason, he fires red lights through the "dog-fight," and all machines should form on him as soon as possible. This requires a high standard of discipline. The chief duty of the leader is to keep a look out for enemy machines, and to keep an eye on the weather conditions. This enables all machines to go ALL OUT till they see the red light fired.

All leaders of formations are experienced men, so that young pilots can safely trust them to know what should be done. There is no advantage in leaving a formation contrary to orders. If any machine is getting a bad time, the leader always goes to his aid. If the pilot gets into this position without instructions from the leader, either he will not be seen, or the leader and the other machines in the formation must come to his aid, and may have to give away all the advantage of height and position for which they have been fighting and manœuvring.

When flying in formation do not do any unnecessary stunting, because there is nothing more annoying for a leader than for him to see one of his machines losing height without reason.

"BRING DOWN YOUR HUN!"

MEETING THE ENEMY.

Getting Position for the Attack.

As in all other forms of fighting, machines should get into position for attack without being seen by the enemy. If the scheme is well thought out this is easier than one would imagine. Machines in the air at a distance of 5 miles are very hard to see, or if they are vertically above or below a distance of about 6,000 feet.

Machines at a distance are usually given away by the sunlight flashing off their planes or struts; therefore no stunting should be done on patrol except for some specific purpose. All turns should be made on as level a keel as possible in order to avoid this.

In cloudy weather one can often see machines crossing in front of the small white clouds which one often finds up high. Great use can be made of these to afford cover from view and A.A. fire.

Always attack, if possible, with the sun behind. This has been the rule in every kind of warfare, because it prevents the enemy from seeing the attackers till too late. There is an exception to this rule. When there is a halo round the sun, machines become very visible. They should then attack from the blue; all the more because the Hun is getting used to the attack from the sun, and will expect it.

In summer, as one rises, a bank of haze appears to rise from the horizon, and keep more or less level with the machine. Machines which attack from the edge of this haze are very hard to pick up, and this especially applies to mono-planes.

It is always better to watch a machine to see what job he is on, rather than to attack without thinking. It is no use getting shot at, when one can down the Hun in safety with a little forethought.

Machines which are coming over the lines to do a reconnaissance usually give a good look round, and then concentrate their attention on our side of the line. They can therefore be attacked from the enemy side of the lines.

Machines, on leaving an aerodrome, circle, then make a bee line for the rendezvous or the lines. Aerodromes therefore can be attacked from far into the enemy's country towards our own lines.

Machines flying near the ground are hard to see, so that it may be worth while, when the enemy machines are at a fair height, to go over low, climb over the enemy country, and attack him from the rear.

Always attack from the enemy's blind side, or in his dead angles. Even if he sees the machine he will not be able to use his gun effectively if this is done.

These angles vary with the different types of machine, so that it is essential for all pilots to study all types of enemy machines.

Then one should consider how the enemy guns are mounted, and also how our machines are armed.

Machines with guns firing ahead can dive on the enemy, but if they are heavily loaded machines, they gather speed so fast that their burst of fire is short.

"BRING DOWN YOUR HUN!"

Machines with guns mounted to fire aft, can afford to let the enemy get astern, and can sink him with the rear gun.

It is of no use attacking where the chances of success are equal. Always attack so that you are sure of sinking the enemy before he can damage you.

The Attack.

First, one must look at the characteristics of the different types of machine.

All scouts are light on the controls and answer quickly. It should be borne in mind that the best use can be made of these light machines only by pilots who have "hands"; and not by those pilots who use the controls too violently and in too great a degree. Remember that use of the controls means added head resistance. This can be tested easily. Try and loop a machine by pulling the elevators moderately, and the machine will obey. Then try and loop by pulling the elevators quickly and as far as they will go, and the machine will stall before it gets to the top of the loop.

There is no scout yet which can fire astern, so that one can try to attack a scout from behind, either above or below. If one attacks from below, one is going at the same speed as the Hun, and the burst of fire is of a good length. If the attack is from above, the burst of fire is not so great, but the machine gathers sufficient speed to climb rapidly and get height for another attack.

If a machine is attacked from below, it should out-turn the attacker. It can lose a little height if it can get behind and under the attacker's tail.

If one can outclimb the Hun machine, one can get behind him and, if he can fire astern, one can use his machine's tail as cover.

As a general rule, keep your height; just as one always kept to windward in the old days of sailing ships.

(a) *The Rotary Scout.*

These machines are very compact, so that all the weights are near the centre of gravity. This enables them to turn very quickly. They have a large mass rotating in front, and great use can be made of this. Owing to the gyroscopic action of this mass, the rotary scouts tend to climb when turned one way and to dive when turned the other. With a suitable use of the engine these machines can be made to turn much faster than the stationary scouts.

(b) *The Stationary Scout.*

This type of scout has a heavy, high horse-power engine, so that the weights are comparatively far from the centre of gravity. This prevents them from turning as fast as the rotaries. On the other hand, they can probably outclimb the rotaries. Their duty is, therefore, to climb and dive, rather than to try and out-manoeuvre the enemy machine.

"BRING DOWN YOUR HUN!"

(c) *The Two-seater.*

This is a heavy machine, and although it can be stunted on occasion just like a scout, this is not the most useful way of using it. It carries two men with guns, so that its chance of hitting is doubled. Because there are two men looking out, their chance of being surprised is halved. As guns are mounted fore and aft, the blind spots and dead angles are few.

On the other hand, the gunner is in the centre of the slip stream, and once the machine can be forced to dive or stunt, the gunner cannot stand up and use his gun. Therefore, in the attack of these machines try and make them stunt, and they become a sitting target.

The whole art in two-seater fighting is the co-operation between pilot and observer. It is likely that a good pilot and observer in a two-seater will beat any single seater. If they do not work together, then the single-seater machine is far the better.

The Fight.

If we can bring down one of the enemy machines in flames the moral effect is good. The enemy sees one of his machines falling, and the others are not at all keen to continue the fight. The enemy does not press the attack, and although very methodical, often gives up, even though he has one of our machines in his power. He does not like taking chances, so there is never any reason for one of our machines to give up the fight, no matter what the odds.

Only very occasionally does one meet a good enemy pilot.

We pass our pilots through a fighting course where they learn to fight selected men, therefore they need not fear to meet the best of Huns. All our new pilots are better than the average Hun, and once they have been through a fight, they are better than any Hun.

As a nation we like fighting, we like working on our own responsibility, and we are not at our best till we are fighting against odds.

In a fight there is no such thing as luck. You often hear a man say he is unlucky because his gun jambed at a critical time. The jamb can in almost every case be traced back to the man himself. If a man takes every precaution, and does not slack, he becomes one of the lucky men, because things always go right with him.

When a Hun is attacked on our side of the lines, he is nervous and his chief idea is to get back to his own side where he can get aid from his own machines or guns. Being a slow thinker he does not stunt much, but opens fire at a long range, and fires a lot of ammunition, most of which is absolutely useless. It is sometimes hard to say whom he is trying to hit.

A bold attack makes the Hun dive away. If he is flying a two-seater the gunner cannot fire, and you have him. If he is in a single-seater, such as the triplane, his wings will usually fall off, and you can save your ammunition.

The Hun is a painstaking creature, so that his gun seldom jambs, and you cannot count on its doing so.

The most important part of the fight is the approach. It is sometimes possible to get one's formation right up under the Huns, for all to select a machine and open fire together.

"BRING DOWN YOUR HUN!"

When you have decided to attack, go ALL OUT. Do not think of anything except that the Hun is coming down. Do not mind which way you are flying, nor where you are. If the Hun can do it, you can go one better. Use your sights, because the Hun is going to use his if he gets the chance, and it is not worth while giving anything to a Hun. He will take every advantage of you if he can.

For the pilot who is coming into action for the first time, Mr. Punch's advice—"Don't!"— is recommended. When you are going to pull the trigger of your guns—"Don't." You will probably be a little excited, and your sights will not be on. Steady yourself and then proceed to down the Hun.

Don't open fire at long ranges. Firstly because you will not hit, and this improves the enemy's morale at the expense of your own; and secondly because you will run out of ammunition at a critical moment if you fire indiscriminately. There is a certain use in sniping the enemy at long ranges, but be careful to husband the ammunition.

It is no good opening fire if you know you are going to miss, so you must open fire only when you know you can hit.

It is much more nervous work having a machine within range of you, which is not shooting, than having the enemy there when he is firing wildly. When he is shooting you know the worst, and you know you can do better. If he is not shooting, you do not know what he can do and get correspondingly nervous.

Fighting range is 200 yards and under. Most pilots under-estimate the range and do a lot of wild shooting. Open fire at 200 yards if you are certain that your sight is correct. If you do not use your sight at this range you will miss.

Machines should aim at working in pairs at least. It is better to work together than to work singly. When you work alone you have an equal chance with the Hun, and the Hun may be a good one. One courses a hare with two hounds, so that when the hare turns he finds a hound waiting for him. To carry this simile further, if the hare uses his head he can out-distance the hounds. The ordinary hare is faster than the hounds on grass and slower on plough. I have seen hares deliberately choose the wrong method and get brought down. A hare can nearly always out-manœuvre a single hound.

When you have decided to attack keep nothing in hand. Be sure that the Hun is going all out in order to get away. Once you are in action it is the little extra determination which counts.

There is a general rule in fighting; always climb on the turn unless you are doing some special manœuvre which necessitates loss of height temporarily. A machine which is turning is very hard to hit, and extra height means speed and choice of attack afterwards. Do not go spinning down, because the enemy can come down quite as fast as you can, and gets a practically sitting shot as you pull out of the spin.

Machines approaching End-on.

Machines which are approaching end-on at the same level, and which see each other, have an equal chance of bringing each other down. Everything depends on the shooting, and this is not a good

"BRING DOWN YOUR HUN!"

way of beginning the attack. If you have to attack, then trust to your shooting.

On the other hand, all Hun machines have a broad fusilage and large engine, so that machines just in front and below cannot be seen. When you do open fire remember that the machines are approaching at a tremendous speed, so open fire in plenty of time to get in a good burst.

There is a manœuvre used with success by a certain pilot, and it depends on the fact that most Huns shoot above one when they approach end-on. When the machines get to effective range, dive your machine till you can see the enemy machine over the top plane. Then pull out and shoot him at an angle from underneath. The pilot is not protected by the engine and should be brought down. If this burst of fire is not successful, stall turn behind the Hun's tail and open fire again. This method is not recommended, unless the pilot is very quick.

Never present your broadside to the Hun as you turn, unless you have an observer, as this allows the Hun to shoot at you and you cannot shoot back.

Machines at an Angle.

If you approach from in front, above or below, and to one side, you come up in the machine's blind spot, and you may be able to open fire before the enemy sees you. As you go past, the observer, if the machine is a two-seater, will find it very hard to get his gun on you. If the two-seater sees you when you are at distance, you must go away and attack again, because he will turn and give the observer a splendid shot at you.

Do not dive from the rear at an angle. This lets the observer of a two-seater get a splendid shot at you, and he will bring you down before you can shoot.

Dive down vertically, if you like, and dive down at some distance away. You can use you extra speed to slip in under the Hun's tail and get into one of his dead angles.

The Two-seater in Attack.

The two-seater in the attack can behave just like the scouts, but it is essential that it should not fly too fast. If it does the observer will be blown out along the fusilage of the machine, and will not be able to use his gun. The same remark applies to stunting. Stunting a two-seater is abnormal, and should be done only in exceptional cases. Co-operation is the secret of the successful two-seater battle.

The Two-seater in the Defence.

If a two-seater is attacked, it must never dive straight away. If the machine is flying in formation, the formation can put up a barrage of machine-gun bullets, which ought to account for some of the enemy. If the attack comes from the front, the two-seater can shoot at the enemy. If the attack comes from the rear, the two-seater can swing his tail from side to side and can give the gunner splendid targets. If the swinging is not enough, the enemy can

"BRING DOWN YOUR HUN!"

avail himself of the cover afforded by the machine's tail. If the swinging is too much, the gunner never gets a fair shot. If the formation is absolutely outnumbered, the machines can circle till help arrives. Circling two-seaters are very hard to attack. Or, else, they can fly in long elipses, the front machines turning back and attacking the Huns in rear, and then taking station in the rear of the formation. The next leaders then turn, and so it goes on.

When the enemy finds that machines are putting up a good defence, he goes away to look for something easier to fight.

The speed of a two-seater in the defence should be as slow as possible.

Escorts.

From time to time machines are sent out to escort others. The escort should fly where they can dive on to any enemy who shows signs of attacking the escorted machines. The artillery machines are not usually escorted, because they can put up a good fight till help arrives.

Beware of the single machine, or of a formation of slow, old machines. The Hun gives nothing away, and they are there for some purpose—probably as bait. Look round and fight the escort, and then you can get the bait as well.

Finding One's Way.

The machine's compass can easily be destroyed by a bullet, and you may want to come home low. If you do not know which way to go, fire one of the Very's lights on to the ground. The smoke will drift away. You knew the direction of the wind when you started out. It is probably the same as then, so that you know the direction of the lines. The particular point of the lines does not matter, as once across you can always land and ask your way.

IN CONCLUSION.

The above notes are not complete, and are not necessarily correct, because procedure changes so fast. They are intended to help the pupils under instruction, and should be regarded in this light.

It is hoped that pilots and observers from overseas will criticise, so that in time these notes will become a more useful work.

1933
'Air Fighting'
from *Royal Air Force Flying Training Manual*
Part II—Applied Flying

Air Publication 928.
February, 1933.

AIR FIGHTING.
GENERAL CONSIDERATIONS.
Introductory Remarks.

1. Air superiority over the enemy confers the greatest advantage and is one of the most important factors in the success of the operations of all arms in war.

2. It is achieved principally by the pursuit of a policy of relentless and incessant offensive against the enemy's air forces in the air and on the ground.

3. The struggle in the air takes the form, as in other fighting, of a series of combats, and it is by the cumulative moral and material effect of a sequence of successes that ascendency over the enemy is eventually gained.

4. It is therefore imperative, in order to prevent the enemy from gaining air superiority, that all aeroplanes, whether primarily designed and maintained for the purpose or not, should be armed for air fighting and their crews thoroughly trained in its principle and practice.

5. Furthermore, fighting aeroplanes will not normally be used to afford direct protection for other types, which must, therefore, be capable of defending themselves against hostile air attack if they are to be successful in the performance of the specific operations for which they are intended.

Characteristics of Air Fighting.

6. The main characteristics of air combat are :—

   (i) The high speed at which it is conducted and the consequent extremely fleeting nature of the opportunities which occur for decisive action.

   (ii) The frequently great disparity in numbers and performance of the opposing aeroplanes.

   (iii) The great physical and moral strain which it imposes upon the crews of the engaging aeroplanes.

   (iv) The high test it imposes upon the qualities of the aeroplane itself.

   (v) Its usually brief endurance owing to the limited ammunition supply.

   (vi) The great moral and tactical advantage which surprise in any form confers upon an attacker.

   (vii) Success is not likely to be achieved except by truly offensive action.

Factors which Affect Fighting Efficiency.

7. It follows from the above that the fighting efficiency of aeroplanes depends :—

(i) On the qualities of the pilot, and of the air gunner or gunners in two-seater or multi-seater aeroplanes, *i.e.*:—

(*a*) Morale.
(*b*) Physical condition.
(*c*) Skill in flying and use of weapons.
(*d*) Understanding of the capabilities of his aeroplane and the ability to use them to the best advantage.
(*e*) Perfect understanding between pilot and air gunner in the case of two-seater or multi-seater aeroplanes.
(*f*) Perfect understanding between the leader and pilots of the other aeroplanes in the case of fighting in formation.
(*g*) Coolness and presence of mind and the ability to make quick decisions.

(ii) On the qualities of the aeroplane, *i.e.* —

(*a*) Performance.
(*b*) Armament and field of fire.
(*c*) Field of view.
(*d*) Power of manœuvre.

Fighting Characteristics of Aeroplanes.

8. The characteristics of service type aeroplanes are described in Chapter I, para. 7. Their fighting qualities vary according to type, thus :—

(i) *Single-seater.*—These aeroplanes are normally designed and maintained primarily for air fighting, and will usually be superior to two-seater and multi-seater types in speed, climb and manœuvrability, but to obtain this superiority entails limitations on their size, fuel capacity and service load. They are essentially the aeroplane for attack, as the pilot has a good view, their small size makes them difficult to observe and recognise at a distance, their performance enables them to gain an advantageous position for attack, and they are usually fitted with fixed guns shooting forward only. In defence, they possess the advantage of being able to break off the combat at will, if necessary, provided they are superior in speed and climb to their adversary; but if not, they must rely on their handiness and power of manœuvring to enable them to obtain position for attack. Their weakest point lies in their liability to surprise attack from the rear, and their vulnerability to attack from that direction and when breaking off combat with two-seater or multi-seater aeroplanes.

(ii) *Two-seater.*—When designed primarily for fighting, these aeroplanes possess many of the qualities of the single-seater, though they will usually be slightly inferior in speed, climb and manœuvrability. They are fitted with one or more fixed guns which fire forward and are operated by the pilot, while the gunner in rear of the pilot is armed with one or more guns mounted so as to allow as wide a field of fire as possible, especially astern. They are thus superior in armament to the single-seater, less liable to surprise and less vulnerable to attack from the rear. Nevertheless, their chief strength lies in attack; and their value will depend largely on the skill, vigilance and determination of the gunner, and on the co-operation between him and the pilot. When designed primarily for purposes other than fighting, these aeroplanes are intrinsically inferior to the two-seater fighter in either speed, climb or manœuvrability, and may be additionally hampered by the requirements for the specific work on which they are engaged, *e.g.* bombing, photography, etc. They will, however, normally be armed in the same way, and, though they may not be able to bring an unwilling enemy to battle, when once engaged, they can, if handled skilfully and aggressively, operate with considerable effect.

(iii) *Multi-seater.*—At present all multi-seater aeroplanes in the Royal Air Force are designed primarily for purposes other than fighting. Their size and weight severely limit their powers of speed, climb and manœuvre in comparison with single-seater and two-seater aeroplanes, and their strength in air fighting depends chiefly upon the weight of fire they can concentrate and their freedom from " blind " spots. In these two respects they are superior to other types as they can usually carry greater weight of armament and ammunition and have the gun positions so disposed as to provide a clear field of fire on aeroplanes attacking from any direction. Close co-operation between the pilot and gunners is, however, more difficult, but these aeroplanes will not usually be required to seek engagement with single-seater and two-seater aeroplanes of superior performance.

TRAINING.

(*Note.*—Attention is directed to K.R. and A.C.I., para. 718).

General Remarks.

9. All commanders, from flight commanders upwards, are responsible for the training and efficiency of their commands, both in war and peace.

10. The squadron commander is responsible for the training of his squadron as a whole, and for the efficiency of his flight commanders, not only as commanders but as instructors. He must train his flight commanders to command and lead the squadron, and must ensure, not only that they are fitted to carry out their duties, but also that they have subordinates in their flights trained to replace them when necessary.

11. The flight commander is responsible for the training of his flight so as to fit it for battle. The basis of his training must be mutual confidence between the flight commander and his subordinates, which is produced by an intimate knowledge of each other's fighting and flying qualities. The flight commander should aim at developing, not only the skill of each of his subordinates as a fighting pilot, but the cohesion of his flight as a fighting unit.

12. The training of pilots and crews in fighting should be progressive and consist of training both in the air and on the ground ; it is divided into :—
        (i) Individual training.
        (ii) Collective training.

Proficiency in air fighting calls for systematic training and constant practice. A definite syllabus of training and a series of progressive practices is therefore necessary.

13. The object of individual training is to fit the crew for war ; it should aim at developing in the pilot dash, self-confidence and initiative, as well as skill, combined with the complete command of aeroplanes and armament.

14. The object of collective training is to render the flight, squadron, or wing, and the larger units and formations capable of manœuvre and co-operation in battle.

Individual Training.

15. It must be borne in mind that success in war is gained largely by moral qualities which may be fostered by training and example. Training should aim, not only to teach pupils how to fight, but also to imbue them with the confidence in their ability and the conviction of their own superiority as fighting pilots.

16. The training should consist of :—

(i) *Ground Training*. A considerable part of fighting training is carried out on the ground ; this ground training, whilst forming a necessary preliminary to fighting training in the air, will continue in its successive stages concurrently with training in the air. Training on the ground should include the following subjects :—

(a) Care, maintenance and mechanism of machine guns and other armament.

(b) Rectification of machine gun stoppages and recognition of faults.

(c) Accurate aiming and use of sights (to [be practised with model aircraft).

(d) Testing and care of ammunition.

(e) Aiming practice with camera guns at aeroplanes flying overhead.

(f) Firing practice at fixed and moving targets.

(g) Recognition of British and foreign aircraft by types.

(h) Theory of the tactics of air fighting.

(ii) *Flying*. Before a pilot can hope to achieve success in air combat, he must be possessed of absolute confidence in his aeroplane, and must have acquired the art of handling it under all conditions. This skill in flying can only be retained by constant practice, which should aim at developing agility and accuracy, more especially in the following manœuvres :—Diving, side-slipping, flat turns, looping, climbing turns and half-rolls. It is of particular importance that manoeuvres, such as climbing turns, half-rolls, steep turns, etc., should be practised to both sides ; instructors should, therefore, insist on the same standard of efficiency for each manœuvre carried out to the left or right.

(iii) *The tactical application of aerobatics.* Skill in the use of the various evolutions of flying, and the methods in which they should be applied in order to out-manœuvre the enemy.

(iv) *Judging distance, accuracy of aim, and skill in the use of machine guns and other air weapons.* Pilots and gunners require a considerable amount of practice in developing their judgment of distance in the air so that they can manœuvre close to the enemy without risk of collision. The utmost skill in flying is, however, of no avail unless pilots and gunners attain complete efficiency in the use of their weapons and sights, and they must receive continual practice in firing and aiming while in flight at stationary and moving targets. (*See* paras. 25 to 33 below.)

(v) *Air tactics.* In order to develop their judgment of the relative speeds of aeroplanes in the air, pilots should be trained in the recognised tactics of attack and defence, and be encouraged to try and develop new tactics.

(vi) *Observation and recognition of aircraft.* The ability to see and identify aircraft at a distance is vital in war, and must be developed by constant practice. Every effort must be made to train pilots and gunners to use their eyes and to develop a sense of intuitive vigilance. A definite system for keeping the sky under observation is necessary in order that the pilot may avoid the danger of surprise attack and that he may reap the benefit of seeing the enemy before being seen. Instruction in recognition of aircraft may first be given on the ground by using silhouettes which the pupil is made to identify from a distance of 15 to 20 yards. These silhouettes must include one of each type of aircraft illustrating its appearance as seen when it is approaching the onlooker head-on. Later, the pupil should be shown how, when flying, to divide the sky into three sectors by means of the top plane and centre-section struts, and examine each sector separately. First the pilot should search the air above and below his tail, examining any blind spots by swinging his tail from side to side, then the sector from port wing-tip to centre section should be searched, then the sector from centre section to starboard wing-tip. The upper sky must then be examined by taking a steady sweep upwards from starboard wing-tip to port wing-tip, each portion of the sky being scrutinised minutely; otherwise a hostile aeroplane approaching end-on may easily escape notice. If this examination is carried out systematically and constantly, the whole sky will be kept under observation. With training, pilots and gunners can sometimes adapt themselves to using wide aperture binoculars of low magnification for observation from the air, and this practice should be encouraged. When flying in formation, crews will be allotted specified sectors which it is their special duty to keep under observation.

17. Fighting-training of pilots in the air should consist alternately of dual-control instruction and solo practices, each lesson being explained and demonstrated by the instructor before

being put into execution by the pupil. Air training is sub-divided into :—
> (i) Elementary training.
> (ii) Advanced training.

18. In elementary training the pilot is taught :—
> (i) To place his aeroplane in any possible position, and have complete and instinctive control at all times.
> (ii) To aim accurately and steadily whilst flying and diving.
> (iii) To manœuvre so as to align his guns on air or ground targets in the shortest possible time.
> (iv) To dive correctly and to turn quickly from any position into a dive.
> (v) To aim correctly at moving targets on the ground or in the air.
> (vi) To rectify machine-gun stoppages in the air.

19. Advanced training should include the following lessons :—
> (i) How to approach various classes of aircraft. In order to train pilots in the art of approaching an enemy, certain aeroplanes, preferably flown by experienced pilots, should be detailed to represent hostile aircraft. The instructor should then take up a certain number of pupils, flying in formation, and order each one in turn to approach and attack an opponent while the remainder of the formation watches from a distance and makes critical notes. By this method, a pupil is taught the various stratagems employed in concealing an approach, and benefits by the criticisms of his instructor and fellow pupils.
> (ii) How to take advantage of background to conceal the approach.
> (iii) How to make use of the sun to screen the approach.
> (iv) How to make use of clouds and mist in order to effect a surprise attack or retirement.
> (v) How to take advantage of an opponent's blind spots.
> (vi) How to co-operate with the back-gunner in a two-seater.

20. In advanced training, the pilot should be armed with a camera gun and taught how to fight another pilot. The pupil should first be taken up by the instructor with dual control. The latter then explains each manœuvre clearly through the telephone, and demonstrates the correct method of approaching and attacking an opponent. During the next stage the pupil takes charge and carries out an attack, whilst the instructor criticises. Great care should be taken to explain the tactics adopted by the opponent, and to point out the correct method of manœuvring.

21. When lecturing to pilots on air fighting, use should be made of photographs, cinematograph films and model aeroplanes, in order to illustrate the following points :—
> (i) The vital spots of an aircraft. These generally consist of pilot, engine and petrol tanks. The instructor should demonstrate how fire may be directed against an aeroplane in such a way as to bring the greatest number of vital spots into the zone of fire.

(ii) The blind spots of the pilot. The instructor should explain and demonstrate how to approach an aeroplane so as to make use of the opponent's blind spots, and point out how these vary with each type.

(iii) The blind spots of the observer, in a two-seater aeroplane.

(iv) Methods of keeping the sky under observation for the presence of other aircraft.

22. While receiving preliminary training in the application of aerobatics to fighting, pilots should be warned against the following faults :—

(i) Excessive speed, which reduces the power of manœuvre, and may cause the temporary loss of eyesight known as "blacking out."

(ii) Losing height unnecessarily whilst manœuvring.

23. When pupils can attack creditably, two of them should be sent up to fight one another, the instructor watching the combat either from the ground or from the air. Careful criticism at this stage is all-important, and can conveniently be classified under three headings :—

(i) Tactics.
(ii) Aim.
(iii) Range.

Tactics can only be criticised from the personal observation of the instructor, but aim and range are shown by the camera gun photographs. If at any time the pupil has difficulty in performing a particular manœuvre, he should be taken up in a dual-control aeroplane and shown how to carry it out.

24. As a final practice, the pupil should be taught how to study his opponent and estimate his weakest points. He should be able to make use of blind spots, and, when attacking two-seater or multi-seater aircraft, be capable of deciding quickly from which direction an attack is likely to succeed.

Air Gunnery.

25. *The importance of accurate marksmanship cannot be overestimated, since it is necessary to hit an aircraft in a vital spot in order to destroy it and in air fighting only fleeting opportunities occur. The use of explosive or incendiary bullets increases the vulnerability of aircraft, but the vital area is nevertheless small in relation to the size of the target. Pupils, both pilots and air gunners, should be encouraged to spend as much time as possible in handling and firing their guns in order that they may learn to use them to the best advantage under all circumstances.*

26. The theory and practice of air gunnery are laid down in the Armament Training Manual (Parts I and III, Air Publications 1242 and 1244), and the pupil will undergo a thorough course of training in these subjects during his preliminary ground instruction. Training in the tactical application of gunnery should be carried out concurrently with other fighting training.

27. The manipulation of machine-guns and the rectification of stoppages and other faults which may occur while firing are far more difficult to perform accurately and speedily in the air than

on the ground ; it is, therefore, essential that pilots and observers should have an intimate knowledge of the machine-gun, and be able to rectify stoppages whenever they occur whilst flying.

28. On the ground, a pupil should be taught to aim and to maintain his aim when firing from a moving fuselage at fixed and moving targets. In the air, a pupil should be taught to combine this knowledge of flying with his knowledge of the machine-gun ; and this training should include the following :—

(i) Grouping practices at fixed targets, *i.e.* how to dive and fire bursts at a target on the ground.

(ii) Grouping practices at moving targets both on the ground and in the air.

(iii) Deflection practice which can best be taught by the use of camera guns, since the film will show an exact record of the pilot's aim at the moment of pressing the trigger.

29. The instructor should explain that in the air a pilot's aim is constantly thrown off, and that it will, therefore, be necessary to re-lay the aim frequently ; this implies that short bursts only should be fired, the aim being re-laid at the commencement of each burst.

30. Before a pilot is permitted to fire his gun from the air, he should first be made to carry out the various practices with a camera gun. By this test, a pupil's progress can be checked and his faults discovered. The camera gun films should show whether :—

(i) A satisfactory angle of dive has been attained.

(ii) The trigger has been pressed at the correct range.

31. A pilot should be trained to accustom himself to different angles and speeds of approach, so that when he attacks he is capable of estimating the deflection correctly.

32. The pilot who is destined to fly a two-seater aeroplane should be taught how to co-operate with a gunner. After he has mastered the use of his front gun in attack, he should be taken up to act as gunner to the instructor ; the latter should then attack another aeroplane, and, during the ensuing practice-combat, manœuvre so as to allow the pupil to use his camera gun. During the combat, the instructor should explain through the telephone how he manœuvres to afford the gunner a good view of the enemy. He should explain how, instead of trying continually to turn towards the hostile aeroplane and use his front gun, he manœuvres so as to allow the gunner to use his weapons effectively. When the pupil has thus experienced the gunner's " point of view," he should be sent up to pilot a two-seater aeroplane carrying a skilled gunner who will instruct him in co-operation, and check him if he does not afford the correct openings for the back gun.

33. At the end of this stage in his fighting training, the pupil should be expert in using his gun in the air, in aiming at and attacking another aircraft, and in defending himself to the best advantage.

Collective Training.

34. When pilots have attained proficiency in individual fighting and have acquired the principles of air drill (which they should be taught concurrently with their individual training in air fighting), they should commence collective training.

35. In collective training the pupil is taught to apply the lessons learnt in individual training, and to co-operate with the rest of his unit under the direction of a leader.

36. Collective training should consist of :—
   (i) Air drill (*see* Chapter III).
   (ii) Instruction in the tactics of fighting in formation.
   (iii) Air manœuvres.
   (iv) Combined manœuvres.

37. The most instructive method of carrying out collective battle training is by a series of schemes in which the air forces taking part are divided into " red " and " blue " forces, a definite line being chosen on the ground which divides the territory occupied by " red " and " blue " troops.

38. If each pilot and, for two-seater aeroplanes, each gunner can be provided with a camera gun, a valuable test of the skill displayed by individuals during the fight can be obtained. At the end of the day the films of all camera guns should be collected, and an approximate idea of the results of the day's fighting can then be arrived at. They should be imparted to pupils in a lecture at which any tactical errors made are pointed out.

39. It is essential that aeroplanes detailed to opposing sides should be of a definite type or types, which should be clearly stated when orders for the schemes are being issued ; by this means pilots will be able to exercise their powers of observation in the air. Practice in the recognition of aeroplanes may be given by handing each pilot a paper, ruled in columns, headed with the designation of various types likely to be encountered, one column being left for those of unknown type. During the flight, at a pre-arranged time, or on a given signal, each pilot should mark down the number of aeroplanes of each type which he can see. The instructor should make a similar note and compare his list with those of the other pilots.

40. During collective training every effort should be made to foster *esprit de corps*, and the pilot who has been taught to fight as an individual will now have to learn to take his place as the member of a unit and to realize that the flight, or squadron, is of more importance than the individuals which compose it.

Training of the Leader.

41. The characteristics of air warfare entail the necessity for quick decision and prompt action on the part of subordinate commanders, and it is, therefore, of the utmost importance that initiative and resolution of purpose be developed during training.

42. The leader of a formation incurs a heavy responsibility, since it is he who determines the course to be steered, decides when to attack and when to withdraw, and orders the tactical disposition of his command ; he should, therefore, have sound air experience, which can only be gained in peace by constant practice, and by thinking out and deciding how best to meet definite tactical problems with which he is likely to be confronted in war. He needs imagination in order to have the power of

anticipating future developments in air warfare, and organizing ability to devise methods to meet them. Prior to carrying out practice air attacks by large formations, the attacks should be practiced in skeleton form, *i.e.* with only the leaders of the sub-formations. In this way leaders may be trained in the approach, the correct position for attack and break-away, and in judging relative speeds and angles of dive and climb.

Training of night-fighting pilots.

43. Night fighting requires special training both in flying and in the use of weapons by night. The tactics employed in night fighting are described in para. 220–227 of this chapter.

44. As soon as a pilot has acquired sufficient skill in flying by night to enable him to find his way and land without difficulty, he should be instructed in approaching another aeroplane and manœuvring to secure a fighting position. This should first be taught by daylight, and practised until the pilot is capable of attaining the position best suited to the types of aircraft engaged. During these preliminary practices the pupil should carry a camera gun, and demonstrate his ability to align his sights and fire an effective burst at decisive range.

45. Practice in approach and attack should then be carried out by moonlight, two pilots being detailed to ascend and rendezvous at 2,000 feet over a corner of the aerodrome, with navigation lights burning. The pilot designated for the role of the attacker will leave his lights burning, and will take up his position. The second pilot will extinguish his lights and fly along on a level course, watching his opponent and making a note of any mistakes committed.

46. Gunnery should be practiced at night, both in the air and on the ground, care being taken to use the same sight on the ground as in the air. It is desirable that a pilot should receive practice in clearing jams in the dark, and that he should accustom himself to handling his gun and manipulating its mechanism entirely by touch.

INDIVIDUAL COMBAT.

General Principles.

47. Independent fighting will often be necessary by individual pilots, sent up either to attack and destroy any small hostile formations or unsupported aircraft they may encounter, or to carry out some special mission ; moreover, owing to the fact that an engagement between two air formations will often resolve into a series of duels between individuals, the general principles of individual fighting will sometimes apply to collective fighting when the battle has developed. Individual attack facilitates surprise, which will often enable a solitary pilot possessing initiative and boldness to achieve success against superior numbers. On the other hand, a pilot acting alone, especially when flying a single-seater aeroplane, will himself be liable to surprise attack, so that only the most experienced and able pilots should be selected for individual missions, see para. 192 of this Chapter.

48. Certain definite principles of air fighting are common to all types of aeroplanes : these are :—

    (i) To discover the enemy first.

    (ii) Altitude confers tactical advantage.

    (iii) The will to conquer, determination and coolness are essential to success.

    (iv) Fire should be opened as close to the enemy as possible to ensure good shooting and to avoid waste of ammunition.

    (v) Accuracy of aim and careful shooting are essential.

    (vi) Every aircraft should be treated as hostile until its identity is established beyond shadow of doubt.

49. After an engagement, pilots should discuss its various phases among themselves; they will thus be able to realize what mistakes, if any, have been committed, and what alternative tactics should have been employed.

50. The direction and strength of the wind should be noted before leaving the ground, as this will assist the pilot in locating his position after a combat. Air pilotage should be cultivated, and is of special importance later when the pilot has to lead his patrol. During a fight a pilot's whole attention is concentrated on the defeat of his opponent, and he has little time to study his map or note the country over which he is passing. At the conclusion of a battle he may thus find himself at a considerable distance from the district over which he was flying when he first engaged the enemy, and must be able to locate himself rapidly and accurately. This ability to find his way without loss of time is essential to a fighting pilot, since it may often make the difference between getting back to his aerodrome or being compelled to land in enemy territory owing to lack of petrol.

51. Air gunnery is complicated by the fact that both gun and target are moving at variable speeds and on variable courses, consequently the period during which a pilot can align his sights on an opponent is necessarily of very short duration; it is therefore of the utmost importance that no opportunity should be lost in battle.

52. The range at which fire should be opened will vary according to circumstances, the guiding principle being that the longer fire can be reserved and the shorter the range, the greater the probability of a decisive result. Pilots and gunners must accustom themselves to judge the range by the apparent size of the hostile aeroplane and the clearness with which its details can be seen.

53. A pilot should endeavour to retain vivid and detailed impressions of every fight in which he takes part. Besides the necessity of recording the details and results of air engagements, a pilot will learn more about air tactics and about the habits of the enemy by careful analysis of his own experiences than by any amount of training.

Observation and Identification of the Enemy.

54. The method of searching the sky for enemy aeroplanes has already been indicated in paragraph 16 (vi) of this Chapter.

55. Observation of an aeroplane in flight is usually considerably more difficult from the air than from the ground. When operating over friendly territory, therefore, pilots should co-operate with ground observers to obtain warning of the presence of hostile aeroplanes and to be directed towards them. Either radio-telephony or ground signals can be used, but a combination of both is preferable.

56. Anti-aircraft artillery fire can also be of great assistance, and, to make full use of it, pilots should maintain close liaison with personnel of the batteries and each should clearly understand the other's methods.

57. Friendly anti-aircraft fire can be used to indicate the direction in which an enemy has gone although he may be out of range, or to warn a pilot that he is about to be attacked or that hostile aircraft are about.

58. The great advantage of friendly anti-aircraft fire is that it immediately identifies the object aeroplane as an enemy, indicates his whereabouts and height, and is, moreover, likely to make him less watchful for attack from the air.

59. A pilot who observes it, even though he may not at once be able to see the enemy aeroplane, has therefore much more chance of achieving a surprise attack.

60. The sudden cessation of anti-aircraft fire will, however, immediately warn the enemy that he is about to be attacked from the air. Attacking pilots should therefore arrange with the batteries that they continue to fire " aiming off," " short " or " over " the enemy until he is actually engaged or observed to have become aware of the attack.

The Decision to Engage.

61. In war, once a pilot has observed an enemy aeroplane or aeroplanes he will normally decide to attack, as this is the pursuance of the policy of obtaining air superiority, *see* paras. 1 and 2 of this chapter.

62. Under certain circumstances, however, he may decide not to attack, viz. :—

(i) It may be more important that he should not risk the loss of his aeroplane and should not divert it from the operation on which he is engaged (see para. 244 of this chapter).

(ii) He may be short of fuel or ammunition, or have already received damage to his aeroplane, guns or crew in a previous encounter.

(iii) His type of aeroplane may be so outclassed in performance by the enemy, or the enemy be so numerous, that there is no hope of his inflicting equal damage to that he is likely to receive.

(iv) It may be apparent that the hostile aeroplane is being used as a decoy to lead him to be overwhelmed before he can hope to achieve a successful attack.

63. Under such circumstances as the above a pilot will usually attempt to evade the enemy (*see* paras. 233–241), or otherwise avoid engagement, but as soon as it becomes apparent that he cannot do so he must assume the offensive at the first opportunity.

The Approach.

64. The first principle of air combat is for a pilot to discover the enemy first and thus obtain for himself the initiative which enables him to adopt his own plan of approach.

65. In approaching an enemy aeroplane the primary object of a pilot having the initiative will always be to arrive within effective range without being observed. This will confer upon the attacker the supreme advantage of surprise.

66. A surprise attack creates a great moral effect upon an adversary ; as a result, a hostile pilot, when taken by surprise, may momentarily lose his presence of mind and either dive or place his aeroplane on such a position as to form an easy target for the attacker.

67. A pilot's ability to carry out a successful surprise approach and attack depends largely upon :—

(i) His superior powers of observation and the facility with which he can observe and identify hostile aeroplanes at a distance.

(ii) His favourable position relative to the enemy aeroplane when observed and identified, or the superior capability of his aeroplane to achieve a favourable position before the opportunity for combat has been lost.

68. If these conditions are present, surprise in approach and attack may be achieved in the following ways :—

(i) By approach from the direction of the sun. When the sun is shining brightly it is extremely difficult to see an aeroplane approaching from its direction owing to the blinding effect of the sun's rays. The reverse is the case, however, when the sun's rays are diffused, as the attacker shows up very plainly. He should, therefore, approach from the opposite direction.

(ii) By approaching from the edge of the bank of mist or haze which in summer appears to cloak the horizon.

(iii) By approaching from behind or above the clouds and seizing a favourable opportunity to dive out of the clouds on to the unsuspecting opponent. In cloudy weather the approach may often be concealed by utilising as cover the small, white clouds which are to be found at a high altitude.

(iv) By making use of the enemy's blind spots. An intimate knowledge of the enemy's aircraft is required in order that full advantage may be taken of its vulnerable points. Pilots should study their opponents' aeroplanes and acquaint themselves with their characteristics, so that they may decide upon the best method of attack.

69. Even when in view, surprise is possible to a pilot who is thoroughly at home in the air, and can place his aeroplane, by a sudden evolution, in an unexpected position on the enemy's blind side, or under his tail.

70. Aeroplanes at a distance often disclose their presence by the flashing of sunlight from the planes or struts ; it is, therefore, important that when approaching an enemy no steep banking be attempted.

71. Hostile aeroplanes which are patrolling at a considerable altitude may sometimes be taken by surprise if the attacker approaches by flying low and then climbs to attack them from the direction of their own aerodrome ; but this method of approach suffers from the great disadvantage that it allows the enemy the tactical advantage of superior altitude.

72. A surprise attack may often be successfully achieved on a cloudy day, because the weather will encourage the enemy to send out aeroplanes on long-distance reconnaissance in the hope that they may escape notice. Cloudy weather, once the enemy has been observed, favours the attacker, who should endeavour to keep out of sight until the very last moment. It should be borne in mind that in such weather it is often of advantage to approach the hostile aeroplane on its own level, when the planes form but a thin line which it is difficult to see.

73. A successful surprise attack enables a pilot to open fire at decisive range before the enemy is aware of his presence ; it should therefore be the aim of the attacker to get as close to the hostile aircraft as possible, and not to open fire until he is quite certain of hitting the mark with his first burst of fire, unless the enemy shows by diving or turning that the attack has been discovered.

74. In war, however, it happens but seldom that circumstances favour the achievement of surprise attack ; and even if they do at the moment when the enemy is first observed, the advantages of this form of attack may have to be sacrificed in order to make certain of bringing the enemy to battle.

75. Careful observation of an enemy's movements and the type of aeroplane which he is flying will often reveal the duty upon which he is engaged and thus afford a pilot guidance as to whether he is likely to be able to achieve surprise attack.

76. For instance, if a pilot discovers a hostile two-seater apparently engaged on artillery co-operation he may be able to choose his time of attack, having previously achieved a favourable position by making use of the sun or clouds to conceal his approach.

77. On the other hand, the enemy may be returning to his base or engaged on some mission such as a bomb raid which it is necessary to intercept. In such cases it will be necessary to attack at once, and there will be no time to gain position, unless the pilot's aeroplane is very favourably located *vis-a-vis* the enemy, or is vastly superior in performance.

78. It may also happen that the enemy will wish to avoid engagement except he be in a position of advantage, and in this case again, a pilot—unless his aeroplane is much superior to the enemy's—may have deliberately to sacrifice any advantage of position he may hold, and approach in a disadvantageous position in order to induce the enemy to engage in combat.

79. In war, therefore, approach tactics will usually be dictated by circumstances, and it is obvious that many opportunities of engaging in successful combat will be lost if pilots endeavour always to gain a position of advantage for approach, and attempt always to have the initiative in attack.

80. Accordingly, it is of the greatest importance that the training of pilots and crews in air fighting should aim at developing their ability to extricate themselves from a defensive position in the initial stages of a combat and to gain the position of attacker.

81. As soon as a pilot has observed an enemy and decided to engage him or that he cannot avoid engagement, he will formulate his plan of approach. In doing this he will take into consideration :—

    (i) His knowledge of the morale, skill and mentality of the enemy pilot.

    (ii) His knowledge of the capabilities of the enemy aeroplane and the duties upon which it is probably engaged at the moment.

    (iii) His observation of the prevailing meteorological conditions.

    (iv) His knowledge of the capabilities and condition of his own aeroplane and crew.

    (v) Any other factors such as his altitude, remaining air endurance and his position *vis-a-vis* the front line which may affect his tactics.

82. During the approach, pilots and gunners will take a final survey and make sure that everything is in readiness for action, and they should be trained to develop a routine drill covering all points which might be overlooked and thus lead to the loss of a fleeting opportunity, viz. :—

    (i) Pilot makes sure that all gunners have seen *all* the enemy aeroplanes.

    (ii) Pilots and gunners check all guns for loading and cocking, and, if likely to be cold, test with short burst, unless surprise is being attempted.

    (iii) Pilot checks that C.C. gear reservoir is charged and Lewis gunners see that full drums are in position and partially used ones removed from guns.

    (iv) Pilots and gunners check that sights are clear of oil, etc., and in working order.

    (v) Pilots and gunners check that fighting and parachute harness is properly adjusted.

    (vi) If their aeroplane has already been engaged, pilot and gunners will carefully look over it to ascertain what damage, if any, has been suffered.

Tactics of Individual Combat.

83. In paras. 47–53 of this chapter the general principles of air fighting were enunciated. It is impossible to lay down detailed tactics to be adopted in attack on, or defence against attack by all the various types of aeroplanes, but the following paragraphs deal with some of the guiding rules which should usually be observed.

84. *Altitude.* During the approach and in the course of the combat a pilot will usually seek to gain superior height to the enemy as this will normally afford him the initiative in the engagement and tactical advantage in attack.

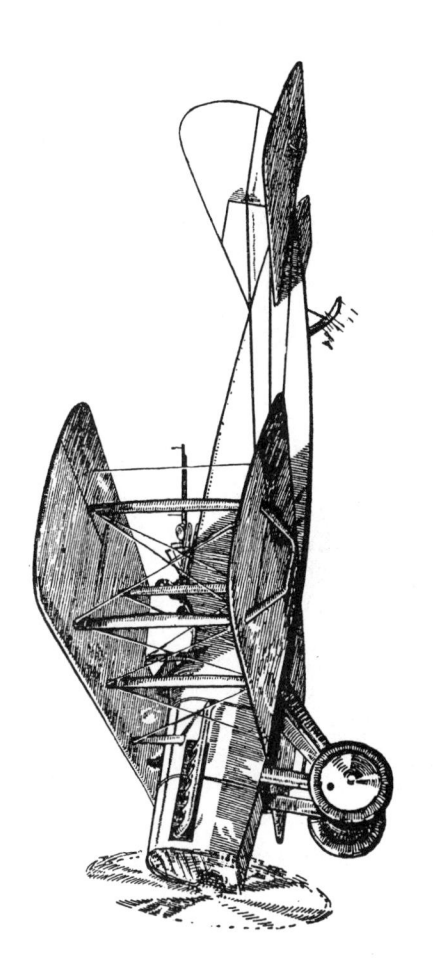

FIG. 11.—Approaching a Two-seater.

85. **Altitude confers a tactical advantage upon the attacker,** because, being above his opponent, he always has a reserve of speed to carry him back into position after a dive. Moreover, being above, he can afford to lose height in a turn, and can therefore more easily out-manœuvre his opponent. Although, as a rule, altitude should be retained by the use of climbing turns, it may sometimes be advisable to go below an opponent after an

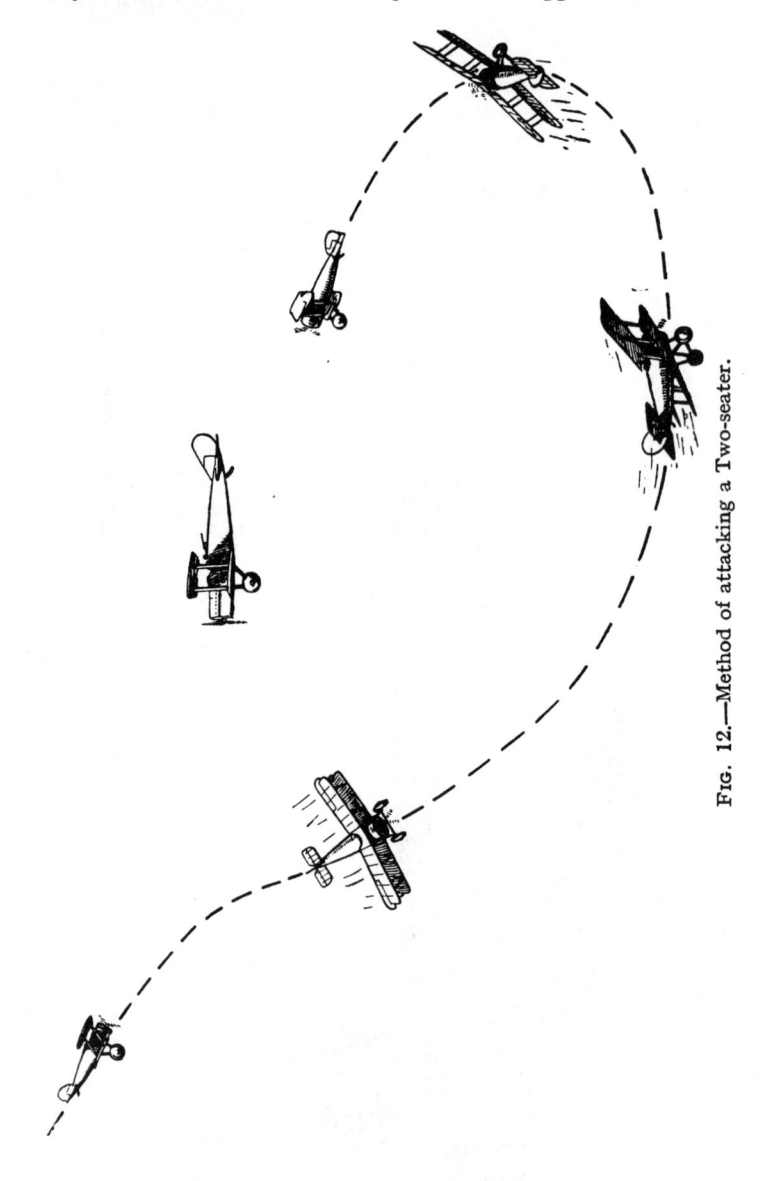

FIG. 12.—Method of attacking a Two-seater.

unsuccessful attack, since many types of aeroplanes have an excellent view above, but, owing to planes and engine, are " blind " below. If, after an unsuccessful dive, the attacker " carries on " below the enemy, the latter will lose sight of him momentarily, and the attacker can seize this opportunity to formulate a fresh plan of attack and regain position.

86. When, owing to circumstances, such as have been outlined in paras. 71–77, a pilot is forced to allow the initiative to the enemy, his aim will be to gain the position of attacker as soon as possible. His chief assistance in this will be his skill in the handling of his aeroplane so as to gain as much height as possible while turning and manœuvring, his coolness in watching for opportunities to seize the initiative and throw the enemy on the defensive, and any knowledge he may have of the enemy's capabilities and usual methods of manœuvre.

87. *Attack on single seaters.* Single-seaters should, generally, be attacked from above and astern, the object of the attacker being to arrive at decisive range before his opponent is aware of his approach. In diving to attack, it is essential to have plenty of engine-power in hand, since the fact that the attacker has a reserve of speed in hand will enable him to anticipate his opponent's next move. With a view to obtaining this advantage, a close watch should be kept on the rudder of the opponent, as it will often afford an indication of the direction in which the hostile pilot intends to turn, before his aeroplane actually responds to the movement of the controls.

88. *Attack on Two-seaters* (*see* Fig. 11). Two-seater aeroplanes should, as a rule, be attacked from below or from any blind angle, the most unfavourable position for the attack being astern and slightly above, in which position the attacker is fully exposed to the back gunner's fire. A skilfully handled single-seater which can attain a position about 100 yards behind and 50 ft. below a hostile two-seater without being observed, is in a position to do most damage to the enemy with least risk to himself. Once in this position, the object of the attacker must be to keep out of the enemy's field of fire and to get to close quarters. The two-seater will endeavour to bring fire to bear on the attacker by turning quickly in order to deprive him of the cover of the fuselage, and great skill is required to retain a position directly in rear.

89. " *Head on* " *attack.* When two single-engined tractor aeroplanes are attacking each other " head on " both pilots are exposed to similar conditions. If the hostile aeroplane has a large engine in front, the attack, even if successful, will in all probability merely damage the engine and not disable the pilot. In this case, therefore, this method of attacking should not be resorted to when the combat is taking place over enemy territory. When, however, the enemy aeroplane is of the " pusher " type with front guns not fixed, or multi-engined, with the engines so disposed that they do not afford protection to the pilot, it is a useful method of attack, as a hesitant enemy can frequently be flustered into turning or diving into a disadvantageous position.

90. A method of attack which may be employed with success against a hostile aeroplane with a broad fuselage and large engine, is to fly straight at the opponent " end on," until within range of

about 500 yards. The attacker should then dive steeply as if to pass under the enemy, firing a burst from his gun to draw the observer's fire to the front, but instead he should execute a quick turn whilst concealed from view by the hostile aeroplane's engine and fuselage ; this turn should bring him into a position from which he is afforded an easy shot from astern and below, with the additional advantage that the enemy pilot is no longer protected by his engine. (*see* Figs. 12 and 13). This position of the attacker under the enemy and flying in the same direction, will give him the opportunity of firing a long burst before the attack can be countered. If the enemy turns, the attacker will be in a position to execute a quick turn and resume the attack. When approaching " end on," it should be borne in mind that the opponents are drawing nearer to each other at great speed, and the time available for manœuvre will therefore be far less.

91. *Diving attack.* When diving to attack, the greater the speed of the dive the more fleeting will be the opportunity for firing, and the less accurate will be the shooting. If, therefore, great speed is not necessary for other reasons, the dive should be commenced with as little speed as possible.

92. Attacks delivered from a flank are often successful, since the vital parts of the aeroplane and the pilot are fully exposed. A flank attack necessitates accurate deflection shooting, the aim being directed in front of the nose of the hostile aeroplane (*see* Fig. 18). In the same way, when an attack is delivered from above and astern, aim should be directed in front of the leading edge of the top plane in order to hit pilot or engine.

93. *Defence.* The primary object of a pilot in defence is to assume the offensive as soon as possible. The chief endeavour of a pilot when manœuvring in defence will be, as in attack, to conceal from the enemy till the last possible moment his own intentions and to anticipate, whenever possible, the enemy's manœuvre.

94. Thus, if a pilot is being dived upon by an enemy a good method of defence will be to continue to climb steadily, while retaining sufficient speed or reserve engine power for rapid manœuvre, until the enemy is almost within effective range. He should then turn suddenly directly towards the attacker. If the latter continues his dive, he will then have the briefest opportunity for fire and will have to increase his angle of dive so acutely and rapidly that he will have a most difficult shot. By carefully watching the enemy's aeroplane as it passes overhead, a pilot will often be able to observe what the enemy is about to do next, and anticipate it. Thus, if the enemy is seen to be about to turn right, the defending pilot by turning left first would get into position behind and below the enemy, whence, if a two-seater, his gunner can open fire, and if a single-seater he can continue to gain height.

95. *Turning.* When under fire or being attacked, a pilot should always try and avoid flying straight. He should, however, avoid turning away from the enemy machine and in or into the line of his fire at the same time. Thus, if an enemy aeroplane is diving straight on to his tail, a pilot should not turn about by means of a half-roll on top of a loop, or if the enemy were diving to his port quarter a pilot should not turn to starboard.

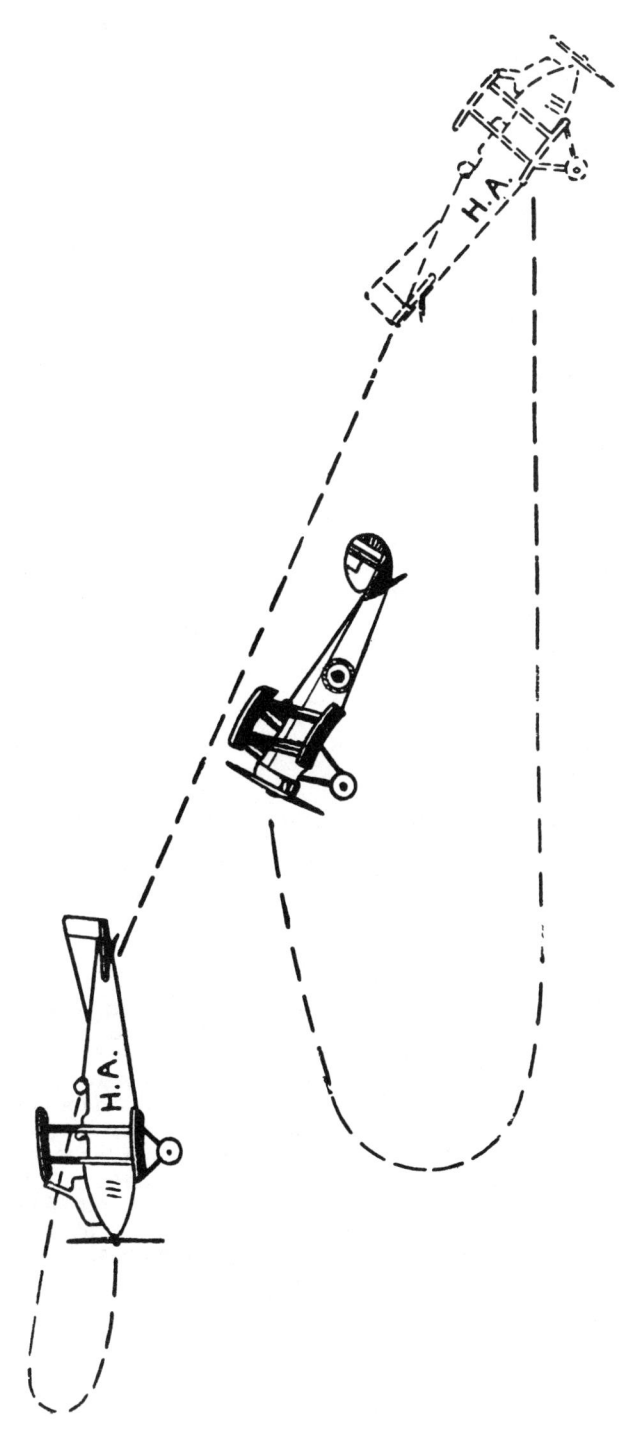

Fig. 13.—Attack of Two-seater from below, showing Turn.

96. *Falling out of control.* Except possibly as a ruse to break off a combat, a pilot should never allow his aeroplane to fall out of control. By so doing, if he is under fire, or the enemy is in position to open fire, he forms an easy target, and when he regains control he will be more confused than the enemy. Falling out of control is also likely to cause a pilot to lose sight of the enemy, and this he must try to avoid at any time, as by so doing he will be unable to watch the enemy and anticipate his manœuvres.

97. *Firing of guns.* Great care must be exercised during a combat that ammunition is not wasted. Not only is the quantity carried limited, but once the engagement is started it may be difficult to break off at will and a pilot may encounter other enemy aeroplanes before he can finally reach his base.

98. Under the stress of fighting, pilots and gunners will be often inclined to open fire before they come within effective range and to continue firing after they have passed beyond it. It is only by much training and experience that they can learn to judge distances in the air and can time accurately the exact moment to open and cease fire.

99. Free guns are usually more difficult to aim and their fire will not be so accurate as that of fixed guns. This is especially so when one or both aeroplanes are manœuvring rapidly. A pilot can therefore take bigger chances under the fire of an enemy's movable armament.

100. Conversely, the pilot of a two-seater engaged in combat will have to decide, in consideration of his knowledge of his gunner's abilities, on the extent to which he will sacrifice his power of manœuruvre and the use of his fixed armament in order to facilitate the gunner's aiming and increase the accuracy of his shooting.

101. *Engine management.* Unless a pilot has acquired complete familiarity with his engine and is thoroughly acquainted with the use of his throttle and altitude control he will commonly experience engine trouble at the critical moment in a fight when maximum speed and climb may be the deciding factors between victory and defeat.

Characteristics of Single-seater in Combat.

102. Single-seater fighting calls for much initiative skill and rapidity of thought. Success will generally be achieved by the pilot who, in addition to the qualities required by a fighting pilot, possesses the ability of adapting himself immediately to varying situations, and is capable of studying his opponent and formulating a tactical plan which, on its execution, will bring the attacker into position to fire before the enemy can counter the attack.

103. Although as a general rule single-seaters do not act alone, yet sometimes when a formation has become disorganized as the result of an engagement, isolated pilots will be called upon to fight individually. Again, selected pilots on the fastest types of single-seaters may be usefully employed on roving commissions, which will enable them to make the greatest use of surprise tactics. As he has no armament fighting astern, the single-seater pilot will have to exercise the utmost vigilance to avoid being surprised, and this will be all the more necessary when he is himself intent upon stalking an apparently unsuspecting enemy.

104. An attack should be delivered with caution, but once attempted should be driven home with resolute determination to destroy the enemy. Pilots who have achieved a number of successes are apt to become over-confident, and should be warned against the dangers of carelessness.

105. When it is necessary to swerve to avoid a collision or to break off the combat temporarily in order to change a drum or rectify a jam, it should be carried out by executing a sudden climbing turn, applying too much rudder, which will cause the aeroplane to slip upwards and outwards. When ready to renew the fight, the attacker should regain a favourable position by manœuvre.

Characteristics of the Two-seater in Combat.

106. Although the general principles of air fighting apply equally to fighting in a two-seater aeroplane, success will depend primarily on the intimate co-operation of pilot and gunner. This close co-operation can only be achieved after considerable practice, and is based on the mutual confidence between pilot and gunner and in the ability to intercommunicate by signs or by some other method, so that each occupant of the aeroplane is always acquainted with the intentions of his companion. It is therefore desirable that the same pilot and gunner should, whenever possible, work together, both in the air and on the ground, in order that mutual knowledge of the methods adopted by each may be developed, and also that the pilot may gain absolute confidence in the vigilance and marksmanship of the gunner, and the gunner in the skill and tactical knowledge of the pilot.

107. In air fighting, the pilot of a two-seater aeroplane is forced to rely just as much on his power of developing fire in all directions as on his quickness of manœuvre. The actual tactics to be employed in two-seater fighting are dependent on the particular type of aeroplane flown and on the requirements of the moment.

108. The pilot of a two-seater should receive instruction in the duties of a gunner, so that he may be familiar with the latter's point of view and with the effectiveness of his fire in different situations. In battle he should resist the temptation to regain position for an attack with his forward guns immediately he passes his opponent, but should know and carry out the manœuvre which will afford to the gunner the best opportunity for the employment of his armament.

109. The air gunner should be in good physical condition and absolutely at home in the air, efficient to a high degree in the use of his weapons, skilled in co-operating with is pilot and in identifying aircraft from a distance, and, above all, vigilant. The gunner should economise his ammunition, and, when fighting at a distance from his aerodrome, should retain a reserve for the return journey.

Attack of Two-seater and Multi-seater Aeroplanes.

110. The attack of a two-seater aeroplane requires forethought, since, owing to its power of developing fire astern, it cannot, as a rule, be approached with impunity like a single-seater. Success will be achieved by the pilot who acquires an intimate knowledge of the "blind angles," of the powers of manœuvre, of armament and other characteristics of his opponent.

111. When a hostile two-seater aeroplane is observed, its movements should be studied in order that the duty upon which it is engaged may be discovered, as this will influence the method of approach. For instance, if from his movements or from ground indications, the hostile pilot appears to be engaged in artillery observation, it may be advisable to delay the attack until both pilot and gunner of the hostile aeroplane gain confidence and relax their vigilance; the enemy may then be approached from the direction of his own territory and surprised when he is least suspecting an attack. On the other hand, hostile reconnaissance or bombing aircraft may have to be attacked immediately, or they will escape.

112. The primary object of the attacker will be to surprise his enemy and arrive within decisive range before the hostile gunner is aware of his presence. This may be more readily achieved by approaching from below, in which position the attacker is partly shielded from view by the fuselage and planes of the hostile aeroplane. If the approach is successful, the attacker should endeavour to keep immediately under the enemy's fuselage and slightly astern, from which position he can open fire at decisive range. If the hostile pilot should alter course while the attacker is in this position, the latter should endeavour by a quick movement to resume his position and renew the attack.

113. An approach from above is more likely to be successful if the attacker executes a very steep dive immediately ahead of the enemy, and endeavours to shield himself from view with the upper planes of the hostile aeroplane. Even if he is discovered whilst diving in this position, the accuracy of the hostile gunner will be impaired by his having to fire vertically upwards.

114. When diving at an enemy from ahead, the attacker, as soon as he arrives within suitable range, should execute a turn which will bring him into position on the enemy's tail, care being taken not to turn too late, otherwise, on completion of the turn, the attacker will find himself some distance astern of the enemy, and will be forced to approach to decisive range in full view of the hostile gunner. (*See* Fig. 14.)

115. The discovery of his approach will be apparent to the attacker, who should thereupon endeavour, by some rapid manœuvre, to place himself in firing position and deliver the attack from an unexpected quarter.

116. The first result of diving at a hostile aeroplane may frequently be to cause the enemy pilot to dive steeply, since this impulse is instinctive in most pilots when taken by surprise.

If this should occur, the attack may be driven home with impunity, as the hostile gunner will be unable to use his gun effectively as long as he is in this position; moreover, the hostile aeroplane will afford an excellent target.

117. Another method of attack from astern is to dive steeply when still out of effective range, and then, when the hostile gunner is expecting the attack from above, to use the extra speed

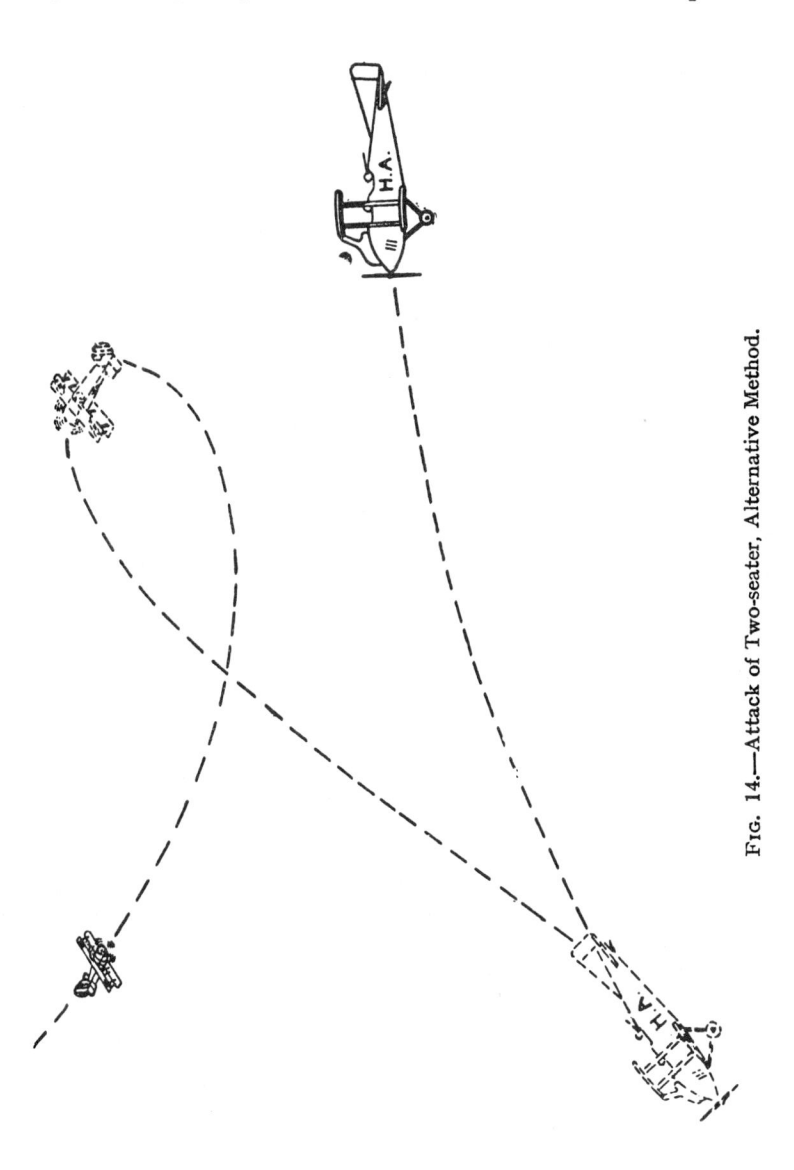

FIG. 14.—Attack of Two-seater, Alternative Method.

FIG. 15.—Attack of Two-seater from Astern.

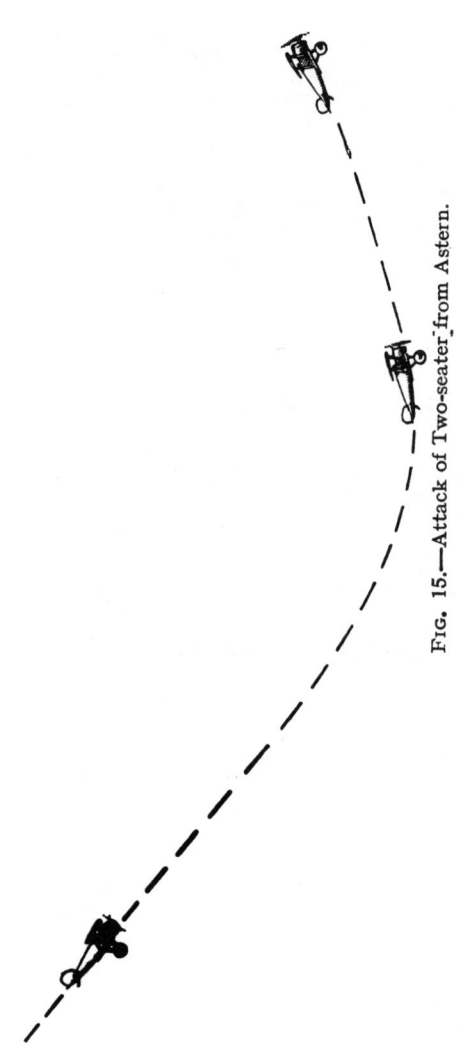

gained during the dive to come up under the enemy's tail. (*See* Fig. 15.) The object of the attacking pilot, once he has been discovered by the enemy, should be to confuse both pilot and gunner of the hostile aeroplane. He can do this by executing unexpected manœuvres and by constantly varying his method of attack. If the attack be delivered from under the tail, the fuselage and tail plane of the enemy may be used as cover from the fire of his rear guns. The gunner will endeavour to prevent this by firing over the side of the cockpit, but his aim may be disturbed by altering position from one side of the fuselage to the other.

118. A hostile aeroplane provided with a gun tunnel through the floor of the fuselage should not be attacked from directly under the tail, but may be approached at an angle.

119. A combined attack against a two-seater by two or more pilots will greatly facilitate success, for, while one pilot occupies the attention of the hostile gunner, the other may deliver a sudden attack from an unexpected quarter. This may be carried out in the following manner :—Pilot No. 1 signals his intention of

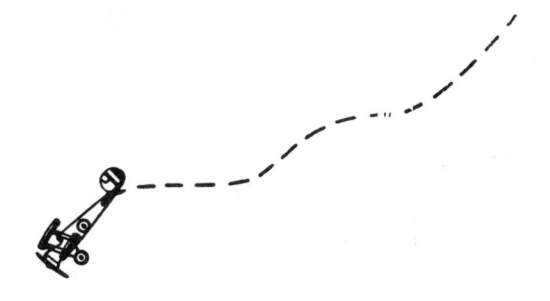

Fig. 16.—Combined Attack.

attacking, and attracts the hostile gunner's attention by executing short dives, at the same time firing his guns. In order not to expose himself unduly, and so as to confuse the hostile gunner, his dives should be irregular. Meanwhile pilot No. 2 makes a detour and endeavours to obtain a favourable position under the tail of the enemy from which he can deliver a decisive attack at short range. (*See* Fig. 16.)

120. When a pilot in a single-seater aeroplane attacks a two-seater, the former generally has the advantage in speed. If this is so, when the enemy alters course, the attacker should take care to avoid over-shooting, and should resume the attack as opportunity occurs.

121. When on a bank in the act of turning, the two-seater will offer a favourable target, if the attacker is quick enough to take advantage of it. A short quick burst at this moment may confuse the pilot and cause him to dive steeply, in which position it will be extremely difficult for the hostile gunner to fire.

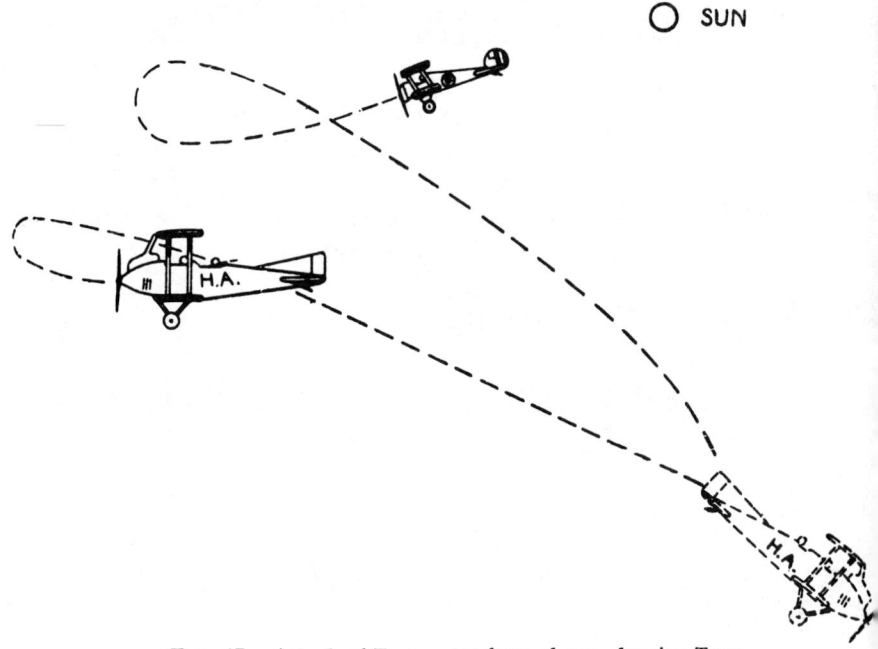

Fig. 17.—Attack of Two-seater from above, showing Turn.

122. Aeroplanes when severely damaged by machine-gun fire sometimes fall to pieces in the air; this point should be borne in mind when closing in on an enemy, especially during a steep dive, in order that the wreckage may be avoided by executing a quick turn or side slip.

123. In the attack on multi-seater aeroplanes the same principles apply, though, owing to their added powers of developing fire, surprise is even more essential to success.

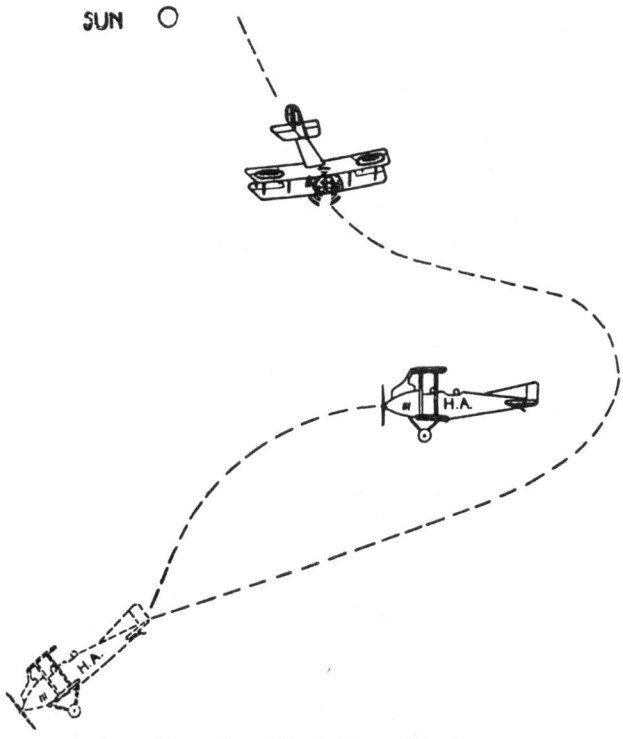

Fig. 18.—Attack from a Flank.

COLLECTIVE COMBAT.
General Principles.

124. The object aimed at in fighting in formation is to enable superior concentration of fire to be brought to bear on the enemy both in attack and defence.

125. This is achieved by :—

(i) Breaking up the enemy formation so that his aeroplanes may be engaged individually,

or (ii) Disposing and manœuvring the aeroplane in a formation so that, while retaining their cohesion, they can bring the maximum number of guns to bear on some portion of the enemy, and/or prevent the enemy formation from bringing its guns to bear.

126. The general principles of formation fighting follow those for individual combat as already outlined.

127. As at present equipped, aeroplanes usually require to engage at close quarters in order to achieve success in combat, and the object of a formation is to develop the greatest volume of fire at decisive range against the enemy's most vulnerable point. Long-range shooting without deflection and with two or more of the object aeroplanes in line may, however, sometimes

prove effective, and may be usefully employed by two-seater fighters to break up hostile formations flying at a higher altitude. Specially aligned sights are required for this attack.

128. Good discipline is of the utmost importance where aeroplanes are fighting in formation. A pilot may be perfect in formation flying and may have distinguished himself in individual fighting, but if he forgets his orders or disregards the leader's signals when he observes an enemy, he will be unfitted to take part in collective fighting. A pilot in a formation is required, not merely to obey orders and signals, but to subject himself to rigid discipline. He must always be in his place, and should be so familiar with the tactics employed by his leader that he can almost anticipate his commands. If he fails in this, he will not only lose his opportunity of destroying hostile aeroplanes but will also hamper the remainder of the formation if it is attacking, and endanger its security if it is in defence.

129. Good leadership is essential to success in formation fighting. A leader must possess a high degree of initiative and skill and be able to judge when and from what direction maximum fire effect shall be brought to bear on the enemy. He must also inspire confidence in the pilots and crews of the formation and have a clear appreciation of their abilities and morale.

130. Surprise attack is more difficult for a formation to achieve than for an individual, but it should, nevertheless, be attempted according to the principles laid down in paras. 68–72 of this Chapter. Successful surprise approach will depend to a large extent on the skill of the leader, who must use his initiative and vary his methods according to the situation.

131. Both in attack and defence a formation must engage the enemy with the utmost determination and aggressiveness, and only the destruction of the enemy or a signal from the leader should end the battle.

132. If a hostile formation superior in numbers is being attacked, it should be done with the greatest determination and dash, which will tend to increase its effect on the enemy's morale. As soon as the leader of the attacking formation observes that the enemy are aware of his approach, he should formulate his plan of attack. The sooner the attack is then delivered, and the more determination shown in driving it home the less time will be afforded to the hostile leader to organize his counter measures.

133. When the fight is joined it is of great importance that all guns which can be brought to bear at effective range should open fire simultaneously.

134. Superiority of fire can usually best be achieved if each enemy aeroplane is engaged by the guns of two or more of the formation. It is, however, undesirable that any hostile aeroplane which is able to open fire within effective range should be left entirely disengaged and free to fire undisturbed. It follows, therefore, that when the enemy formation is equal or greater in number it should be attacked as far as possible from a direction which will mask the fire of some of its guns. Conversely, a formation being attacked will endeavour to manœuvre or alter the disposition of the aeroplanes so that as few guns as possible are masked.

135. Pilots flying in sub-formations should act together. They may either attack simultaneously the same objective from different directions, or if approaching in close formation, targets sufficiently far apart to minimize the risk of collision due to converging courses. If this is carried out effectively the hostile formation will tend to become disorganized, and may be destroyed in detail. (*See* also para. 160.)

136. Once the fight is in progress great difficulty will be experienced in maintaining communication with the members of a formation, and pilots will have to rely chiefly upon the initiative and intelligence of the sub-formation leaders, their knowledge of the methods of the leader and a sound understanding of the principles of fighting in formation.

137. A pilot whose engine is running unsatisfactorily should drop out of a formation and return to his aerodrome, if possible, before the formation starts on its mission. If he attempts to continue with a failing engine, not only does he run the risk of being cut off himself, but he may greatly hamper the leader when in face of the enemy. Any pilot who experiences engine failure when over enemy territory should make the necessary signal (*see* Chapter III, para. 61) and turn for home, whereupon if the leader so decides he may be escorted back to safety. A pilot with a failing engine should not attempt to keep at the same altitude as his escort, or of the formation if it is accompanying him, at the expense of his speed, but should maintain course flying vertically below.

Importance of Co-operation.

138. The success of a formation in battle will depend largely on the effective co-operation of its component parts, which can only be achieved as the result of mutual confidence and practice.

139. During a severe engagement, as the result of which both sides suffer numerous casualties, cohesion will be greatly facilitated if the sub-formations maintain their organization. As soon as the battle has terminated, or the formation leader issues the order to re-form, these sub-formations will collect, each sub-formation joining on to the next until reorganization is complete. Isolated pilots should endeavour to form up with another pilot or sub-formation.

140. When a formation is subjected to heavy fire from the ground, the leader may occasionally alter course in order to confuse the enemy's range-finders, but any tendency on the part of individual pilots to fly an irregular course should be checked, as this tends to disorganize the formation and afford hostile aeroplanes the opportunity of a concentrated attack against an isolated portion of the force.

141. The leader should invariably check his speed before initiating a fresh manœuvre, and should issue a warning signal whenever he meditates a change of direction, so as to allow his formation to close up.

142. The ability to replace casualties without becoming disorganized is of primary importance. If both leader and deputy leader have been forced to drop out, the next senior pilot should take over command.

143. No pilot should leave the formation on his own initiative to attack hostile aircraft, however favourable the opportunity may seem; it is his duty, however, to warn the leader of the presence of any enemy which appears to have escaped notice.

144. In a general engagement, the breaking-up of a formation is sometimes inevitable; it is therefore of the utmost importance that definite instructions as to rallying and re-forming after a battle should be issued and understood by all.

Responsibility of the Leader.

145. The duty of the leader of a formation in battle consists, not in gaining a personal victory over a hostile pilot, but in achieving decisive success with the force which he commands. His responsibilities during the battle include the following:—

    (i) To lead, direct and control the formation.
    (ii) To manœuvre for position.
    (iii) To decide when to attack.
    (iv) To decide when to withdraw the formation with a view to reorganizing.

146. It should be clear to the commander of a formation that his mission is not only to fight but also to lead his force in the attack, and having initiated the battle, he should watch the progress of the fight, and if a change occurs in the tactical situation, such as the arrival of hostile reinforcements, he must be capable of withdrawing his formation with the object of re-forming or of gaining height.

147. A leader is responsible for the security of his command. He must watch over his pilots and know where they are and what they are doing. He must be able to realise the capabilities of some and the weakness of others, and must estimate the fighting power of his formation as a whole. Before deciding to attack, he should note the altitude, numerical strength and organization of the enemy, and should not forget that an error on his part in overlooking other hostile formations in the vicinity may seriously jeopardise his chances of victory.

148. The leader should regulate his approach in such a manner as to arrive with all his pilots together, and should regard the stern of his formation as his own tail and guard it accordingly.

149. During an engagement, the enemy may detach a sub-formation or even a single aeroplane which will endeavour to climb to a higher altitude with the object of resuming the attack at a tactical advantage. As soon as the leader becomes aware of this manœuvre, he should counter it by climbing to a higher level with a sufficiently large force to deal with the hostile detachment. The duty of preventing hostile detachments from climbing out of a battle to gain a tactical advantage may, by pre-arrangement, be delegated to a subordinate, so as to leave the formation leader free to control the decisive attack.

Organization of Formations.

150. The fundamental principles which apply equally to all aeroplane formations and sub-formations are laid down in Chapter III.

151. Formations may be divided roughly into two classes, *i.e.* :—

(i) *Fighting formation*, whose primary duty is to fight and destroy the enemy's aircraft ;

(ii) *Bombing or other formations*, that have other duties, such as bombing or reconnaissance, to perform, and whose primary object will usually be to complete their mission and return to their base with the least possible delay.

152. Generally speaking, the organization of formations and sub-formations will vary according to the type of aeroplane employed and the numbers available, the duties upon which it is engaged and the strength and nature of the enemy opposition to be anticipated. It is therefore intended that the principles of formation organization and tactics given in this manual should serve as general guides rather than as rigid rules of procedure.

153. Thus, a formation of fighting aeroplanes will normally be so disposed as to be able to develop the maximum volume of concentrated fire against any objective which it may attack, and a bomber-reconnaissance formation will endeavour to fly so that the individual aeroplanes afford each other the best mutual support ; but, owing to force of circumstances, either before or during an engagement, both these formations may be forced to alter the number and disposition of their aeroplanes.

154. The basis of all formations, however large, is the sub-formation (*see* Chapter III, para. 9 to 15), and on this sub-formation devolves the greatest responsibility for success or failure in an engagement.

155. The closest understanding is required between the members of a sub-formation : the pilots should always be trained together and, as a general rule, not employed to make up deficiencies in flights other than their own.

The Formation in Attack.

156. The tactics of a formation in attack are of necessity dictated by the circumstances at the time, and no rigid rules can therefore be laid down.

157. The principal factor will usually be the performance of the aeroplanes relative to those of the enemy, and, in the case of formations whose primary rôle is fighting, it is to be anticipated that their aeroplanes will usually be equal or superior in performance to the enemy formations they attack.

Single-Seater Fighter Tactics.

158. The larger a formation is, the more restricted will be its power of manœuvre. Formations of single-seater fighters which have the initiative in attack or are superior in performance to the enemy, and can thus afford to split up and attack by sub-formations, should therefore do so, as this confers increased performance and manœuvrability and, in some cases improved fire effect.

159. The most promising method for a large formation to adopt in attack is usually by sub-formations from different directions and from different planes. The ability to repeat this form of attack is governed by the margin of performance available to the attacker. Careful timing of the attacks by the sub-formations is essential in order to ensure that no one sub-formation comes under the concentrated fire of all the enemy at any one time.

160. When aeroplanes are attacking in formation or sub-formations each attacker should be in a position to open fire on an aeroplane of the enemy formation. It is therefore best that the attack should be started in close formation, which will tend to open out as the enemy is neared. If the attack is started m very open formation, there will be a tendency to close up as the enemy is neared, thus incurring risk of collision and distracting the pilots' attention from the attack.

Fighter Tactics for both Single and Two-seaters.

161. Sub-formations will normally be stepped up, the highest sub-formation being usually in the nature of a reserve. The principle governing the employment of the reserve is that the enemy should be attacked with great vigour as soon as they appear to lose cohesion as the result of the engagement. If the enemy is surprised, it is of the utmost importance to increase the demoralisation which will already have been produced, by utilising the maximum available force. On the other hand, if a small enemy formation be encountered, the formation leader may decide to attack with only a small portion of his force. This will generally be the lowest sub-formation and while it delivers its attack, the remainder will patrol above ready to deal with further opposition.

162. Decoy tactics are sometimes successful and may be usefully employed against an enemy numerically superior. Thus, by alternatively attacking from long range and retreating, some of the enemy sub-formations may be induced to pursue until out of reach of their main body. A leader may detach one sub-formation to draw a hostile formation on to attack, while he retains the remainder at a greater altitude, ready to surprise the enemy should the apparent opportunity be seized. The sub-formation going down as a decoy must not be more than 3,000 or 4,000 ft. below the main formation, or it will run the risk of being attacked by superior numbers before the remainder can come to its assistance.

163. During an engagement, if the hostile formation scatters, attention should be concentrated on the stragglers, and if they dive, only a portion of the force should pursue them, the remainder being retained as a protection against surprise from above.

The Formation in Defence.

164. The considerations which affect the disposition of aeroplanes in bombing or other formations are somewhat different from those which influence the organization of fighting formations.

165. In the first place the formation will usually be engaged on some mission and may not be able to divert its course or delay to engage in combat. In the second place the enemy aeroplanes will probably be superior or equal in performance and will have the initiative in attack.

166. In the initial stages of the engagement, therefore, they will be on the defensive and may have to fight long rear-guard actions. They must, then, be so organized as to be able to develop the maximum concentration of fire against an aggressor attacking from any direction, and especially from the rear.

167. Certain dispositions of the aeroplanes within a formation may be required for the work in hand, *e.g.* bombing or torpedo attack, but if such formations are unsuited to the needs of possible combat they should be adopted only when the operation is actually in progress, and a formation suitable for defence should be assumed on the way to and from the objective.

168. The most favourable organization of a formation for defence will depend primarily on the field of fire of the guns and the field of view obtainable by both pilot and gunners. This will vary with different types of aeroplanes, but it is most important that pilots should always be able to see the aeroplane acting as their guide.

169. As in fighting formations, the exact interspacing between and disposition of aeroplanes in a bombing or other formation will vary according to the type and size of the aeroplanes and the tactical situation.

170. In nearly all types of day bombing formations, it is essential that during combat the aeroplanes should be kept as close together as possible without unduly masking the fire of each other's guns. When cruising, sub-formations should be allowed to open out so that the strain of close formation flying may be relieved, and sub-formation leaders enabled to locate their position on the map.

171. During an engagement, a pilot should avoid flying directly above another aeroplane in the formation. Apart from the probability that he will not be able to see it, there is the danger of collision if he is shot down or otherwise forced to dive suddenly.

172. Close formation has two essential advantages :—

(i) It places the attacker within effective range of the maximum number of the defending aeroplanes of the formation at the same time.

(ii) It renders it impossible for a hostile aeroplane to force its way through the formation and thus prevent pilots and gunners from opening fire on account of the danger of hitting each other.

173. As in fighting formations, the principle of the sub-formation will be adhered to in bombing or other formations. A formation in defence will make every effort to avoid becoming disorganized, but if forced to do so, the sub-formations can retain their cohesion and afford each other mutual support.

174. Formations in defence, as compared to attacking formations are more restricted in the variety and scope of their tactics. For this reason each member of a formation acting defensively is required to display initiative and execute timely offensive movements as opportunity offers.

175. When a formation of two-seaters engaged in bombing or other operations is attacked by a hostile formation it must depend primarily for its defence on the rear gunners. Close formation must be retained throughout the engagement and advantage may be taken of defensive manœuvring. When the attackers approach within range every possible gun will be brought to bear on them.

176. The gunners, however, must have a clear understanding of the system of fire and must know when they are to concentrate their fire on the leader of the enemy formation or sub-formations and when they are each to select different enemy aeroplanes for attack. The system must vary in accordance with the type of formation adopted by both the attackers and the defenders and numerous other factors. As a general rule, however, when the enemy is observed to be in a very good formation, fire, in the first attack, should be concentrated by all gunners upon the leaders of the sub-formations nearest to them. This, if successful, will cause the maximum disorganization of the enemy's attack and will ensure that if the enemy is attacking by sub-formations from different directions at the same time the attackers will always be met with fire. If the enemy aeroplanes are in bad attacking formation or have become disorganized, they are less formidable and may be engaged individually by the gunners of the defending two-seaters.

FIGHTING PATROLS.

General Principles.

177. Fighting patrols by night are dealt with in paras. 206–227 of this chapter. By day there are three types of operations on which aeroplanes are employed in war specifically for fighting, viz. :—offensive patrols, defensive patrols and escort duty.

178. The strength and composition of patrols will, of course, vary according to the general conditions of the war, the nature of the duty, the number and type of aeroplanes available and the anticipated strength of the enemy. It will seldom be possible, however, to be certain that any one patrol will be sufficiently strong to achieve complete success, and on this account it is important that means of communication between patrols, either in the air or on the ground, should be developed with a view to obtaining co-operation.

179. Effective co-operation between patrols and the effective operation of the patrols themselves calls for careful ground organization and a high state of training of personnel in the routine of preparing to start on patrol, leaving their base and gaining position in formation or on patrol.

180. A formation on patrol must take all possible measures to ensure that no hostile aircraft in the patrol area escape observation, and pilots must be trained to adapt their methods of observation to the varying conditions imposed by the state of the sky,

the time of day, etc., and should learn how to take advantage of cloud or other background such as desert which may facilitate observation.

181. In a cloudless sky enemy aircraft above a patrol which is facing into the sun may not be observed even though engaged by anti-aircraft artillery fire. When not facing the sun, however, a patrol can more easily observe hostile aircraft from below, either against a clear sky or high cloud.

182. For tactical reasons, however, the position of a patrol at a higher altitude than the enemy is desirable, and if the ground affords a reasonably good background or, as sometimes happens, there is a slight haze low down, enemy aeroplanes passing beneath should be observed, and a position higher than the enemy should, therefore, usually be adopted by a patrol, if possible.

183. It is the responsibility of all pilots and crews engaged in a patrol to keep a sharp look-out for hostile aircraft and to notify the leader by the recognised signal when any are observed. It is, therefore, desirable that the aeroplanes should cruise in sufficiently open formation to free pilots from the necessity of constantly watching the aeroplanes next to them and to avoid obstructing the view of the pilots and crews, but the formation should not be so open as to render rapid concentration difficult.

184. In cloudy weather it is desirable that observation should be kept above and below any cloud layer near which a patrol is operating. A patrol leader must, however, avoid the risk of his sub-formations losing touch and being unable to concentrate rapidly for attack, and, if this risk exists, he should not detach more than one or two aeroplanes at a time.

Offensive Patrols.

185. An offensive patrol is one carried out by individual aeroplanes or formations either over enemy territory or the sea. It may be with the general object of obtaining air superiority over the enemy, or have some more particular object, such as affording protection to the operations of friendly aircraft, or denying freedom of operation to enemy aircraft.

186. The immediate aim of the aeroplanes of an offensive patrol will be to seek out and destroy enemy aircraft, and their success will depend largely upon the initiative of the patrol leader, which should be restricted as little as possible by the orders he receives.

187. Before starting on a patrol, however, all pilots should receive explicit instructions concerning :—

(i) The object of the patrol.
(ii) The time of starting and ending.
(iii) The method of relief, if it is to be relieved.
(iv) The area or locality to be patrolled.
(v) The number and types of friendly aeroplanes it is anticipated will be in the area at the same time.

The height at which the patrol will fly and the disposition of the aeroplanes within it should be left, when possible, to the leader to decide in accordance with the prevailing conditions of weather, the object of the patrol and information he may have concerning the enemy, or the operations of friendly aircraft.

188. Much importance attaches to the disposition of the aeroplanes of a patrol to the best advantage for the observation of hostile aircraft, bearing in mind that the assistance of ground observers and anti-aircraft artillery will not normally be available. If he can do so without unduly weakening his strength, a leader should dispose his patrol in sub-formations at different heights.

189. Towards the end of the period of an offensive patrol it may not be possible to pursue or attack hostile aircraft observed, unless the aeroplanes have a margin of air endurance over and above that required for return to their base. The patrol will thus become less effective unless this is taken into account in its operation orders.

190. The duration of a patrol is usually counted from the time aeroplanes leave the ground to the time they leave the area or line they are patrolling.

191. In war, the areas in which offensive patrols operate, and the times of day, should usually be varied in order to prevent the enemy taking measures to avoid them or overcome them with superior forces.

192. It will sometimes be possible for an individual aeroplane to operate on offensive patrol with a " roving commission." In such cases the pilot must be one of exceptional ability and have great experience of the theatre of war, as he will depend for his security on his superior powers of observation and his ability to escape if surprised by superior forces. The actual method of carrying out the patrol will be left to the pilot's initiative, but he will usually cross the lines at a high altitude, and his success will be facilitated if he is in possession of the fullest information concerning the activities of friendly and hostile aircraft in the vicinity.

Defensive Patrols.

193. A fighting patrol is known as a defensive patrol when it is required to operate over friendly territory with the primary object of preventing the operations of enemy aeroplanes and intercepting them in approaching or retiring from their objectives.

194. This method of employing fighter aircraft confers the advantage of the initiative upon the enemy, and should not therefore be resorted to, except in the following circumstances :—

(i) When offensive patrols cannot operate owing to the distance of enemy territory, or suitable objectives.

(ii) When, owing to the close proximity of a defended area to the enemy, there is insufficient time for fighters, held at readiness, to take-off, intercept and defeat an attack, before the latter reaches its objective.

(iii) When, as at night or in cloudy weather, information from the ground observers of a local defence system, is not sufficiently comprehensive or reliable to ensure the requisite number of interceptions by aircraft held in readiness.

195. Defensive patrols work on the same general principles as offensive patrols and have the same immediate aim, *i.e.* to locate and attack enemy aeroplanes in the patrol area.

196. As compared to offensive patrols, defensive patrols have the advantage of assistance from ground observers and anti-aircraft artillery in locating the enemy aeroplanes. They may, however, be more restricted in their tactics—especially in home defence, as the line or area of patrol will be more strictly delimited and it will usually be necessary to attack on sight in order to prevent the enemy achieving his object. For this reason, defensive patrols should normally be stronger than offensive patrols in relation to the anticipated strength of the enemy.

197. The advantage the enemy has over a defensive patrol is that he may be able to select any direction or height of approach to the patrol area, and a time when weather conditions, etc., are most unfavourable to the defenders. He may also be able to make use of ruses or feint approaches to confuse and distract the defensive patrol.

198. To overcome these advantages of the enemy, a careful organization of the system of defensive patrols is required, embracing an elaborate scheme of ground observation and methods of communication with aeroplanes in flight and on the ground, and necessitating a well-organized procedure for the despatch of patrols from their base and for their return to re-fuel, and re-arm.

199. When plain language is used in inter-communication with patrols care must be exercised that the enemy are not enabled to intercept information upon which they can act with advantage.

200. A defensive patrol will usually be given a patrol line which, it is calculated, will lie on the line of advance of the enemy, and the enemy's height, strength and direction of approach will be communicated to the leader if and when they become known. It will then be the duty of the leader to select the height of patrol and the formation on the patrol line in such a way that every pilot can easily watch the sky and yet be able to concentrate at once in preparation for attack.

201. It will usually be necessary for defensive patrols to approach and attack the enemy in the shortest time possible in order to prevent him achieving his object. Patrol leaders, therefore, must endeavour to anticipate the course of enemy aeroplanes sighted, and fly in a direct line to the probable point of interception. There is usually a tendency to under-estimate the distance ahead of this point. After contact is made the time available for attack may be so short that patrols will be unable to choose the direction or method of attack.

202. On the other hand, the pilots and crews of a defensive patrol operating over friendly territory enjoy considerable moral advantage over the enemy in that they have nothing to fear from a forced descent in their aeroplane or parachute, and should, therefore, attack with much greater dash and determination than can the enemy, who may have a long and difficult flight still before them.

Escort Duty.

203. Fighting formations are seldom employed for the close escort of aeroplanes or formations engaged on special missions, since better results are usually obtained by sending offensive

patrols to operate in the area where opposition is likely to be encountered. In these circumstances offensive patrols must endeavour to act with great vigor so as to attract the attention of any enemy aeroplanes which may be in the vicinity.

204. Should an escort patrol be provided, however, its primary duty will be to enable the escorted aeroplane or formation to accomplish its mission, and it should not fight except in execution of this duty.

205. The escorted aeroplanes should fly in a separate formation and should be expected to deal with any minor opposition they may encounter, the escort patrol being there merely to attack and drive off hostile offensive patrols which may seek to interfere with the duty in hand. The escort should generally fly above the aeroplanes to be protected, in such a position as to be able to keep them constantly in view, and at the same time have freedom to manœuvre in any direction.

FIGHTING BY NIGHT.

General Remarks.

206. Owing to the difficulty of observing hostile aeroplanes, fighting at night will usually be effective only when over friendly territory and with the co-operation of an organization on the ground embracing sound rangers, searchlights and anti-aircraft guns. Night fighting over hostile territory will usually be confined to areas such as enemy aerodromes which are known to be active, and will be possible only on clear or bright nights.

207. Fighting patrols at night will usually be carried out by single aircraft operating in definite areas and within definite limits of height. For this reason fighting at night will usually be between individual aircraft.

Observation of Aircraft by Night.

208. Aircraft illuminated by searchlight can best be observed from below on dark nights and from above on bright moonlight nights. If not illuminated they can best be observed from below on both dark and bright nights.

209. It follows, therefore, that defensive patrols on dark nights should fly below the supposed height of the enemy ; and on bright nights they should fly above, unless searchlights are not available or the weather is unfavourable for their use.

210. Offensive patrols operating over an enemy aerodrome should fly low, not only to assist in observation of the enemy aeroplanes but also because their most favourable opportunity of attack will frequently be just as the enemy aeroplane is about to land and is silhouetted against the ground or wing tip flares.

211. The main consideration in defensive patrols is to ensure efficient co-operation with the searchlights and anti-aircraft batteries. If clouds prevent the searchlight crews seeing the enemy aircraft, they will endeavour to " point " the searchlights, that is, to concentrate a small number of beams as near as possible to the position of the enemy as determined by means of sound locators, etc.

212. An experienced searchlight crew can generally estimate the approximate altitude at which a hostile aircraft is flying, even if they fail to illuminate it at once ; pilots should, therefore, estimate the altitude of the first apex of beams and climb or descend to that altitude whilst searching.

213. On dark starlight nights it is possible to observe aeroplanes silhouetted against the sky as far off as 200 yards, and, on a bright moonlight night, as far as 600 yards. At these distances, however, all that can be seen is a dark shadow and it is rarely possible to determine if an aeroplane is hostile or friendly at a greater range than 100 yards. Pilots and crews should, therefore, make a careful study of the types of enemy aircraft and their silhouette form from all angles. They should note, in particular, the position and type of the enemy's engine exhaust pipes, as these act as one means of identification by appearing red at night and sometimes emitting sparks, which must not be mistaken for tracer bullets.

Defensive Patrols by Night.

214. The chances of encountering aircraft in the dark are small, and defensive patrols depend for their success on efficient co-operation between pilots and the personnel in charge of searchlights and anti-aircraft guns.

215. When a pilot observes hostile aircraft held in concentration of searchlights he should signal to the anti-aircraft gunners his intention of attacking. Upon receipt of this signal, anti-aircraft guns should cease fire, but searchlights should continue to hold the enemy aircraft in their beams.

216. Pilots should limit their activities to their own sector and should not normally leave it to search a concentration of searchlights in another area.

Offensive Patrols by Night.

217. Owing to the difficulty experienced in locating aircraft at night without the assistance of searchlights, it is usually best for offensive patrols to stand by until intelligence reports of hostile air activity are received. These reports may be obtained by information supplied by reconnaissance pilots flying over the enemy's country or by reports from advanced troops or observation posts.

218. As soon as information has been obtained as to which hostile aerodromes are active, the patrol should be sent off to one of them and should remain in its vicinity until the hostile aircraft, on their return from their mission, disclose their presence by switching on navigation lights or by endeavouring to signal to their aerodrome, when they can be attacked.

219. The moral effect of destroying hostile aircraft over their own aerodrome is very great, and this is increased by attacking the hangars, anti-aircraft defences and searchlights, especially if the attackers are armed with light bombs which can be released as soon as a hostile aeroplane is seen to be attempting to land.

Two-seater aeroplanes in which the observer can use his gun while the pilot is occupied in manœuvring the aeroplane are better suited to this form of attack than single-seaters, since diving near the ground is rendered more difficult at night owing to the dazzling effect of searchlights and the flash produced by the attackers' own guns.

Tactics of Night Fighting.

220. The methods of approach and attack of hostile aeroplanes at night are restricted owing to the ease with which the enemy may become lost to view.

221. Apart from the natural difficulty of keeping in view an aeroplane which starts to manœuvre rapidly in darkness, the glare of searchlights may cause a pilot to lose sight of the enemy, and the flash of his own machine guns, even when shielded, will usually impair a pilot's sight to such an extent that after the first few rounds have been fired he will lose sight of his target.

222. It is, therefore, of the utmost importance in night fighting that the first burst of fire should be effective. To minimise the dazzling effect of machine-gun flash, it is desirable that only a small proportion of tracer bullets should be fired from the pilot's guns, and, if the aeroplane is a two-seater, the rear gun should be used as the primary weapon.

223. To ensure that the first attack is effective, fire should not be opened except at very close range. When a hostile aeroplane is observed, therefore, the object of the attacker will be to approach within decisive range without disclosing his presence.

224. Range at night is very deceptive, and pilots are prone to under-estimate it. Fire should, therefore, not be opened until the attacker is close enough to distinguish the outline and principal characteristics of his opponent; this will ensure :—

    (i) That fire is opened at effective range.

    (ii) That a friendly aeroplane is not attacked by mistake.

    (iii) That a friendly aeroplane engaged in attacking the same opponent is not hit by wide shots.

225. The most favourable position for attack is from the rear, and slightly below the enemy aeroplane. From this position searchlight glare will not cause the attacker to lose sight of the enemy, and his reduced relative speed will enable him to fire a long burst at close range.

226. Every effort should be made to take steady aim and to make sure that the first burst of fire strikes the hostile aeroplane in a vital spot. Great coolness and self-control will be required to overcome the tendency to open fire erratically or at indecisive ranges.

227. Before opening fire it is essential to establish the identity of the object aircraft without possibility of error, as a friendly aircraft may easily be mistaken for an enemy in the dark at long ranges.

REAR-GUARD ACTION.

General Principles.

228. Although in air fighting the offensive spirit is essential, there are many occasions upon which rear-guard action may become necessary owing to the nature of the mission which is being performed. Moreover, owing to the fact that limited fuel capacity forces an aeroplane pilot to return to his aerodrome after the lapse of a certain length of time, he may be compelled to retreat in order to avoid the possibility of a forced landing.

229. The methods to be employed in fighting a rear-guard action must necessarily vary according to the type and number of aircraft engaged in the battle, and will depend on the mission, the performance of which is the immediate object of the flight, but there is one rule which is applicable to all methods, *viz.* : " The best method of defence is to employ aggressive tactics." This does not mean that an isolated pilot, or even the leader of a formation, should fly out of his course to attack any enemy observed in the sky, but that whenever an encounter is imminent, the enemy should be met and fought in the same spirit as that which animates the attack, *i.e.* the determination, not merely to drive him away, but to defeat and destroy him. It should not be forgotten that the attacker invariably possesses a moral advantage, though his advantage may to a large extent be nullified if he be met with determination, and, when his attack has failed, counter-attacked with vigour.

Individual Rear-guard Action.

230. Owing to lack of armament aft, a single-seater pilot forced to fight a rear-guard action is extremely vulnerable, since he can only use his guns by turning to face his aggressor. The nature of his mission, or lack of fuel, may compel him to fly towards his aerodrome, but, even if he is attacked by superior numbers, his best defence is to counter-attack with such skill and determination that the enemy may leave him to resume his course unmolested.

231. A good method of counter-attacking an enemy diving from astern, is to turn suddenly in his direction and, as he flattens out to avoid a collision, fire up at him, and then execute a climbing turn on to his tail.

232. If attacked from below, a sudden zoom and turn, executed so as to terminate in a dive on to the enemy's tail, may sometimes be successful. Care should be taken to carry out this manœuvre so as to surprise the attacker, otherwise he will counter it by changing direction.

233. A single-seater pilot who runs out of ammunition, or finds himself with his guns out of action, can defend himself only by manœuvre. If attacked by a pilot flying a similar type of aeroplane, he should endeavour to outclimb his attacker. If the attacked pilot fails to outclimb his opponent, he may succeed in out-manœuvring him by keeping at the same altitude and

flying parallel to him, so that the opponent, unless he possesses great advantage in speed, will not be able to gain a firing position without turning and losing distance. By manœuvring skilfully in this manner and seizing every opportunity afforded by the enemy to edge closer to friendly territory, a retreat may be successfully achieved.

234. Unless as a means of gaining a position of advantage, the straight dive away from an opponent should not be used, as by doing so, the attacker obtains an easy shot even if outdistanced.

235. If there are clouds near at hand, an enemy may be shaken off by diving into them. It is not advisable to spin unless over clouds, as a straight dive is necessary to regain control, when the attacker, if he has followed, will obtain a no-deflection shot.

236. A quick climbing turn, carried out generally with too much rudder, is the best method of escaping from an unfavourable position, since this manœuvre does not entail loss of height, which would afford the enemy the opportunity of resuming the attack with a tactical advantage. A pilot, even when short of ammunition, may succeed in driving off a hesitating attact by showing a bold front.

237. If a pilot is forced to abandon the combat when flying at a low altitude, the best method of escape is to go right down and fly back on a zig-zag course as close to the ground as possible. Even a determined attack may be driven off by skilful flying and by dodging round obstacles such as trees and houses.

238. A rear-guard action is more easily fought with a two-seater aeroplane owing to its ability to develop fire astern, and success will depend very largely on the skill and alertness of the back gunner, whose primary duty is to avoid being taken by surprise.

239. Although the general tactics, described above, to be adopted by a single-seater pilot in fighting a rear-guard action apply equally to a two-seater pilot, the object of the latter when attacked should be to manœuvre so as to disturb the enemy's aim, and at the same time to facilitate the fire of his own back-gunner, while being himself ready to seize any opportunity that he may be afforded of destroying the attacker with his front gun.

240. For a two-seater to dive or spin away with the object of escaping from an enemy is just as fatal as it is for a single-seater to do so, since in these positions the back gunner is hindered in the use of his weapons. On the other hand, an upward spiral affords the gunner an opportunity of firing, and renders the attacker's target extremely difficult to hit.

241. The same fire tactics as are laid down for the pilot apply equally to the gunner, except that as the latter is generally provided with a larger quantity of ammunition, he can use his gun more freely and open fire at longer ranges. A gunner should, however, delay the opening of fire until the enemy arrives within effective range; otherwise he will merely expend ammunition without result. Nevertheless, one or two short bursts at long range will sometimes deter a hesitant enemy or cause him to open fire too soon to be effective.

Collective Rear-guard Action.

242. The ability to fight a successful rear-guard action depends, for all classes of pilots on well-disciplined formation flying. (*See* Chapter III.) Once a formation has become disorganized, especially in the face of superior enemy forces, the leader will experience difficulty in collecting his scattered force, and the enemy will thus be afforded the opportunity of destroying the formation in detail.

243. The leader of a formation which is attacked by superior numbers from above, should warn his pilots to hold themselves in readiness for a change of direction as soon as he observes the enemy's approach to be imminent. As the hostile leader dives, a turn in his direction should be executed ; if the change of direction is carried out at the right moment, the hostile formation will overshoot, and possibly leave itself open to a counter-attack.

SPECIAL MISSIONS.
General Principles.

244. Although the general principles of air fighting, both in attack and defence, are applicable to all types of aeroplanes, it is often necessary to employ aeroplanes for duties other than fighting, and combat should not then be sought. Thus if a formation is required to carry out an important reconnaissance or bomb attack, it is obvious that the fulfilment of the duty in hand may be the primary consideration. On the other hand, the execution of such duties in the face of a hostile air force will not generally be possible without fighting, and it is therefore essential that the formation undertaking it should be organized for defence.

245. Success in the performance of operations under these conditions may be achieved even in the face of attack by superior forces. Determined and skilful leadership, combined with good formation flying may cause the enemy to delay his attack in the hope of obtaining reinforcements, and thus give time for the duty in hand to be accomplished.

246. When attacked, the primary object of the formation will be to retain its cohesion, to do which it must be able to fight a rear-guard action and prevent the enemy from delivering a concerted attack against one or two aeroplanes at a time and thus destroying the formation by a series of isolated engagements.

247. A formation which has been well trained and is capable of flying in close order, even in difficult circumstances, should be able to contend with any normal opposition and to inflict such heavy losses on the aggressors that they will hesitate to renew the attack.

1940
Forget-Me-Nots for Fighters
by No. 13 Group, R.A.F.

FORGET-ME-NOTS for FIGHTERS

by

NO 13 GROUP
RAF

FOREWORD

"All for one and one for all"

THIS BOOK is the outcome of discussion amongst the Training Staff, on the best and simplest way to bring to the notice of new Fighter Pilots certain salient points in air fighting, which it is essential that they should master before taking their places as operational pilots in Fighter Squadrons.

The various points illustrated are by no means fully comprehensive, and it must be clearly understood that only the main points which a new Fighter Pilot should know before going into action are included. These have been compiled on the advice and guidance of many well-known and proved Fighter Pilots, who have willingly co-operated in placing their knowledge and experience at the disposal of their younger brother pilots.

In selecting the motto of "The Three Musketeers" to put at the head of this Foreword, I have done so because it expresses what should be the creed of every Fighter Pilot. Never forget you are an essential cog in the wheel, and if you break or fail it will let down your brother pilots, and the grimness of war allows for no such weakness.

Air fighting is a combination of skill and courage, which, allied with confidence and experience, makes the Fighter Pilot master of his trade.

Good luck to each and every one of you.

R. E. Saul

Air Vice-Marshal,
Air Officer Commanding, No. 13 Group.

The need for vigilance

Never stop looking round. Many pilots shot down never saw the enemy fighter that got them. Out of every five minutes on patrol four should be spent looking over your shoulders. Whether you are by yourself or with a hundred others, never stop looking round. Mirrors are useful, but not infallible.

Start looking round as you taxi out to take off, and do not stop until you have taxied in—people have been shot taking off and landing.

NEVER STOP LOOKING ROUND

SOME PILOTS NEVER SAW THE ENEMY THAT GOT THEM

LOOK — WHEN TAKING OFF

AND LANDING

Search Formation and Weaving

The object of Search Formation is to provide the maximum and most effective look-out for enemy aircraft. Remember that your Leader can't always be expected to sight the enemy first, as he is a busy man. This responsibility must be shared by ALL members of the formation, and all your lives depend on the vigilance of your look-out. The Leader, and in some cases other Pilots are detailed to watch the area in front of the leading edge of their main planes, but there are always some Pilots whose duty is "Weaving," and it is on them that the responsibility for keeping a watch to the rear depends.

Weaving is to enable you to keep a good look out for enemy aircraft both behind and above; the best position for a Vic of three is 50 to 100 yards apart; if in a section of four, the man in the box should do most of the Weaving.

THE LEADER IS A BUSY MAN

THE MAN IN THE BOX

Always keep above your Leader: it will help you to come into formation quickly. This is vital for formation attacks. The man who is late lets the team down—sometimes right down. Try and weave alternately with your opposite number, and do not stop until you are over the base. Several times formations have been surprised after the order to "pancake." Take it for granted there is a HUN behind you. There often is!

Attacks

The advantage of height is half the battle. Always try to achieve it. Remember that the initial attack is the most successful. Keep together for it, and if possible after it; you may have another chance to go in together.

Attack forward of the Beam; it is the most effective, and you don't get hit often. Your breakaway must be a "HAM" manoeuvre downwards.

THE LATE MAN LETS THE TEAM DOWN

THERE OFTEN IS

THE ADVANTAGE OF HEIGHT.

Always stick together for as long as possible—you can then help each other when dog fights ensue.

When you have got separated from your Leader, individual attacks must be largely left to your own judgment, but here are a few tips:—

DON'T rush in without thinking how you are going to attack, but on the other hand, DON'T hang about trying to work out something very clever, as there is probably a "Messerschmitt" very close, and it would be such a pity if you didn't see him.

ALWAYS STICK
TOGETHER AS
LONG AS POSSIBLE.

DON'T HANG ABOUT
THINKING UP SOMETHING CLEVER.

The Almighty provided the Sun and Clouds for several reasons, take advantage of both. Remember there is no such thing as a " sitter."

The range is invariably twice what you think it is, so save your ammunition, and DON'T open fire too soon. You will probably need all your ammunition in a few moments.

Aim at 12 o'clock on your target, and use a head-on attack if possible against a formation. When using deflection always allow twice as much as you think necessary.

A three seconds burst is normally sufficient to shoot a German down, so look behind you every three seconds.

THERE IS NO SUCH THING AS "A SITTER"

YOU MAY RUSH IN WHERE YOU WILL, A FEW MINUTES LATER, 'FEAR TO TREAD' —

Evasive Tactics

A barrelled aileron turn is very effective with fighters. An increasing rate of turn prevents the enemy getting his sights on to you, and will usually give you a shot at him. Try and face an enemy fighter who is above you. Climb into the Sun: this will also give you an attacking position.

Remember that the Sun can be your best friend, and your worst enemy. Used correctly he is your friend; neglected, he can be your worst enemy.

When out of ammunition DON'T hang about, but dive steeply with rocking turns to right and left. If you put your stick forward quickly the engine will cut out for a few seconds. This is not recommended.

If you have been really surprised by an enemy fighter on your tail, and if his bullets are getting uncomfortably close, do a quick barrel half roll, pulling the stick back firmly when you are on your side, and then rudder into a steep dive with aileron turns.

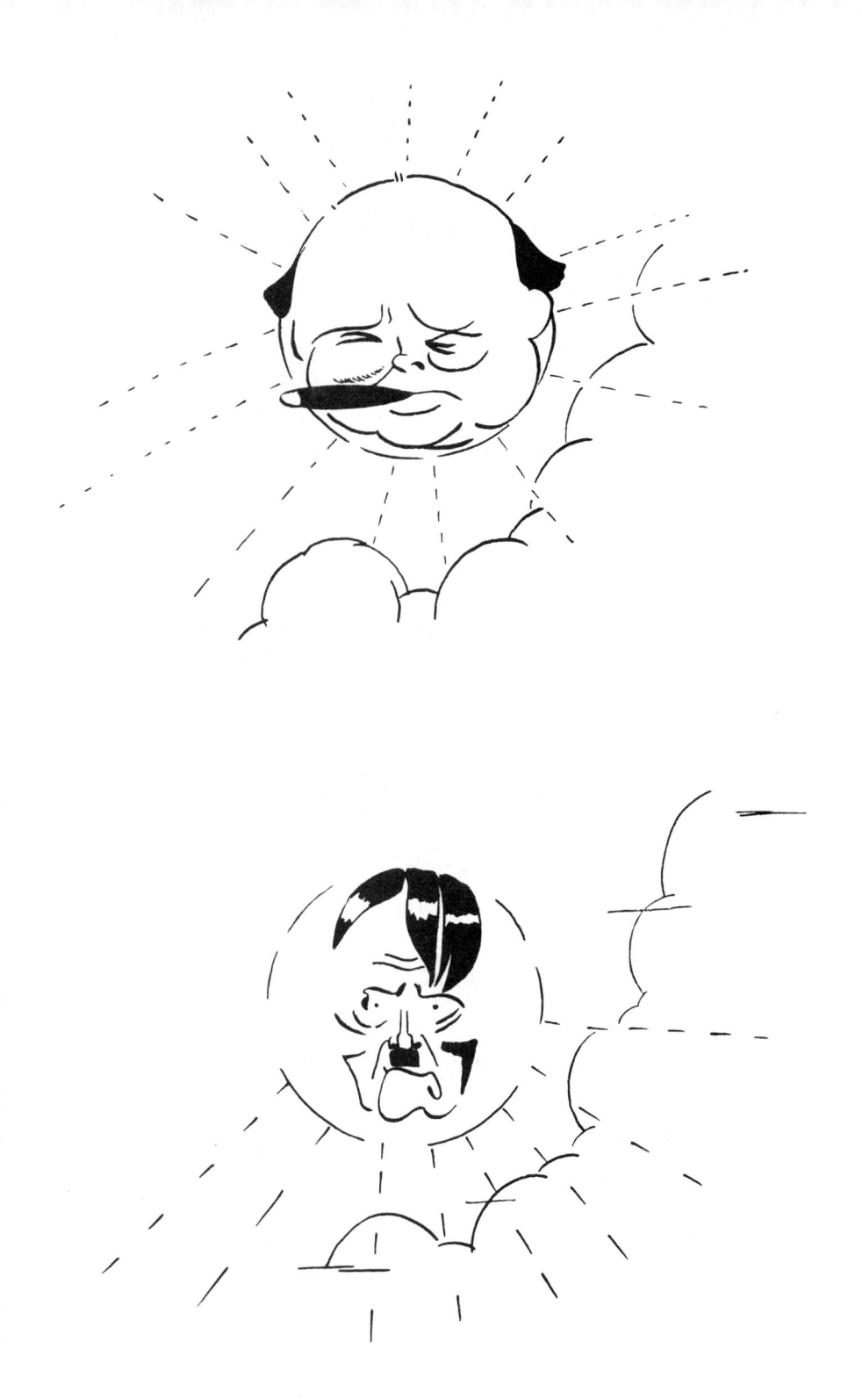

Reporting of enemy

DON'T get excited, and DON'T shout. Speak slowly and into the microphone. Report ALL hostile aircraft, not one group, and then a few minutes afterwards another one below or above.

If you see a formation of enemy aircraft look all round it, and report its escorts at the same time, using the clock system, and giving their height above or below you.

It is also quite a good idea when you have finished, to put your R/T set on to receive.

Remember that ACK-ACK bursts are often a useful indication of the whereabouts of enemy aircraft.

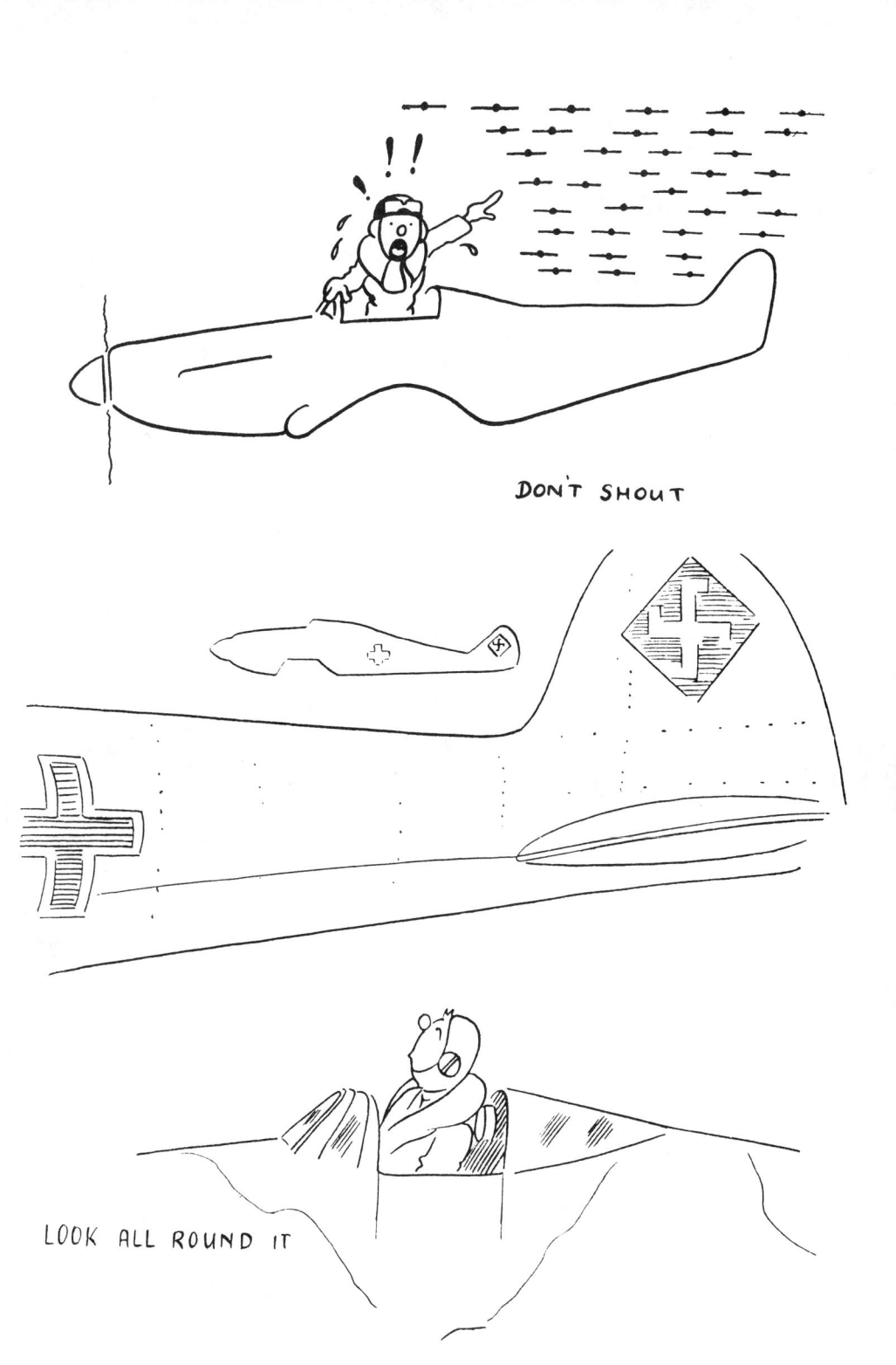

DON'T SHOUT

LOOK ALL ROUND IT

R/T

Remember that "Silence is Golden."

Maintain R/T silence unless you have something important to say. Always say who you are; speak slowly—if it is really important speak slower than usual. This is quicker than having to repeat.

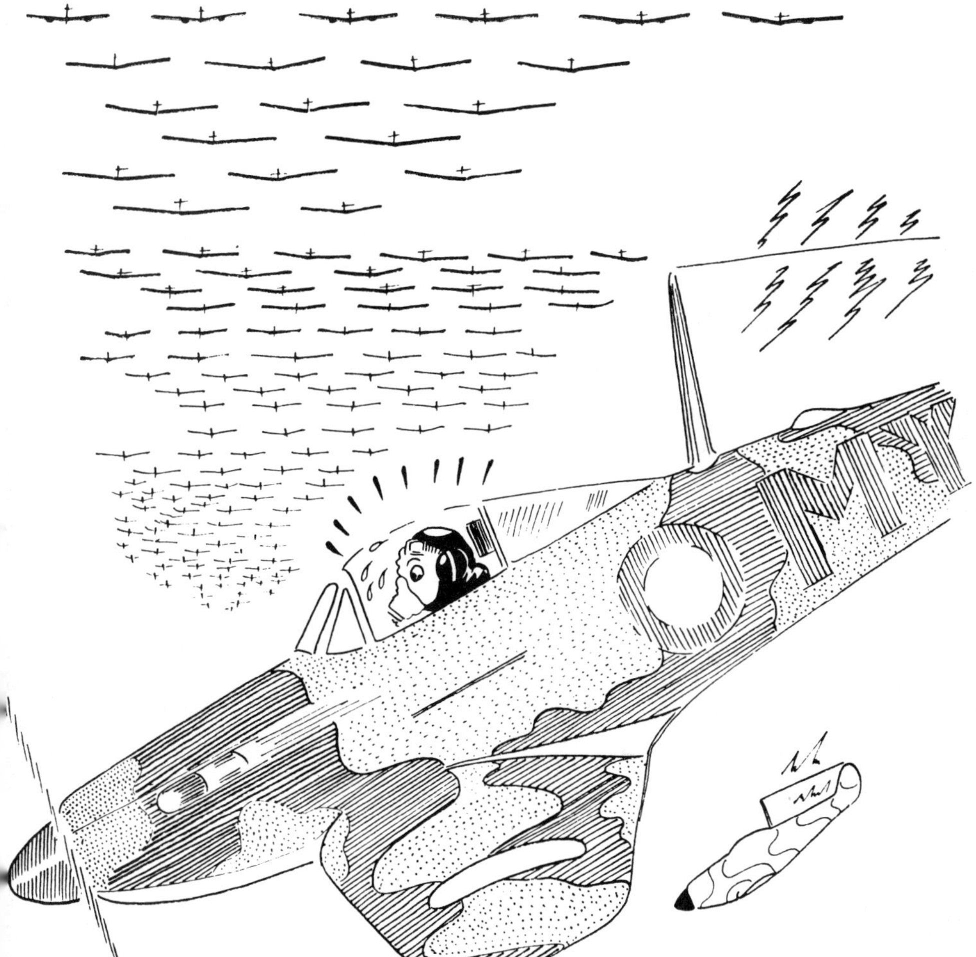

Use hand signals if you can. Remember that the Leader will tap his microphone if he thinks you have left your transmitter on. If you are guilty you had better avoid him when you get home.

USE HAND SIGNALS IF YOU CAN —

DON'T LEAVE YOUR TRANSMITTER ON!

IF YOU DO — AVOID THE LEADER WHEN YOU COME HOME.

Baling out

The sequence of operations is most important, even if you are in a hurry. First, lift your seat to the full up position, slide back your hood and lock it fully open. Undo your harness, take hold of the parachute rip cord, and then either stand up on the seat and put the stick forward, or roll on to your back. Our old friends gravity and centrifugal force will have done the rest before you know they have started. If the aircraft is spinning get out on the inside of the spin.

If you are on fire DON'T open the hood until the last moment, as it will draw flames into the cock-pit.

If your clothes are soaked in petrol, switch off the engine switches, and leave the throttle open, otherwise as you get out the sparks from the exhaust may act like the flint in your cigarette lighter.

LOCK YOUR HOOD
FULLY OPEN.

DON'T OPEN YOUR HOOD TILL
THE LAST MINUTE.

Keep hold of the rip-cord as you leave the aircraft, but if you are very high there is no need to pull it for the time being. Pilots who have pulled the rip-cord immediately after getting out in a high speed dive have been badly injured. You will fall more slowly out of your aeroplane than in it, so do a delayed drop whenever you can. The "109" will also find you harder to hit with the umbrella shut than open. You only fall 1,000 feet in 5 seconds so there is really plenty of time.

If you have failed to keep hold of the rip-cord as you left the aircraft, it is quite easy to look down and find it. If for any reason you cannot see, pass your right hand down the centre of your chest till you come to the quick release knob, then move it left along the wide strap and you will find the rip-cord.

Flying boots, leather gloves and goggles will protect you if your clothing or the cock-pit should catch fire.

Your gloves are most important, as if your right hand were to get burnt you would not be able to feel the rip-cord.

THERE IS PLENTY OF TIME

General

If your aircraft has been hit, test the hydraulic system at a safe height. If it has broken you can nearly always get your wheels down by diving and pulling out quickly, or by rocking the aircraft with your rudder. If it still won't come down ask for orders over the R/T, since it might be possible to land with wheels up at your Maintenance Unit.

If your wing surface has been damaged by a cannon shell, or a panel has been lost, remember that the wing will stall first when holding off to land, so be ready for this, and try and do a wheel landing.

If you have been wounded and feel you may pass out before you get home, turn the oxygen full on—it will help you a lot.

TEST YOUR HYDRAULIC
SYSTEM AT A SAFE HEIGHT

ROCK YOUR A/C
WITH YOUR
RUDDER.

IT MAY BE
POSSIBLE TO LAND
WITH WHEELS UP AT YOUR
MAINTENANCE UNIT.

Don'ts

NEVER follow down a machine you have shot; there may be a kick still left in the air gunner, or he may have a pal in a M.E. 109 just behind you.

DON'T approach a friendly aircraft from astern; come in from the side, so that he can see your markings.

DON'T get out of your Leader's sight. He hates playing hide and seek.

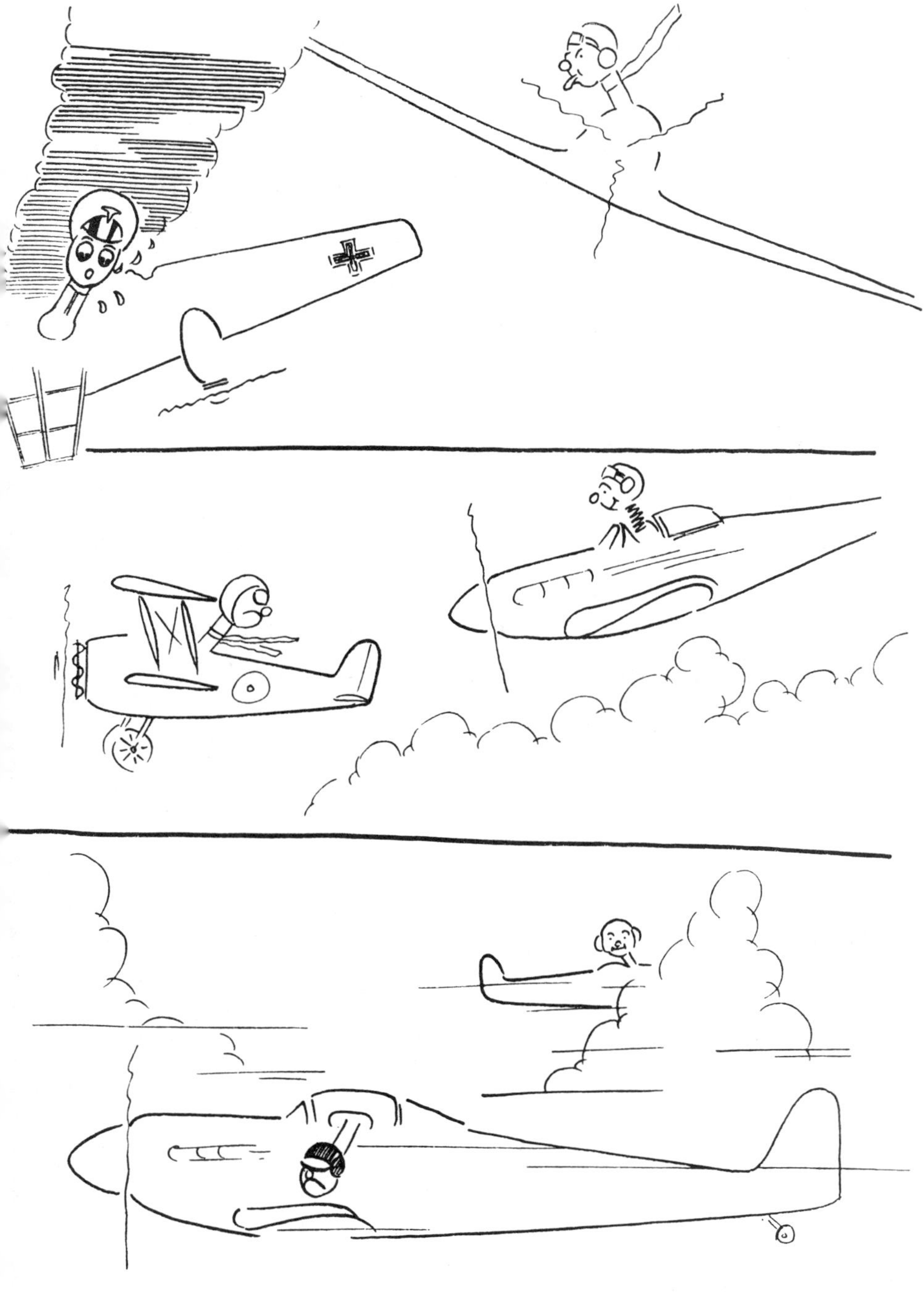

DON'T open fire unless you are certain it is an enemy aircraft. If you are within range you can always see his markings.

NEVER break formation to do an individual attack. He who hunts on his own won't live long to enjoy it.

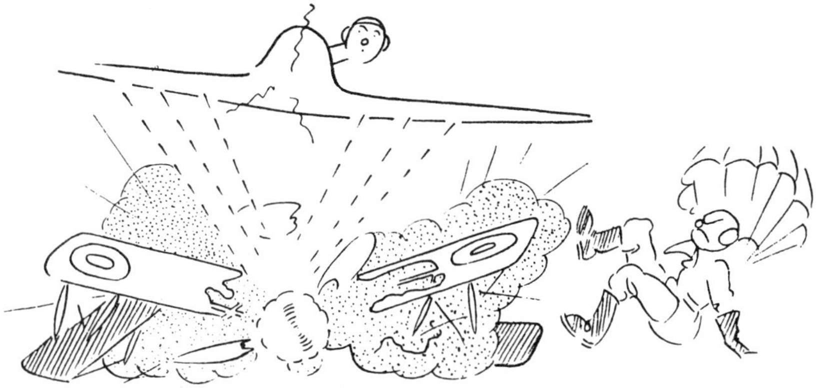

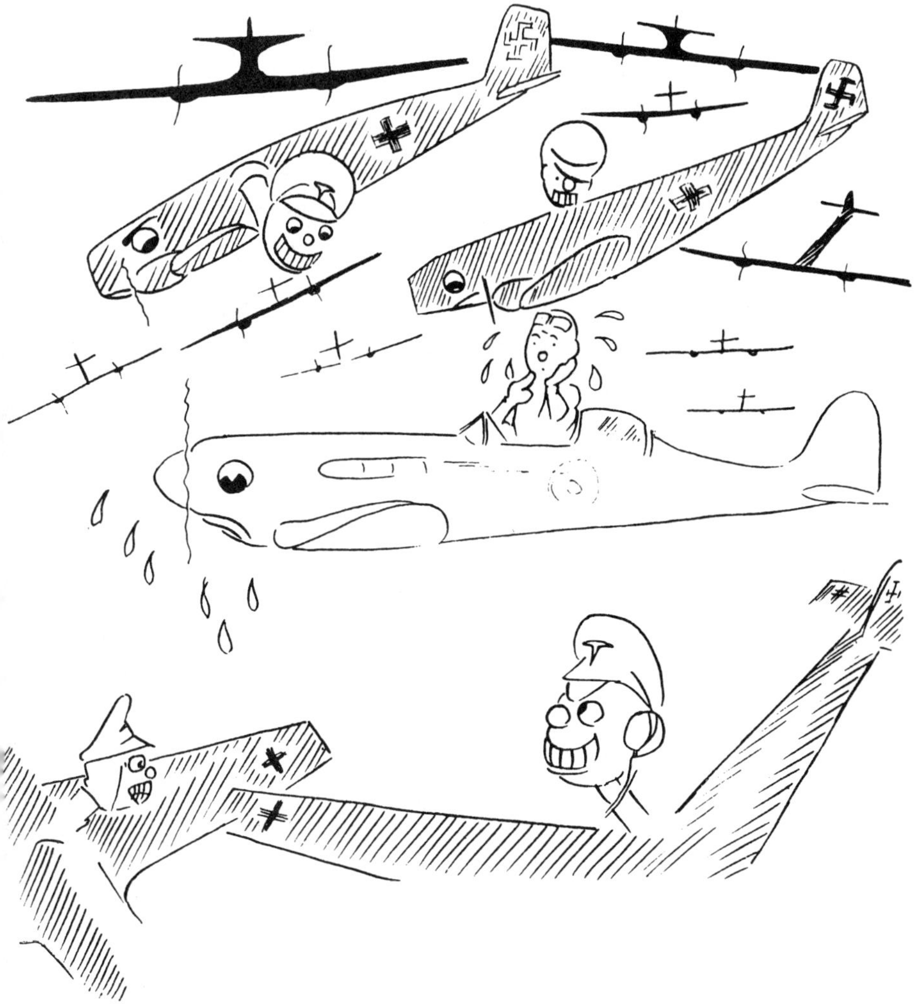

DON'T imagine that an enemy aircraft is "finished" if you see black smoke pouring from his engines.

DON'T forget to turn the firing button on to "FIRE."

DON'T forget your radiator; remember that your guns need keeping warm.

DON'T forget your oxygen at night; you need more, and you need it from the time you leave the ground.

FIRE

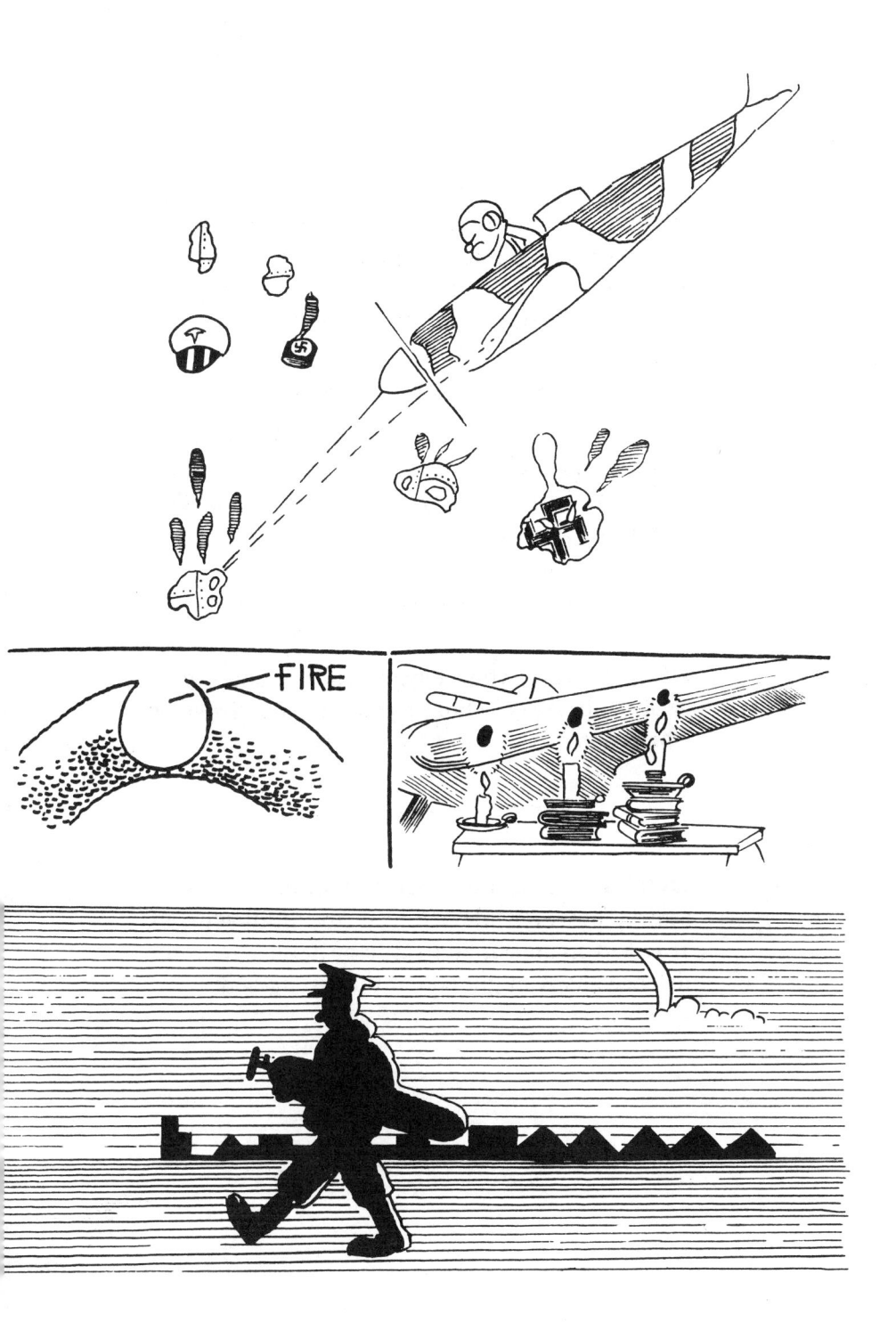

DON'T go into a combat without goggles over your eyes. Splintered glass is not good for them, and some Pilots are now paying extra Insurance Premiums for their cars.

DON'T go off without your goggles, gloves and flying boots. They are a great help in case of fire in the cock-pit.

DON'T wind your oxygen tube around your neck. It may choke you if you have to "bale out."

DON'T "beat up" the aerodrome on your return, however pleased you are with yourself. It is bad manners, and some of those aerodrome defence chaps might take it the wrong way.

DON'T FORGET THESE

DON'T land with your wheels up after an exciting and successful combat. Some have.

NEVER forget that the HUN is listening to nearly everything you say either on the R/T or in the "Local."

Be careful what you say on the former, and always resist the temptation of describing even your most successful patrol at the latter. It would be very hard to do so without telling HITLER something that he would like to know.

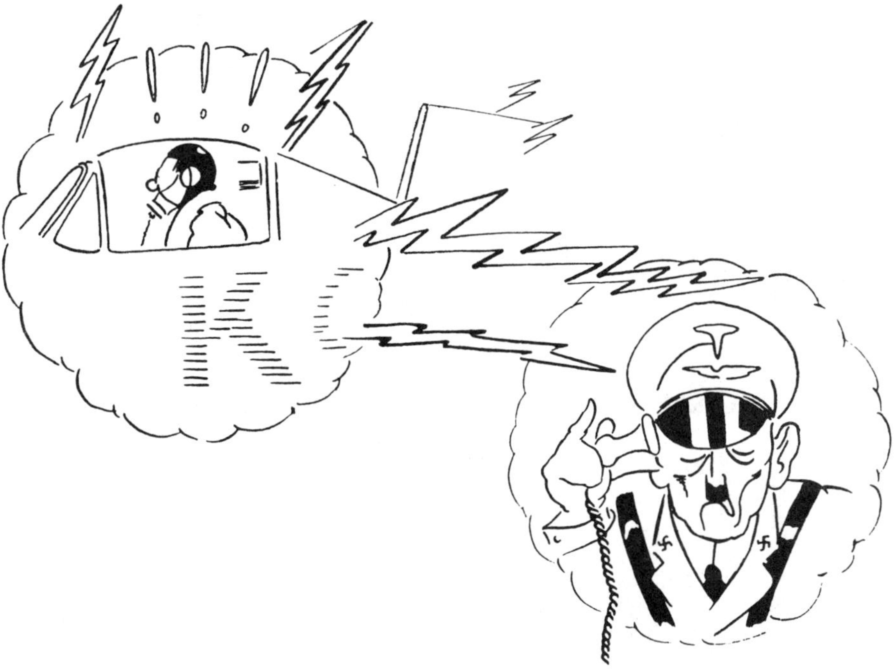

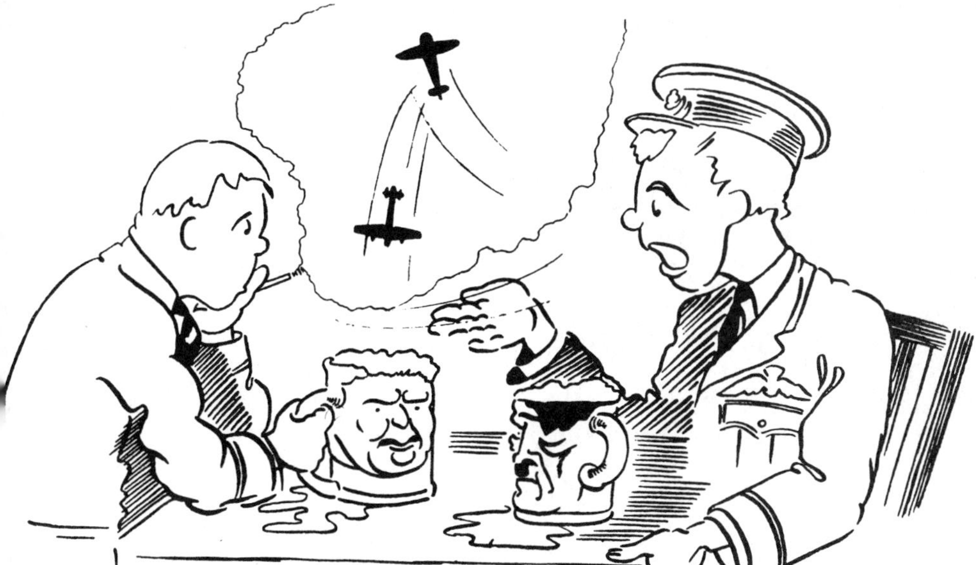

DON'T get shot down. YOU SHOULDN'T IF YOU TAKE THESE HINTS!

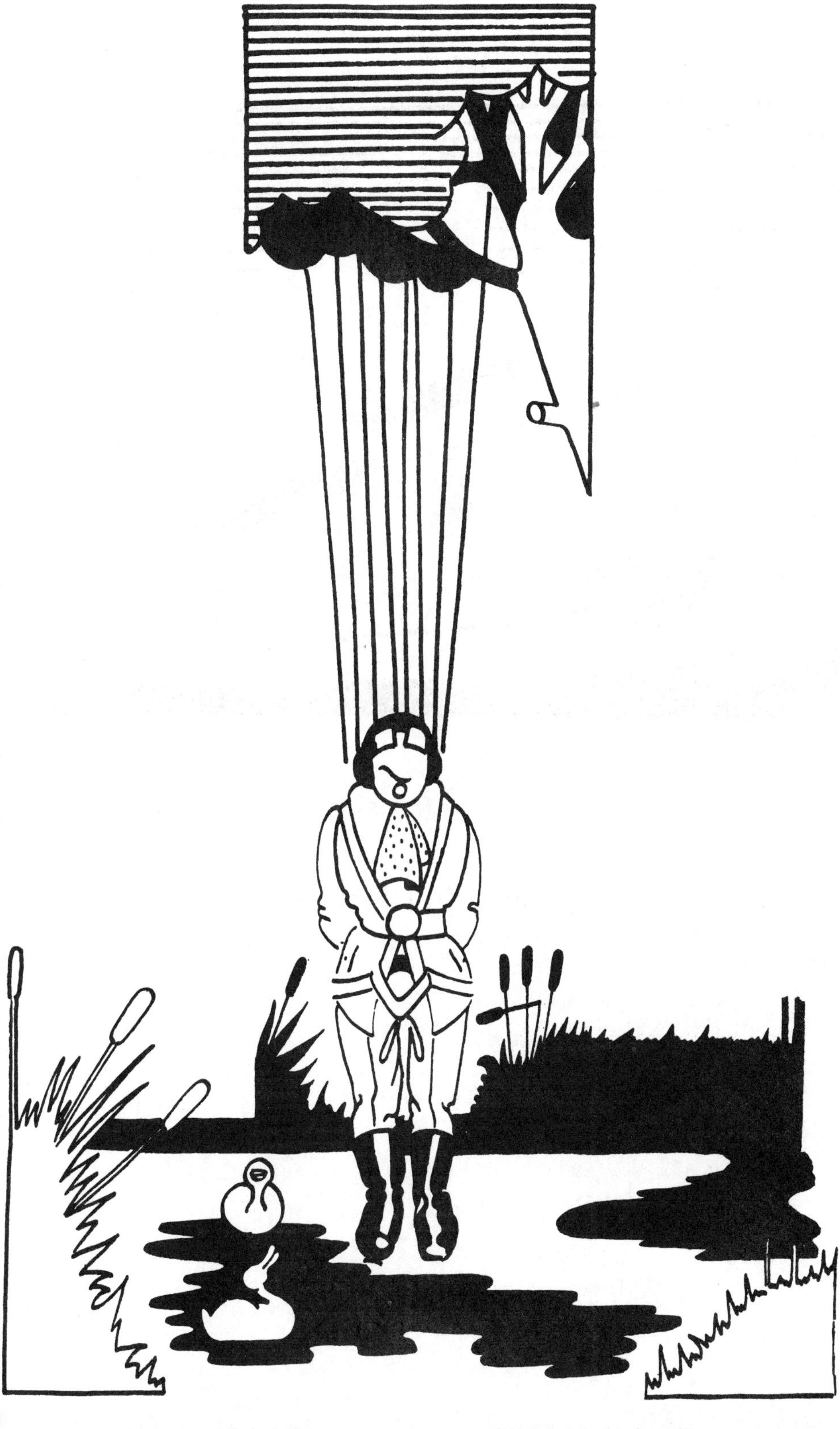

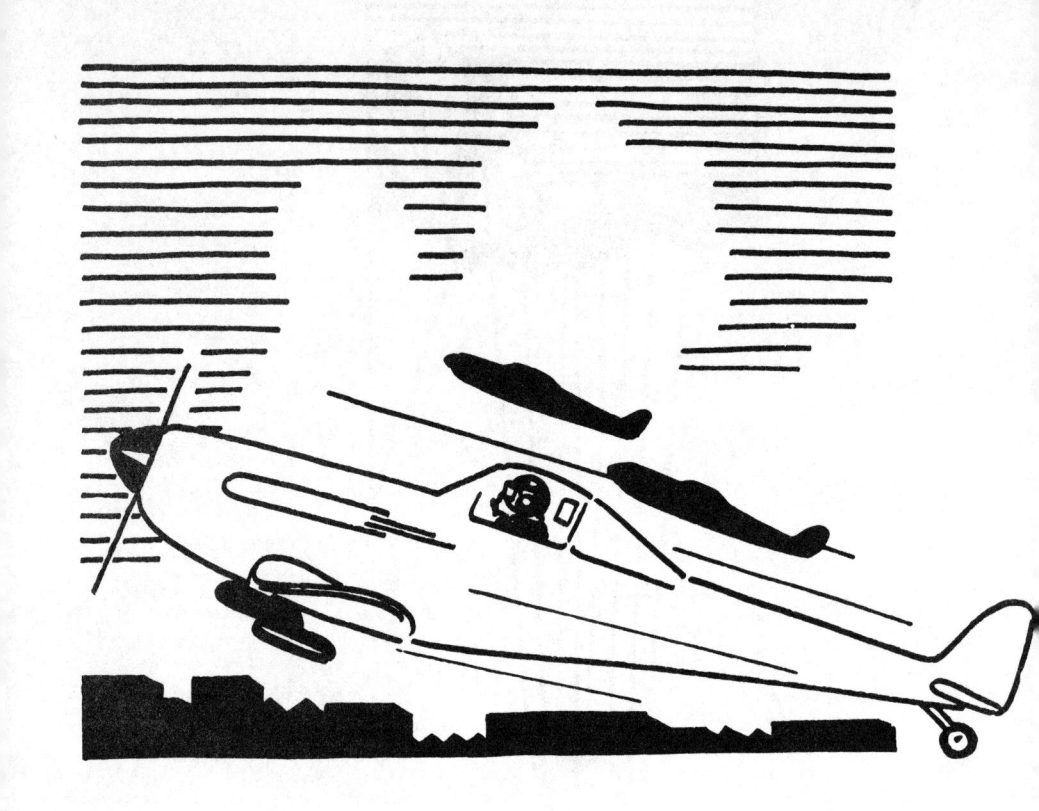

GOOD HUNTING!

1943

Notes on Air Gunnery and Air Fighting

by Wing Commander E. M. Donaldson,
D.S.O., A.F.C., R.A.F.

GENERAL NOTES ON AERIAL GUNNERY

FIXED GUNS IN FIGHTERS.--The guns are fixed in the aircraft and harmonized so that they fire along the fore and aft axis of the ship. So that to aim the guns, it is necessary to point the whole ship, and aim the ship with the sight provided directly on your target at the correct range.

SIGHTING.--When shooting at a stationary target one merely has to aim directly at the target and pull the trigger in order to hit it. But should the target be apparently moving (that is, not flying directly to or from you, or is a stationary target on the ground) then several complicated points arise. You as a pilot have to judge:
    (i) The distance from the target.
    (ii) The speed of the target.
    (iii) The distance to aim ahead because of the speed of the target to allow for the length of time the bullet takes to get from the gun to the target.
    (iv) The angle that target is cutting with your own course.

Suppose the pilot has only an aiming point to direct his fire by, he has to then judge all the above points accurately. Supposing, however, he has a ring and bead type of sight (an explanation of which follows) he need not trouble about the point number (i) the distance from the target; or point number (iii) the distance to aim ahead of the target because the ring at once gives him an angle instead of the two distances. Your problems with a ring are therefore reduced to:
    (i) Speed of the target, and
    (ii) Angle of target's course to your own.

THE RING AND BEAD SIGHT.--The ring and bead sight consists of a bead sight mounted well forward toward the nose of the aircraft and a double ring sight mounted fairly close in front of the pilot's eye. The inner ring of the back sight is just larger than the bead of the foresight and thus if you, as pilot, align the inner ring of the back sight with the bead of the foresight, onto the target, you will then be aiming along the fore and aft axis of your aircraft, or, in other words, along your line of flight. With the same alignment, from your eye onto a target, the outer ring gives you an allowance basis for targets moving at any angle to your line of flight. The size you have the outer ring is immaterial but experienced pilots have preferred a ring designed for target speed of 100 miles per hour when flying at right angles to their line of flight. In other words if you are using a 100 m.p.h. ring sight and are approaching a target which is flying on a course 90º different from your own, you should, while holding your eye and the bead centralized in the inner ring, maneuver your aircraft so as to place the target on the outer ring of the sight but flying directly at the center bead. If you hold this aim, you should hit the target. The angle between the line of the pilot's eye and the outer ring to target and the line through the inner ring and the bead (which is the path of the bullets) is called the angle of deflection. So when a pilot fires at a target moving other than directly toward or away from him, he must allow an angle of deflection. Or as the Americans call it, he must LEAD the target.

The size of the outer ring can be calculated on certain standard data as follows:
    (i) The distance you wish to have between your eye to the ring sight, in feet.
    (ii) The average speed of the bullet, in feet per second.
    (iii) The speed of the target in feet per second.

In this way:

$$\frac{\text{The distance from the eye in feet}}{\text{Bullet speed in feet per second}} \times \text{Speed of target in feet per second} = \text{The size in feet of the outer ring.}$$

An electrical sight designed on the basis of the ring and bead sight just described, shows a lighted image on the windshield of the ring and bead. This is called the Ring and Dot Reflector Sight. The Reflector sight has many good points over the ring and bead sight but the ring and bead sight has to be retained in case of failure of the electrical side of the reflector sight. To enumerate, these points are:
    (1) In the ring and bead sight, because of the size of the outer ring has been calculated according to the distance the pilot's eye is from the ring sight,

it is essential that he places his eye at this exact distance otherwise the basic allowance given by the outer ring will vary. For instance, if the distance of the sight from the pilot's eye be eight inches, a movement of two inches towards or away from the sight will give an error of 25 feet at 400 yards. This is not so with the reflector sight which automatically compensates for any distance the pilot may place his head from the sight.

(ii) In the ring and bead sight the pilot must align the bead of the fore sight in the inner ring of the back sight in his eye for every type of shot otherwise his "line of sight" will be incorrect. For instance, if the eye is 1/8" out of line it will give an error of 20 feet at 400 yards. Again this is not so with the reflector sight which, so long as it's image is visible on the windshield, it again automatically compensates for the position of the pilot's head.

(iii) The eye like a camera has to be in focus to see the object clearly, hence if the target is in focus the sights must be out of focus and are not seen distinctly. Not so with the reflector sight which gives the pilot the vision of the dot and ring's image being superimposed on the target.

DEFLECTION ALLOWANCES AND DIFFERENT ANGLES OF ATTACK.--When the target is flying at an angle of less than 90° to your aircraft the amount of deflection to be taken varies with the sine of the angle of attack. This is best shown diagramatically.

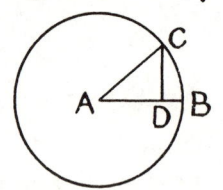

In the above diagram an aircraft flying across the ring sight from A to B at 90° to your course would therefore have to be positioned at the point B to allow for the target's movement during the time of the flight of the bullet over the target range. The distance AB is the full deflection allowed by the sight. An aircraft attacking along the line CA would be at 45°, would at first sight appear to be 1/2 that of 90°. This is not so, and it can be seen from the diagram that the allowance for 45° is DA, which is considerably more than 1/2 the line AB. That distance is of

410-2F-42

course allowed along the line of flight of the target.

But $\frac{AD}{AC}$ = sine 45º

and AC = AB which = full allowance

∴ AD (the allowance required) = full allowance X sine the angle of attack.

The following values for the sine of various angles may be studied at this point in order to derive what I consider the most important factor when shooting with deflection.

Sine 90º = 1		Sine 45º =	.71
80º =	.98	30º =	.5
70º =	.94	20º =	.34
60º =	.87	10º =	.17
50º =	.76	5º =	.1

The factor that stands out from this is that from angles of 90º to 60º one still has to take the full allowance of deflection. I cannot emphasize sufficiently how important this point is. No pilot ever seems to take sufficient lead.

DENSITY.--When you fire at a target moving at an angle to your line of flight, you must turn your aircraft continually so that you hold the target at the correct deflection and sighting while you fire your guns. If you do not hold the aim, bullet hits the front of the airplane by the time the second bullet covers the distance to the target the target would have moved on its course 12 7/20 feet which equals 7 1/2 feet behind the first and the third round 7 1/2 feet behind the second, etc. From this you can see how important it is to hold your aim during your burst. IN OTHER WORDS YOU MUST TURN WITH THE TARGET AND KEEP YOUR SIGHTS ON. I realize, of course, that the fitting of multi-guns to fighters does produce a heavy concentration of fire at any moment, but modern aircraft are robust and heavily armored and it requires a great many hits to disable them. Likewise they would be going a great deal faster than 100 mph that I have shown in my example, so the faster the speed of the target the less is the concentration of your fire if you do not keep your sights on.

ACCURATE FLYING WHEN FIRING.--Even if you are able to take good aim and place your sights in the correct line ahead of your target, it is still very important indeed to fly accurately. ON NO ACCOUNT MUST YOU USE RUDDER ALONE TO CORRECT YOUR AIM. Your turns while keeping your sights on, must be accurate turns; that is the indicator bubble must be dead center. If you make either of these two faults; your airplane must have a slight sidewise velocity which obviously is imparted to the bullets as they are fired, this is sufficient to take them quite clear of the target. There is another natural tendency for your aircraft to turn out of line of its own. This is due to the fact that the airflow from the propeller rotates around the fuselage in a clockwise motion. To counteract this the makers of the ship place an offset fin. This allows your aircraft to fly hands off at its cruising speed. Should you dive or zoom in your ship, there is an immediate tendency due; in the first place, to the airflow straightening out, and the second place to the tightening of the corkscrew motion, around your fuselage as your propeller starts to thrash, for your ship to turn out of line. This must be corrected immediately by application of rudder. To fly your aircraft accurately without skidding requires infinite practice and skill. Practice doing this without altering the position of the trimming tabs, in combat with continual changes necessary, you will not have time. So practice without, and continually watch that slip bubble--always keep it dead center.

SKIDDING OF YOUR TARGET.--It has been pointed out that the line error in a deflection shot is caused by the pilot's failing to position the target aircraft so that it is flying towards the center of the sight or by failing to make accurate turns, or by using rudder alone to correct aim, when sighting or firing. The pilot must also be able to estimate the line of flight of the enemy, who may in extreme cases in individual combat, be skidding violently so that his aircraft is not in fact flying along the line in which the nose of the aircraft is pointing.

Unfortunately in a modern streamlined ship the application of rudder does not change the course of your ship, but only turns the nose of the ship away from the course. The ship in actual fact still proceeds along its original course slipping to one side. Therefore when firing at a ship try not to heed the direction the ship is pointing when deciding your line of sight, but try and access its general direction. When duck shooting in a high cross wind it is no use aiming ahead of the direction their beak and neck are pointing; because the duck, due to the high cross wind, is not actually proceeding in that direction at all. The same with an enemy aircraft flying with rudder applied. It is not easy to position the target in the sights so that it is flying towards the center of the target and a line error frequently occurs. This is a gunnery fault that firing with tracer ammunition will cure, as it is easy to see which side of the target your bullets are going. (See: Firing with Tracer.)

RANGE.--Range is one of the most important things of aerial gunnery. Obviously it is not quite so important when firing with only one gun mounted near the gun sight but with any form of guns carried in the wings which are considerable distance from the sight base, range is vitally important. The guns are harmonized so that all the bullets meet at a certain point in order to give you a concentration of fire which is the real reason you have this multiple armament. Therefore the range which the guns are harmonized to meet, is the best range to shoot. In practice you must do what you will have to do in combat; that is you must fire at your correct harmonized range. After ranges of more than 300 yards your bullets, even 50 caliber, start to lose their powers of penetration, and bullet drop enters into it. Another point to consider is the scattering of the bullets due to the vibration of the guns, this increases as the range increases. Against all this if you were close to any range of under 150 yards to an enemy bomber carrying rear gunners, I maintain that your chances of living to tell about it will be very slender. The danger point arises when you start your break-a-way after your attack. Firstly, because you are no longer firing at the bomber, this tends to buckup the courage of the rear gunner, and secondly because you are turning your unarmored flank towards the gunner. I maintain that 150 yards is a minimum range for the attacking of bombers.

GRAVITY DROP.--An object is drawn towards the earth at an acceleration of 32 Ft. per second, per second, so that the bullets fly in a slight curve depending primarily upon the initial velocity. However, no allowance need be taken on any firing ranges up to 250 yards.

Owing to the fact that most of your guns are mounted below the line of sight, they must be canted up if they are to meet at the point of harmonization. This allows for considerable bullet drop when your ship is level about its horizontal axis, but when banked one must remember to aim up, and not ease the stick back to raise the nose, as this of course pulls the nose around the horizon and not up at all. It is recommended that no firing takes place at ranges of more than 300 yards.

BULLET GROUP.--Because of the slight inaccuracies in the gun itself, slight movement in the mounting and vibration of the aircraft, the bullets fired will roughly cover a circular area of approximately 20 feet in diameter at 400 yards. Without very careful thought, do not speed your guns when harmonizing them to get extra spreadage or you will loose too much concentration and your fire will be ineffective. A chapter of this manual gives guidance on this problem.

LINE OF SIGHT

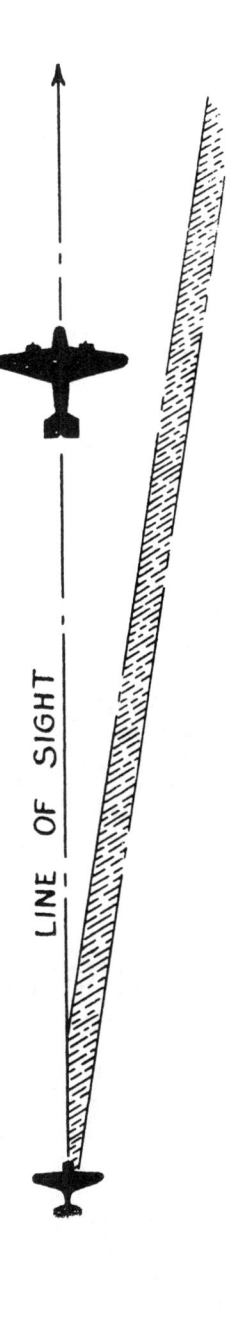

Although pilot took good aim this is path of bullets. Owing to fact that fighter pilot has failed to counteract correctly the tendency of his aircraft to swing to starboard whilst diving on target, this allowed the aircraft to attain a sideways velocity which is obviously imparted to bullets.

NOTES OF AIR FIRING PRACTICES (Fixed Gun)

Air Firing Practices against towed targets are not designed to teach potential fighter pilots any tactical methods of approaching hostile aircraft, but rather the final run onto the target, which includes (1) Judging of Range, (2) Aiming, (3) Firing, (4) Holding the sights on, (5) Correct deflection, (6) Correcting of flying faults. All the practices and exercises, however, have a very definite bearing on air combat and are essential in teaching the actual hitting of targets before the pilot has to go into action. These gunnery exercises must be made as realistic as possible.

There are two most important points which remain constant whatever the attack or exercise. In the case of deflection shooting (See Notes on the importance of deflection shooting) - it is obviously absolutely imperative that a pilot be able to assess automatically the angle between the course of the enemy aircraft and that of his own aircraft. Now in air firing against towed targets this is comparatively a simple task, as the towing aircraft, cable, and target give the attacker a definite indication of the direction in which the target is traveling. Unfortunately this is not as simple in combat, as the enemy aircraft need not necessarily be traveling in the direction in which he is pointing. For instance an enemy pilot might apply full rudder (and opposite stick to prevent banking and a turn) and point well to one side of the track he is making good. See diagram A I and A II.

In the case in diagram A II, it is most tempting for the fighter pilot to take a proper deflection shot at the enemy, assessing the amount of deflection on the APPARENT course of the enemy aircraft. So it is essential, through practice and experience, to be able to assess the amount of deflection to take by judging the amount of GENERAL MOVEMENT of the enemy compared with the fighter pilot, rather than by noting the direction in which the enemy aircraft is pointing.

Now there is the other important point and this point is absolutely vital whether in actual combat or on the practice range. This point is the "skidding" or "slip"

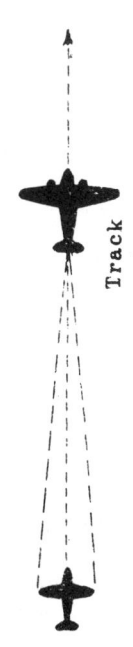

Track made good and actual direction enemy is pointing

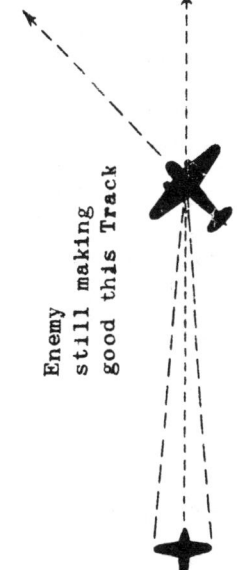

Enemy pilot applied rudder and is now pointing at X but is still making good original track as in A I. Fighter pilot would be very tempted to take a full deflection shot.

Enemy still making good this Track

but fighter pilot still takes no deflection shot.

of the fighter aircraft. This can be caused in two ways, both are serious and must be overcome by instant action on the part of the pilot. Firstly a single engine fighter is drawn through the air by an airscrew, which to impart a forward movement to the aircraft, has to rotate. In rotating the airscrew sets up a corkscrew flow of air backwards and ROUND the fuselage. This corkscrew motion of air, strikes the side of the rudder and tends to turn the nose of the aircraft around its vertical axis. In other words the aircraft starts to "skid" or "slip". To keep the aircraft straight the pilot must apply rudder. However to avoid having to make the pilot fly around with continual pressure on the rudder bar, the makers of the aircraft fit a fin. This they "offset" enough to counteract the the corkscrew airflow motion; but of course this must be fixed. It is fixed so that the aircraft flies hands off at normal cruising speed, so that if any changes of air speed occur the pilot has to counteract either with rudder bias adjustment or by application of rudder. For instance, should the pilot dive his aircraft, the corkscrew airflow motion past the fuselage tends to straighten out; the fin, being offset (to counteract the normal corkscrew airflow) tends to swing the aircraft out of line. In other words the aircraft starts to "skid" and no longer proceeds in the direction in which it is pointing. This has to be counteracted at once by application of rudder. Another instance would be when the pilot starts to climb. At once the airscrew starts to thrash, blasting the air in a tighter corkscrew motion around the fuselage, so that the fin being set for a lesser "side blast", catches this extra blast from the side which tends to swing the nose of the aircraft, causing a skid to the opposite side. This again must be counteracted by application of rudder. See diagrams B I, B II and B III. This is the most IMPORTANT POINT IN AIR FIRING, FOR THIS REASON.

When an aircraft "skids" it has a speed to one side or other of the direction in which it is pointing. One can skid in a turn by having applied too much or too little rudder for bank applied. Therefore when the guns (which are fixed and fired dead down the line of the fuselage) are fired the bullets which come out of the guns have a velocity to the side of the same amount as that at which the aircraft is slipping to that side.

so that however careful your aim, the bullets you fire whilst slipping can never hit what you are aiming at, owing to the fact that they have this sideways velocity which, even though it be slight is enough to take them quite clear of the target. One can imagine that any combat at all, be it against bombers or fighters, must of necessity be one of continual dives, zooms or level flying. A fighter pilot must take great care that he is able automatically to counteract just sufficiently the slip caused by the offset fin. See diagram C I page 17. I must now take this argument a step further.

I HAVE MADE OUT IN THESE PRECEDING PARAGRAPHS THAT THIS SLIPPING AND SKIDDING WHICH OCCURS WHEN ONE DIVES AND ZOOMS IS VIOLENT, BUT THE DANGER IS THAT THEY ARE ACTUALLY INDISCERNABLE.

SECOND METHOD OF CAUSING "SKID".--Suppose you are taking the correct action to counteract this natural tendency of the aircraft to skid whilst zooming or diving to attack. As you approach your target and are all ready to open fire and are concentrating on aiming, you may find the sights are to one side or the other of your target. The natural tendency is to push on rudder in order to bring the sights to bear. This is a useless practice, as quite obviously, (although you actually bring your sights on to the target), you cause the aircraft to "skid". In other words the aircraft immediately has a movement to the side; this, of course, throws the bullets clear of the target. If one finds that one's sights are not dead on, one must use "bank" and rudder to bring them to bear.

B-1

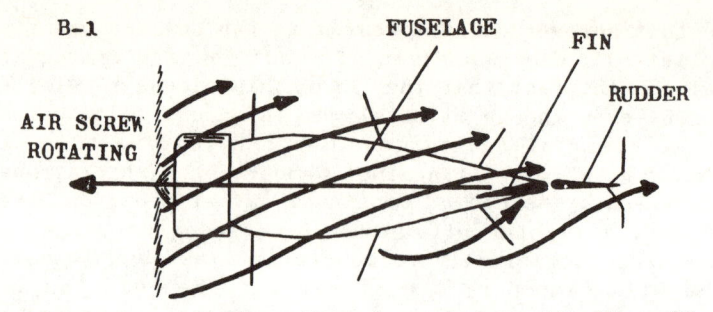

AIR SCREW ROTATING — FUSELAGE — FIN — RUDDER

Corkscrew airflow Normal cruising with fin off set to counteract.
Fin counteracting any tendency to swing.

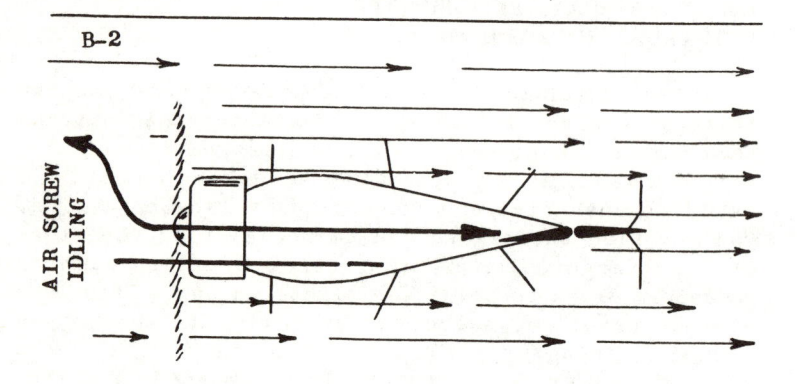

B-2

AIR SCREW IDLING

Aircraft diving airflow straightened out and striking off set fin swinging nose to starboard.

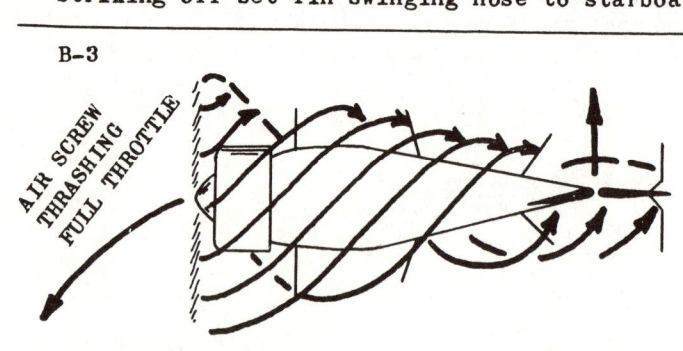

B-3

AIR SCREW THRASHING FULL THROTTLE

Aircraft climbing, airscrew starts to thrash more, corkscrew tightens, airflow airflow strikes side of fin which is not off set enough tending to swing to port.

THE IMPORTANCE OF DEFLECTION SHOOTING.--Since the dead astern or no deflection shot appears so easy you may wonder why it is ever necessary to learn to fire with deflection at all. The reasons for learning deflection shooting are briefly:

(i) It gives you technical freedom in attack, that is it allows you to attack any member of an enemy formation from any direction. This would allow you to attack in such a way as to screen with the target you select the rest of the enemy formation so that their supporting fire would be useless.

(ii) All the bullets fired from the side at enemy aircraft will enter into unarmored parts and therefore be very much more lethal.

(iii) In fighter vs. fighter combats, owing to the constant maneuvering, the no deflection shot seldom if ever, occurs.

Therefore, it is essential that you learn and be able to fire from the side. Any target you select which has an apparent movement to one side or the other of you (that is, not flying directly to or from you) one has to aim ahead of, in order to allow for the length of time which the bullets require to travel that range. The angle between the line of sight, that is the line you are aiming along, and the line between your ship and the target is called the amount of 'lead' or the 'angle of deflection'. There are four points which a pilot has to estimate. These are:

(i) The distance he is from the target.
(ii) The speed of the target.
(iii) The distance to aim ahead of the target because of the speed it is traveling at to allow for the length of time the bullet takes to travel that range.
(iv) The angle that the target is cutting to your own line of flight, however, this may be assessed as general sidewise movement, as for instance, a target traveling at 330 m.p.h. at right angles to your path would require the same amount of 'lead' as a target traveling at 200 m.p.h. at 45° to your own line of flight.

There is a fifth point which is always known to you which is your bullet speed and your own airplane speed;

that effects the length of time the bullet takes to travel the range that you have selected. The length of time is roughly 1/4 of a second for 250 yards, the airplane speed making no appreciable difference in this length of time.

With a ring and bead type of sight, be it electrical or standard iron ring and bead fixture, gives you the angle of deflection rather than the distances mentioned in point (i) and point (iii) above. The theory of this is well discussed in the opening chapter of this manual. There are one or two practical applications which the fighter pilot will find useful in combat. These points are as follows:

I. THE FLY-THROUGH METHOD.--Suppose that you are on beam at 250 yards range, flying in a straight line, at right angles to the enemy and that fire is opened whilst the allowance made is still too large and continued until the enemy has flown through the bullet stream. The fuselage of a bomber is about 50 feet long and, if its speed is 250 m.p.h., the bullet group sweeps the whole length of the fuselage in 0,14 seconds.

During this time four 20 m.m. guns fire 6 bullets so that the best that can be done by this method, even supposing that none of the bullets pass either above or below the enemy, is to put six bullets through the fuselage or 1 in 40 sq. ft.

Fire by this method cannot therefore be very effective though it may occasionally achieve a lucky success. Rather greater success may be expected from the method when fire is from a small angle from astern, since the bullets pass more lengthways through the fuselage and have more chance of doing damage. It is clear, however, that the adoption of the "fly-through" method amounts to a confession of weakness, since it throws away the much greater concentration of bullets than can be obtained by following through.

II. THE FOLLOW-THROUGH METHOD.--The alternative is to endeavor to follow the enemy, making throughout the correct allowance. If this can be done, the bullet group remains on him for the whole duration of fire and very much greater concentration on the target is, of course, obtained.

The difficulties of this method are of two kinds. In the first place it is necessary to have a much clearer idea of what the allowance should be, for if it is wrongly estimaged the bullets may miss all the time. In the second place the act of following him requires you to fly on a curve, the curvature of which may be greater than can be conveniently applied, owing to the effects of G and limited field of vision in a steep bank due to the length of the nose of certain fighter aircraft.

Now the allowance or deflection required to hit him is dependent upon his speed and either the angle between you and his direction of flight or the range. That is to say, the deflection can be judged either by estimating that he will have moved a certain distance during the time of flight of the bullet.

(a) THE ANGLE-OFF METHOD.--Estimation of the deflection by angle-off from the target is that recommended because it is nearly independent of range. If the bullet flew at a constant speed the deflection would be exactly independent of range, for if the range were doubled the time of flight would be doubled and the distance travelled by the target in this time would be doubled, leaving the deflection angle unchanged.

Actually the bullet slows up a bit at the longer ranges so that the allowance is slightly bigger than at short ranges, but this difference can be safely neglected in comparison with the much larger errors which you are likely to make in judging the angle from astern.

Estimation of the angle off the target can only be done by constant practice against model aircraft, by studying photographs, by use of the various characteristics of the aircraft in order to obtain this angle, e.g. tail aligned with wing tip.

Estimation of speed requires appreciation of the performance of the aircraft being attacked, and also of your own aircraft, under varying conditions.

The allowance required is obtained by multiplying the speed of the target by the sine of the angle-off. Obviously such a sum cannot be done in the air and pictures should be prepared showing the appearance of various targets for 1/2-ring, 3/4-ring, 1-ring allowance, etc.

(b) **THE LENGTHS-AHEAD METHOD.**--Some pilots prefer to use the lengths-ahead method of aiming. They decide to hold their aim at a point which is some chosen number of times the fuselage lengths ahead of the target, the number of lengths depending on the mean range at which they expect to fire. The more usual method of using the ring, described above, gives better results, but as the lengths-ahead method has some points in its favor it is worth consideration.

The idea behind this method is that at a given range the time of flight of the bullet, and therefore the the distance flown by the target in this time, is roughly the same for all angles. If therefore, the number of lengths ahead can be correctly chosen to suit the range and target speed, the aim will be correct for all angles.

The defects of this method are:
    (i) The numbers of lengths ahead depends on the length of the target fuselage.
    (ii) It gives the wrong answer when the range is different from that supposed and, futhermore, it depends on the range remaining constant during an attack.

ALWAYS REMEMBER: FEW PILOTS EVER TAKE TOO MUCH LEAD, NEARLY ALL TAKE TOO LITTLE. BEGINNERS: TRY AND TAKE TOO MUCH, AND YOU'LL BE ABOUT RIGHT.

RANGE.---when a bullet is fired from a fixed-gun fighter flying at 400 m.p.h. it has a very high velocity (something of the order of 3,000 ft. per sec. or over 2,000 m.p.h.). This velocity, however, is very rapidly lost due to air resistance and half is lost when the bullet has traveled about 600 yards. This means a considerable decrease in hitting power at long ranges and your bullets would fail to penetrate the thinnest armor plating. It follows then that it is a waste of time and energy to open fire at excessive ranges.

As the range of the bullet increases so does the 'gravity drop'. A bullet takes more than twice as long to travel 600 yards as it does to travel the first 300 yards because it is slowing up at an increasing rate. This means that the pull of gravity has more than twice as long to act over 600 yards than over 300 yards, and thus the gravity drop at 600 yards is more than four times that at 300 yards because the gravity has an acceleration of 32 feet per sec., per sec. Now your sight and guns are not harmonized to allow for gravity drop at 600 yards, so if you do open fire at 600 yards you must make an additional allowance for this greater gravity drop by an amount which, at best, you can only guess.

When four guns are harmonized they are so arranged as to give some pre-arranged pattern at a definite range (usually 250 yards). This pattern is designed to to give the best chance of effective shooting from point-blank range up to some optimum range outside of which your chance of success rapidly deteriorates. With any type of gun the bullet pattern spreads out as the range increases. This means that the area of the pattern produced at 400 yards, say, is four times larger than that produced at 200 yards. This may at first sight appear a good thing, but it is necessary in addition to remember that the pattern area will contain practically every bullet fired. So, in terms of bullet density, the pattern at 400 yards contains only 1/4 of the number of bullets per square foot contained in the pattern at 200 yards. For example let us suppose that certain fighter in 1 sec. burst fires 200 rounds, his gives us approximately a bullet density at 200 ards of 12 bullets per square foot, at 400 yards the ensity is reduced to 3 bullets per square foot.

Correct deflection allowance is also bound up with correct range estimation especially if you use the lengths-ahead method described in Part II on deflection shooting. If you allow, say, three lengths for opening fire between 400 and 300 yards and then, by an error in range estimation, open fire at 600 yards, your deflection allowance will be insufficient and your bullets will pass behind your target.

From the foregoing it will be seen that shooting at excessive ranges produces:
    (a) Loss in penetrating power of bullets, and thus loss in effectiveness of shots (even though your aim is correct).
    (b) Increase in gravity drop which leads to an additional allowance which you must guess.
    (c) A very thinly distributed bullet pattern and this means you have to fire a much longer burst to have the same effect as at short ranges.
    (d) Errors in deflection allowances.

It follows from all this that successful air combat might well hinge on your ability to estimate range correctly. In fact it is not an overstatement to say that range estimation is one of the most important aspects of air fighting. It has this disadvantage, however, in that you must teach yourself, and to that end continuous practices on the ground with scale models must be carried out in addition to regular air-practices--at least one a week of both cine camera gun practices and air firing against towed targets.

AIR EXERCISES
AIR FIRING AGAINST GROUND TARGETS

TARGETS.--10 feet square (white) lying at an angle of about 50° to the ground. (Aluminum sea markers, or smoke floats, just thrown into the sea make very good targets). It is preferable to have the 10 foot targets located on soft sand or in shallow water in order that the pilot firing may see the results of his firing at the time.

This firing at ground targets is very useful work and must be conscientiously carried out as follows. If on fixed targets, fly to a position at right angles to the target, at a height of 2,000 ft. and so that a dive at an angle of 30° would take you into the target; throttle back, turn on to target and commence shallow dive. Get sights on immediately and open fire. Continue to fire, until at 700 feet. Cease e. Then open up the engine and climb up and round into position to repeat. Check carefully any rough movements of the controls, paying particular attention to rudder. Do not fire with aircraft skidding.

When flying with dual control the effect of correcting errors in aim by using rudder alone, and the effect of wind on firing results are demonstrated.

QUARTER ATTACK (Carried out on A-B Target lines along airfiring danger area).--This is carried out with towed target over a course of approximately 1½ miles. Approach the target aircraft head on but about 400 feet higher up and the radius of an easy turn to one side; when approximately 500 yards ahead of drogue, start turn towards line of path of target. As early as possible sights should be got 'on' allowing correct deflection, fire open at 250 yards and held until angle decreases to 20 degrees. Break away downwards, turning in opposite direction to that of target and get into position at other end of two line so that exercise is repeated in the opposite direction.

The instructor will demonstrate: (i) How to keep (with bank and rudder) the line of sight dead in line with the path of the target. (To assist beginners the towing cable can be used as a rough check on this, although he must try to accomplish it without this artificial aid. It is a very bad habit to make use of such aids). (ii) The correct deflection and how this is gradually decreased as the angle of attack decreases and attacker falls astern of target. (iii) Minimum angle of attack so that pupil will know when he has reached the dangerous angle and bullets might prejudice the safety of towing aircraft. (iv) Check any tendency to keep sights 'on' by use of rudder alone. (v) Check roughness on controls.

ASTERN ATTACK (C.D. line).--This is possibly the easiest of all attacks and is carried out against a three-foot cone target towed so as to fly below and to one side of the towing aircraft. Never go lower than the cone. This rules out any possibility of the towing aircraft being hit.

You will be shown a three-foot cone target on the ground before taking off, and what it looks like from various ranges. Approach to the cone target is made from a position dead astern of the actual towing aircraft. This means that the target cone lies some 300 feet below, 300 feet to one side, and the attacker is approximately 500 yards astern. Throttle is eased back as soon as nose of aircraft is depressed, sights 'on' at once and open fire at 350 yards. Fire is opened as soon as target crosses danger area and firing only takes place in one direction, that is, into the danger area. If pupil flying aircraft with dual control, the instructor will demonstrate ranges. Watch bullet drop if using tracer. This is important and is one of the few practices which demonstrate effectively the amount that bullets drop over ranges of more than 200 yards. Any rough corrections with rudder should be checked and sights always kept 'on' by application of bank and rudder together.

The attacks should be repeated at various overtaking speeds.

During astern attacks, there is a danger of the attacking aircraft flying into the cone target if the towing cable breaks. For this reason a minimum range to which attacking aircraft may approach is laid down. Broadly speaking, this minimum distance is 200 yards when approaching at 160 m.p.h., 250 yards at 200 m.p.h., and 300 yards at 240 m.p.h.

HEAD ON ATTACKS (Camera Gun Only).--These are most important attacks because in spite of the very short length of the time in which one has to get the sights 'on' and fire, the enemy presents a fairly easy no deflection target, and every bullet that hits goes into the unprotected fuselage of the enemy with usually disastrous results.

When practicing these attacks strict orders must be laid down, and one aircraft must always be TARGET and whatever happens he must never alter course. If he does so he might easily alter it to the same place as the attacker had decided to pass; in which case a head-on collision results. Fire must be opened at a slightly greater range, otherwise one is inclined to leave it too late so that it is not possible to open fire at all. This attack invariably meets with little opposition and often one can carry out such an attack without even being fired at. If enemy turns, the attack can immediately be developed into a '$\frac{1}{4}$' attack or an 'astern' attack.

EMPLOYMENT OF FIGHTER SQUADRONS
STRATEGICAL AND TACTICAL CONSIDERATIONS OF THE TASKS WHICH MAY BE ASSIGNED TO FIGHTER UNITS

In the order of importance, the tasks which may be assigned to a fighter unit are as follows:

1. Home Defence.
2. The offensive sweep patrols over enemy country.
3. The maintenance of air superiority over a given position at a given time in order to allow Naval, Military, or Air Operations to take place without interference of enemy force. This is sometimes referred to as forming a mushroom of fighters, a good example of this would be the British evacuation from Dunkirk.
4. Escort for bombers.
5. Ground straffing.

1. HOME DEFENCE.--Home defense is a very wide and varied task. It includes individual day fights, mass dog fights, individual attacks against bombers and synchronized and carefully planned squadron attacks. It is obviously impossible under this heading to discuss details of all the tasks mentioned above. However, certain principles do remain constant without going into detail of how the actual attacks take place. The principles I shall endeavor to outline below:

When working in a country with such a highly specialized defense system such as Great Britain, one is inclined to become careless regarding the presence of the enemy as normally one receives so much warning of the exact position of enemy aircraft. This is entirely wrong. One must always expect the enemy. Pilots taking off from English aerodromes have been shot down by German fighters. Keep your eyes open the whole while, as a matter of habit, looking for enemy. It is essential that the squadron sticks together from the moment it takes off until it returns to the aerodrome again. The squadron must work as a squadron and not as individuals. Pilots are only to attack when told by their squadron commander to do so. They must not break formation for any reason whatsoever, unless told to do so by their squadron commander. The squadron commander must always place his squadron in an advantageous position with regard to the enemy before he orders any attack. He must insure that he:

      a. Has the advantage of the direction of the sun.
      b. Has altitude over the enemy.
      c. Notes carefully cloud formations and makes the best use of them.
      d. Makes up his plan of action at once without any loss of time, gives his orders to his squadron as clearly and concisely as possible.
      e. Launches and presses home the attack with determination. A timid attack is useless.

After attacking, if possible without too much hanging about, the squadron should reform or at least get together, but under no circumstances hang around trying to get into formation with each other in the vicinity the attack was made. Escort fighters will deal very severely with you if you so do.

    2. OFFENSIVE SWEEPS.--The aim of these sweeps is to destroy enemy aircraft in the security of their own country. Obviously it is a fairly hazardous procedure unless properly carried out. The danger lies in being surprised and attacked by overwhelmingly superior enemy forces. In deciding in what formation one must fly, one has to consider these points. You are supposedly in offensive action, therefore, your formation must be one which can instantly be developed into any form of attack you might wish to make. The men who are in constant danger are the men who are at the back of the formation. So from this point of view, one would get the impression that the ideal formation would be a flat one so that everyone is well up and there are no 'back' persons. However, a formation of this sort is entirely unwieldy, as in the slightest turns, you get stragglers, owing to the difference in speeds between the persons on the outside and those on the inside. Once one crosses enemy territory, one automatically comes under fire from antiaircraft batteries; so you cannot fly straight with safety.

    The most important point in the type of formation, must be its maneuverability. There are many types of formations used but I think the best is a squadron of 12 ships divided into flights of 4, each flight in line astern formation. These flights move out when passing through enemy antiaircraft fire and weave independently, they don't need to move out any great distance but just enough to break down the mass target effect. When over enemy territory, they must weave continuously and at no time fly straight for more than 30 seconds. Defensive and offensive tactics must be practiced continuously. In case of defensive tactics some maneuver must be executed in which the whole squadron supports each other. In the offensive tactics, always leave 1/3 of your strength up over you as a guard when you go down to attack.

Whatever occurs while over enemy territory, one essential is that you stick together. If the squadron is attacked and the formation broken, the pilots must remain in the same piece of air. Do not run away and leave your squadron for your own safety as well as theirs. There must be no straggling of any sort, any straggling is dearly paid for as the straggler is bound to be destroyed.

Owing to the fact that the serious danger lies in the squadron being surprised, possibly by a larger formation of enemy fighters, it is best to adopt this system:

The squadron commander searches for enemy targets to attack and also concentrates on his navigation.
The leaders of his other flights concentrate on maintaining positions and do what searching they can.
All the remainder of the squadron keep the sky above and behind and especially up sun carefully searched.

Radio silence must be strictly maintained. The squadron commander should be the only person to use the radio and he only uses it to give orders regarding attacks. If, however, the squadron is surprised, any person in the squadron who sights enemy fighters which might appear to constitute a menace, he is to warn the squadron on the radio at once.

3. MUSHROOM COVERING.--The strength of the mushroom covering is dependent on the strength of the opposition expected. It is obvious that the strength of the fighters must be considerably greater than the maximum strength that the enemy are able to muster in that area.

The fighter squadrons should be allotted to certain areas and altitudes and must strictly adhere to their allotted positions. Squadrons should be evenly spaced in their definite altitude between 5,000 feet and the ceiling of their particular aircraft.

The squadrons should patrol to the 'up sun' side of the locality. In this manner enemy aircraft are more easily seen should they enter the zone, and also it gives one the advantage should attack be necessary. Great care should be taken that you are not drawn off the zone. One must always bear in mind the area one wishes to guard; and when enemy aircraft enter, ATTACK but in no circumstances allow yourself, through overkeeness, to be drawn off in an extended pursuit. Radio silence must be maintained and only broken by the issue of necessary orders. The officer commanding the mushroom covering should be in the squadron at the lowest altitude.

Always detail the minimum number of aircraft to attack so that always the greatest number possible are ready to most further attacks. No one must attack without Commanding Officer's orders. The lowest squadron should look after the immediate air over the zone; the other three squadrons should be solely responsible for their own safety. This is most important, as the feeling of doing a job of work at 5,000 feet and not being certain that at any moment a horde of enemy fighters will descend upon you, seriously impairs the ability of the low squadron to carry out its task.

The high squadrons must not allow themselves to be drawn off in pursuit of the enemy. They must only attack enemy aircraft which attempt to interfere, and not rush after enemy aircraft away from the zone.

If could covering is 10/10 it is not necessary to patrol above, as it is impossible to maintain one's position and this covering to a great extent precludes enemy surprise attack as they are seen so easily the moment they break cloud cover and are not difficult to see as aircraft are at great heights up sun.

4. ESCORT OF BOMBERS.--The strategy of escorting bombers remains the same whatever the strength of the fighters available or the strength of the bombers to be escorted.

The bombers' should fly in a fairly compact formation, I think spread out in depth rather than width. The escort should divide itself as follows: One squadron for close escort, these should fly half a mile astern and a 1,000 feet or so above the bombers. The next squadron, if available, flies some 5,000 feet above and to the side of the first squadron. If other squadrons are available, they take up their positions besides and above the bombers until the air all around the sides, behind, and above the bombers are filled with friendly fighters.

The bombers' whole safety lies in whether or not the fighters are able to maintain these positions. As soon as the escort are engaged, they almost invariably have to turn and fight leaving the bombers unguarded. They must endeavor to ignore all enemy aircraft except the ones that actually attack or those obviously just about to attack and even then only engage them long enough to drive them off and on no account should leave the vicinity of the bombers. The control of the fighters must be rigid and the commanding officer must be careful, if he thinks it necessary for the bombers' safety, to order the minimum of the escort to engage the enemy at once, always holding the maximum in reserve.

One must bear in mind that there are always many more aircraft about than one can see. The escort wing must discuss a comprehensive scheme on the ground before taking off so that the minimum number of words need be issued on the radio.

When the target is reached, fighters should circle above the bombers to keep the air clear while the bombers go about their dangerous task of running up and bombing the target. As the bombers start for home, so the fighters take up position again and the same procedure is adopted. The fighters should remember that the bombers will be flying several miles per hour faster than on the outward journey owing to the fact that they have got rid of their loads of bombs. They must anticipate this and not allow themselves to get behind and become ineffective as escort. Another fatal mistake is to allow oneself to lose vigilance towards the end of an uninterrupted flight. One must remember that there is 70 percent more chance in being intercepted on the way home than there is on the way out. Once the bombers have started to stir up trouble you can expect the sky to be filled with enemy.

5. GROUND STRAFING.--The term 'Ground Strafing' is more commonly applied to attacks by fighters from a very low level delivered against enemy infantry or motor transport concentrated along roads or in camps. During these sorts of attacks there is only one rule which must be rigidly adhered to, and that is to keep as low and as fast as possible. Try and place between yourself and the enemy as much of the countryside as possible, that is take advantage of all trees, buildings and hills by keeping down below them if possible. One must climb a little at times in order to check one's whereabouts and to be able to make some sort of shallow dive on the targets you select; however, this climbing should be cut down to the barest minimum.

On the other hand, one might be assigned to the task of shooting up one definite target and after shooting it up to return home. I think if this be the case one should approach the target at some 15,000 feet and actually pass some five miles beyond it so that the attack may be delivered from a more unexpected direction and the get-a-way made easier. After passing some five miles beyond the aerodrome the squadron should be echeloned to one side or other and on the order to attack should peel off in turn, following within, but not at a greater distance than 600 yards. Actually this distance should not be less than 500 yards as it might not give the aircraf ahead full powers of maneuvering. For this approach the throttles are shut back and altitude is lost so that one makes contact with the ground some two miles from the target. These two miles are passed in very quick time owing to the extra speed gathered in the dive. As one approaches the target, one should climb slightly to three or four hundred feet in order to get a good view and be able to select profitable targets. Attack them as fiercely as possible opening fire at about 400 yards and continuing to fire to point blank range, turn immediately you pass the target so as to present a more difficult target yourself. By turns to each side shoot at as many targets as you can possibly find, but waste no time in circling or going back on your tracks. If you do this, you will only embarrass the aircraft following you. Make your get-a-way at ground level. Throughout the whole of this approach, attack, and get-a-way, watch carefully behind, and see thet the aircraft following you is indeed a friend.

FORMATION FLYING IN CLOUD.--A pursuit squadron commander in leading his squadron into combat must make use of all the elements to achieve his aim (which is the destruction of the enemy) and only in so doing can can he hope to be successful. In air warfare surprise is the greatest of all weapons. It is very difficult to achieve complete surprise, but in certain weather conditions it is possible to attain certain important advantages by judicious use of cloud. Of course when cloud is non-existent the only possible way to attain surprise is to maneuver to attack from the direction of the sun, but when certain cloud conditions prevail, it is very important that a squadron be able to maneuver through the cloud into such a position that an attack can immediately be launched without any loss of time thereby a degree of surprise can be attained. On the other hand, if in so maneuvering through cloud the squadron becomes detached and on coming out of the cloud the squadron commander finds that he is on his own and that his squadron has disappeared, he is naturally in a very embarrassing position. To be able to maneuver through cloud requires a great deal of practice and the more polished the squadron becomes in the art of formation in cloud flying, the more maneuvering the squadron commander may do.

The most successful formation to fly through clouds is the three aircraft in "Vic" and if the four aircraft section is favored the fourth aircraft takes up station close astern of No. 1. The other two or three sections, as the case may be, follow the section ahead. It is important that the leader of the squadron flies extremely accurately and it is better that he throttles his engine down considerable so as to give the pilots following a greater chance of catching up should they get behind. Of course cloud flying in squadron formation should not be attempted until pilots are proficient in maintaining station on their leader in section formation. To attain this proficiency the leader takes off with the two pupils, one on each side. He flies around with them at 4,000 feet carrying out steep turns from one side to the other, smoothly and without a break. When this is done successfully, these turns can be combined with dives and zooms until the two pupils can keep stationed accurately in any of these maneuvers. This "warming up" stage should last approximately ten to fifteen minutes. It is an important stage and it is certainly not advisable to take new pilots straight off the ground into cloud without first carrying out some form of practice flying such as I have outlined above. The selection of cloud for formation practice is important; it is realized that in America the opportunities for this practice are not so good as they are in countries which are naturally nine-tenths covered in various types of cloud. However, I think advantage can be taken of any of the other types of cloud except thunder cumulus cloud which should be avoided. Do not keep the pupils in the cloud too long to start with. They should be made to fly at not more than half a span distance from the leader; anything closer then this is dangerous and anything more distant the leader would be invisible. They should be informed that if they lose sight of the leader, they are to break away outwards and under no circumstances are they to attempt to reform in the cloud. Straight and level flying should be carried out until the pupils become proficient--after this slight turns may be attempted and then climbing and gliding. Of course for gliding the leader must take care not to completely close down his engine as the pupils will shoot ahead.

AIR FIGHTING AT OPERATIONAL ALTITUDES.--Nowadays very few combats are ever fought at altitudes of less than 17,000 feet. Many combats take place up to 38,000 feet so it is essential (since conditions at altitudes above 17,000 feet are so dissimilar from those at lower altitudes) that as much practice as possible should take place at operational altitudes--that is above 17,000 feet.

Firstly, it is absolutely essential that a serviceable oxygen mask be used. The best form of oxygen mask is one which fits tightly over the nostrils and mouth and under the helmet straps so that all the rarified atmosphere is excluded, the oxygen pipe flowing into the mask directly besides the mouth and flowing out directly opposite. This mask can also contain the microphone for the radio. Flying at oxygen height, if care is not taken to guarantee adequate supply of oxygen, is extremely dangerous. As everyone knows too well the danger of the shortage of oxygen lies in the fact that the pilot so suffering is completely unaware of the fact, as one minute he feels perfectly all right and the next second without any warning he can pass out. It might take many thousand feet before he recovers consciousness. In fact, it is seldom that such an incident doesn't end in the pilot striking the ground before he does recover.

Following are a few points which might help pursuit pilots who are to carry out exercises at above oxygen heights:

1. Before taking off.--Check the pressure gauge and see that sufficient oxygen is in the bottle. Check the flow meter to insure that oxygen is passing from the high pressure to the high pressure systems; this can be done by placing one's thumb on the outlet pipe and seeing that there is sufficient pressure behind the flow. Turn off the flow and listen carefully when the engine is not running for any leaks. Normally any leak of consequence can easily be heard as it makes an audible hissing noise. Plug in your oxygen lead and see that the flow passes into the mask--this is done in the same way and can actually be done at the same time as the item mentioned before. Make absolutely certain that your oxygen mask fits correctly.

2. Just after taking off turn on oxygen flow to 5,000 feet. Keep the flow meter well in advance of the height at which you are. Breathe quite normally the whole time.

3. At altitudes above 17,000 feet the pilot will notice that everything he does is more of an effort than it is when he is on the ground. Constantly check the flow meter and pressure gauge. See that the pressure gauge readings do not drop too fast; this will indicate that the system is leaking and the pilot must return to his aerodrome at once. It is imperative that one must not remain above 17,000 feet when the bottle pressure falls below the 'red line' minimum.

4. The pilot will notice that formation flying station keeping is more difficult as the aircraft has lost considerable amount of the sensitiveness of the controls, the control column and the rudder have to be used more violently as they are less effective and the throttle must be opened and closed more violently as the aircraft accelerates and deaccelerates very sluggishly. This is all due to the rarified air, and of course the higher one goes, the worse the conditions become.

5. Great care has to be taken to avoid collisions, both whilst maneuvering and during attacks because of the delayed action of firstly your mental ability and secondly because of the insensibility of the controls. One has the impression that one is thinking just as quickly as one does normally on the ground; this is a dangerous delusion because in actual fact one's mental power has deteriorated and one's brain functions a fraction of a second slower.

6. The stalling speed of the aircraft goes up. Care should be taken not to carry out maneuvers of too violent a nature or at too slow a speed. As a matter of interest and for quick reckoning one's true speed can easily be worked out from one's indicated speed at altitude by a very simple formula which is: add to indicated speed one mile per hour per 60 miles per hour for every thousand feet of altitude so that an indicated speed of 120 m.p.h. at 30,000 feet would in actual fact be a true speed of 120 + (2x30) which equals 180 m.p.h.

7. When diving to attack an enemy aircraft flying along straight some distance below, pull out of the dive in good time or you will sink a great deal farther below than you intended. Also one must start one's break away slightly earlier for the same reason.

8. Always remember that one cannot have too much oxygen and that it is fatal to have too little, so whenever in doubt about the amount you are receiving being adequate always turn on a little more for safety's sake.

9. Do not get flustered or make any physical effort in the cockpit as this will make you very short of breath. Take everything easily but think quickly.

GETTING OFF THE GROUND QUICKLY

QUICK-GET-AWAYS.--The importance of pursuit pilots being able to get off the ground in the shortest possible time is too great for me to have to emphasize. The reasons also, for having to leave the ground in such drastic hurry are so obvious that I think I can leave them unsaid. Suffice to say that cutting seconds off the time taken from the signal to take off and the actual time the aircraft leaves the ground may easily mean the difference between a successful interception or a complete failure, and I go so far as to say in certain circumstances where the enemy attack is directed against the pursuit aerodrome, it might end in disaster. To get off the ground quickly requires very careful planning. A set drill must be enforced both for the starting of the airplane engines and also for the quick dressing and seating of pilots in cockpits and the taxiing out and take off. It is impossible to keep pilots at an advanced state of preparedness for any length of time, to do so would put an unnecessary strain on them and severe fatigue would result. One has to remember that wars go on for years and so one must set a standard of alertness which can be carried on throughout the period of the war. In order to relieve pilots of unnecessary strain due to being kept in a high degree of alertness for long periods, the following states of preparedness have been arranged, and in practice have proved most satisfactory. It is a squadron commander's constant task to practice and practice in order to cut out seconds in the time to get off the ground after the order to do so is given.

1. "RELEASED". Pilots in this state are permitted to go wherever they choose and will not be required under any circumstances until the time the "released" period expires. Squadrons are always released until a definitely stated time. After this time they automatically revert to the next stage which is "AVAILABLE".

2. "AVAILABLE". Pilots in this state are required to be able to leave the ground within fifteen minutes from the time they are ordered into the air. This means that they must remain near a telephone or loud speaker system somewhere on the post reasonably near

their dispersal areas where their aircraft are parked, so that on the word "take off" they can rush to their aircraft and be in the air in the required time. From this state pilots may be required to come to the next state which is "READINESS"--ten minutes is allowed for this.

3. "READINESS". Pilots in this state are required to be able to leave the ground within five minutes. They must remain in the vicinity of the aircraft and be dressed in their flying clothing. They may be required to come to the next state which is "STAND-BY"; for this three minutes is allowed.

4. "STAND-BY". Pilots in this state are required to be able to leave the ground within two minutes. They must remain in their cockpits with the engines running. It is obvious that this high state of preparedness is governed by the length of time an aircraft engine can stay running on the ground without overheating. Of course pilots remaining for any length of time in this state become most fatigued. Quite normally this state is usually dispensed with as nearly always pilots are ordered into the air from the state of "readiness".

Of course these times stated above against states of preparedness are the absolute maximum times permitted. With practice the squadron should be able to cut them all down by about 75 percent. No squadron should be satisfied with the time they take off the ground from the word "go" and should constantly strive to improve this time.

I intend not to go through these states of preparedness and try to give some detail as to the points one ought to watch. Starting with the state of "RELEASED". The squadron is released say until 14:00 hours. At 13:45 hours all pilots and mechanics should report to their dispersal areas. The squadron commander should check his pilots to see that they know which is their allotted aircraft and it is their responsibility to see that everything is in order. The mechanics, assuming that the airplanes have had their daily inspections, etc., give the aircraft a quick check over and then start up the engines. The engines are warmed thoroughly, run-up and checked and then switched off.

The squadron can then report that they are now available. It is important that this be done before the time that the released period expires.

During the next state, "AVAILABLE", the aircraft crews should remain resting somewhere in the vicinity of the aircraft. The pilots are permitted to leave the immediate vicinity but must always remain in hearing of the loud speaker zone so as that they may return to their aircraft in the matter of a minute or two. All pilots' flying clothing must be laid out carefully so that the pilots can put them on in the least possible time without any trouble.

The next state, "READINESS", is the most important of all the states of preparedness and it is from this state that the most practice is required. Aircraft crews must remain handy. A definite starting drill must be enforced so that every man knows exactly what is required of him and the aircraft engine is started at once when the order to do so is given. The pilots must don their flying clothing and remain in the vicinity of the squadron operations room. When the order "take off" is given the pilots must run at their greatest speed to their aircraft, the engine of which should have been started by the time they reach there, strap themselves in, check all the instruments and other gadgets in the cockpit, make certain that the bulb in the reflector sight is functioning; if this is not functioning, it should be changed at once with one of the set of spares. (Many pilots have taken off and have even entered combat and then have switched their reflector sight on only to find that the bulb was fused.) The aircraft are then taxied out in such a way as to leave the aerodrome always clear for the leading aircraft to take off at once. Whilst it is the aim to take off in squadron formation, the squadron commander and flight commanders should not wait around for the squadron to form up on the ground, but take off immediately and by keeping their enginee throttled back allow the squadron to form up in the air. It is important though that the squadron should take off in a definite order, otherwise considerable maneuvering and shunting results. A sharp lookout must be maintained when taking off in case an enemy aircraft is ready to attack. It is vitally important that the squadron gets into its correct formation with the least possible delay.

The next stage, "STAND-BY", is very seldom used. The reason it is included in the "take off" itinerary is that sometimes one is not certain what the enemy is going to do and therefore it might be necessary to have a number of squadrons standing by in different parts of the country rather than have one squadron carrying out an extended stern chase. From "STAND-BY" to "TAKE OFF" is really the latter part of the "READINESS" to "TAKE OFF" drill, so needs no further enlarging.

QUICK LANDINGS.--It is very important that a squadron returning from a patrol or combat on reaching the aerodrome should be able to get out of the air on to the ground, taxi to the dispersal areas where the aircraft crews are waiting to refuel and to rearm, in the shortest possible time for these reasons:

1. Any number of aircraft seen circling a point on the ground by enemy aircraft would at once give the enemy aircraft an exact indication as to the whereabouts of the aerodrome. The enemy quite obviously must be kept in doubt as to which aerodrome the fighter aircraft are operating from; this can only be done in forward areas by cutting down this circling to the minimum.

2. The aircraft should remain non-operational for the shortest possible time, and quite obviously after combat or patrol duties a squadron returning without gas and perhaps without ammunition it is very definitely non-operational.

To get a squadron on to the ground and to the allotted positions for rearming and refueling in haste requires some definite drill for the approach, breaking up, landing and taxiing in. The most successful drill for carrying this into effect I have found is as follows:

When about three miles from the aerodrome, leader notices which direction the wind is blowing and knowing which side of the field his dispersal area is situated he plans to land so that he ends his run as near as possible to this dispersal area. With this aim in view he orders his squadron to echelon to a side so that on landing he does not have to taxi across the path of the remainder of his squadron coming into land. For instance, if during the final run into wind the dispersal area should lie on the right, the squadron would have ordered echelon to port; this allows aircraft to land in very quick succession and taxi straight to their dispersal areas without any delay or danger. So during this final three miles the leader makes a long sweep around the aerodrome gradually losing height with wheels and flaps down coming into land on the area he has selected as near to his dispersal point as possible. The squadron follows in quick succession. The taxiing to the dispersal area is done before the landing run is completed, pilots merely watching that the aircraft immediately ahead is clear; they do not worry at all about the aircraft following. At the dispersal areas the crews of the aircraft a e standing by with ammunition and gas all ready. Pilots taxi straight to their allotted positions and switch off the engines, the crews immediately getting to work. I cannot describe in detail the refueling and rearming operations as each type of aircraft has a different best way to be refueled and rearmed.

THE GUN SIGHT

BRITISH TYPE

TYPES.--One may say now that the old types of ring and bead, and aldis sights are obsolete. Anyway their construction is so simple as to need no special notes. The latest type of sight is the reflector sight. Instruction on this is amply covered in the manual dealing with the sight, but perhaps a few extra notes on the sight from the practical experience point of view might be appropriate. One of the snags about the sight is that it is lighted by an electric bulb and this bulb burns in a very small compartment in the sight and consequently is inclined to get very hot. I am not trying to say that the sight is in any way unreliable because of this point, but it is of the utmost importance that before taking off on patrol duties, the pilot does switch the bulb on to see that it does light. If it does not do so, it must be changed at once. Spare bulbs must always be carried and pilots should see that the spare bulb holder is carrying the two spare bulbs it should. The other snag is the very small base anchorage of the sight. I don't suppose the base anchorage is more than some 1 1/2 inches in diameter. You can see that the very smallest fraction of an inch movement on this small base would throw the sight some feet off the target at 200 yards, so it is of the greatest importance that the lining or harmonization of the sight with the guns is checked frequently. For some reason or other the sight makes a very attractive article at which to clutch in order to help one get out of the cockpit; all the mechanics invariably do this and one does find oneself reaching for the sight to help one out. Of course the sight must not be touched at all once it is correctly lined. Pilots should refrain from hanging their helmets or any other articles of clothing over the sights bearing in mind that the sight was not designed as a hook for such articles. After each flight the windshield of the aircraft should be wiped off; if this is not done it seems to hinder the effectiveness of the reflection.

OPERATION.--The reflector sight is absolutely fool proof and all that a pilot is concerned with in the air is the switching on of the bulb and the setting of the range bar. Personally, in combat I have never used the range bar as a range finder, but in practice I find it invaluable as a check of the range that I am opening fire at and I find with this practice in combat I am able to judge the range very accurately. However, I do recommend that a range be set on the sight and I think that range should be for a 60 foot target on 300 yards, this being the size of the average bomber target. I say 300 yards because one is inclined to watch the enemy until it fills the range gap and then open fire so that in actual fact one is always very much closer when the trigger is pressed than the range one has set on the sight. This means that one opens fire at the best possible range which is 250 yards.

I think also it advisable to leave the reflector sight light switched off when not in use. It has a very intensely bright bulb and if left on for any length of time will run the battery down if the generator is not functioning correctly. I have known generators to fail in the air and because the sight is left on the battery becomes quickly discharged and the sight useless.

HARMONIZATION.--There is no question that the careful and correct harmonization of the sight and guns is the most important of all the points in air fighting. It would be a pathetic state of affairs for a pilot to enter a combat and fight his hardest, firing his guns and yet achieve nothing because his guns are not pointing where his sight is aiming. The pilot himself should make it his personal responsibility to harmonize the sights and guns on his own aircraft; under no circumstances whatever should he delegate this responsibility to anyone else.

The procedure for the correct harmonization of sights is laid down in the appropriate manuals and should be strictly adhered to.

In this connection I should like to mention, not how to harmonize the guns, but at what ranges for the most effective fire one should set the harmonization point, that is the point at which the guns' bullets should meet. The greatest difficulty a fighter pilot has to contend with when firing wing-mounted guns is range, therefore anything which gives him more latitude in judging of range is bound to be helpful.

I have found it most effective to harmonize the two inboard guns to say 200 yards, the next pair at 225 yards, the next pair at 250, and so on according to the number of guns carried. If one draws a plan of the paths of the bullets from each gun, one will see that with a five foot target you have practically covered with a maximum density of bullets all ranges from 175 yards to, if using twelve guns, 325 yards.

NIGHT OPERATIONS.--I am not certain that I am qualified to voice any opinions on this subject, never having been successful at night. However, perhaps a few notes on the subject in general might at any rate be interesting.

Firstly, I am certain that fighter aircraft are most effective at night when used individually and not in formations. I cannot see any advantage of using more than one aircraft, but there are many disadvantages in so doing. The main disadvantage is that it is so easy to become detached from one another in the dark and this invariably ends in one fighter launching an attack on the other, or at any rate wasting valuable time in chasing each other. All the fighters should have definite zones to work in and should rigidly stick to them. The areas should be divided into zones for altitude as well.

I think recognition at night is still one of the most difficult and yet important tasks - great care should be taken to recognize what you are about to fire on - remember it is infinitely more desirable to let one enemy bomber escape than to shoot down one of your friends.

Fly with ALL lights off. This of course includes all interior lighting. This will facilitate search and also prevent the enemy seeing you first.

The new British device (which of course cannot be mentioned here) will bring you well into attacking range. However, do not open fire until you have placed yourself in a very favorable position to insure the enemy is destroyed in your first burst. Remember if you miss, in all probability that will be the last you will see of the enemy, who will not wait around and allow you another shot. So MAKE CERTAIN that FIRST burst is a good one.

Always place yourself in the best position with regard to the light available. Get the enemy silhouetted against some light patch - the moon or clouds; sometimes it is possible to pick them out against a moonlit sea. Fighter pilots have had great success in cruising over a large fire. The Germans invariably, once they have set something on fire, empty all their bombs into the fire. So if you remain over a fire you are certain to get a target. They show up well silhouetted against the flames.

On returning to the airfield waste no time circling-- get down at once. Keep a careful watch behind the whole time. After landing get off the flare path at once, you may have been followed home by the enemy and if you remain in the flare path you might get hurt.

The lighting of flying fields is very much in the throes of redesigning. The Drem electrical system seems to be coming in, although I personally think that this is too much of a good thing for war time. Roughly, the system is as follows: All the lights are hooded so as to be invisible above 1,500 feet. There is an outer ring of lights about 3 miles from the perimeter of the airfield and then a funnel of lights leading you into the first touch down light. During the approach in your altitude is guided by lighted totem poles about 15 feet high, the procedure being that after permission to land is given, the lights are switched on and the pilot makes a circle of the outer ring until he comes to the lighted funnel and turns in, approaching into the funnel, checking his altitude on the totem poles touching down on first flare light. The whole system is then switched off immediately.

There are other systems, not so elaborate. Up to now we have used a flare path of ordinary hooded goose necked flares laid out in the form of a Tee. There are five flares one hundred yards apart and a sixth fifty yards, forming the long arm of the Tee (450 yards) and two flares 100 yards and at right angles to the last one in the long arm forming the cross of the Tee. A flood light is placed 75 yards to leaward of the first flare and is only used in an emergency. Beside the flood light is placed an important device called the "Angle of Glide Indicator". This only shows to a pilot coming into land if he is dead right in this angle of approach and shows a green light. If, however, he is too high an amber light appears, and if he is too low a red light appears. If he is too far to one side or other of the flare path the lights are invisible. Marking the extreme boundary of the safe landing point are two amber glim lamps of ordinary indirect flashlamp brilliance. Likewise marking the limits of the runway each end are placed two red glim lamps. No. 3 flare is a double one, so that if a pilot is not running along the ground as he passes this flare he must open up his engine and go around again. The whole lighting system is invisible from above 1500 feet. Sufficient crews must be standing by to douse all lights should an emergency arise.

Of course on moonlight nights no lighting is required other than perhaps two white glim lamps placed into wind some 600 yards apart on the best landing area.

Homing of returning fighter of course is highly secret and cannot be mentioned in these notes, but suffice to say that the procedure adopted is absolutely infallible and always 100% effective and brings one always back dead over the airfield.

There are many strategical methods of employing fighters at night, but as these are highly secret it is impossible for me to go into them in this manual. A night fighting pilot is usually specially selected and trained for the task.

It is hoped, however, that these few notes may be of use in a tactical sense.

ANTI-AIRCRAFT GUNNERY

I do not intend to go into any of the technical details of anti-aircraft gunnery, or even into the principles of the control or location of guns, in these notes, but rather into the question of the effect of this gunnery on you as pursuit pilots.

Firstly I might mention that I consider anti-aircraft gunnery entirely useless, unless used on the barrage principle. The direct firing of guns at aircraft at whatever altitude is, in my opinion, the question of good or bad luck as to whether a hit is obtained. Whether this will remain so in view of improvements of gun laying, etc., remains to be seen. Personally I think that anti-aircraft gun fire will always remain ineffective from pursuit pilot's point of view. During the last year of the war I believe that I flew many more than 100 hours over German territory and was continually under fire from the ground during the whole of that period and was always accompanied by at least 11 other fighter aircraft, yet I only lost one airplane during the whole of this time.

The most dangerous of all anti-aircraft fire is the quick firing light guns from 20 mm. to 37 mm. cal. Sometimes as many as eight 37 mm. guns are mounted as one gun, aimed and fired by one man. However I believe the effective ceiling of these guns is at the most, 10,000 feet. I also say that as they are rather on the heavy side for quick swinging around that they become ineffective at targets overhead at low altitude. I do not recommend flying under 10,000 feet over enemy territory unless it cannot be avoided. This is exaggerated if the base of the cloud is below 10,000 feet, as aircraft show up in bold relief and make such excellent aiming marks. So avoid flying over these types of gun under those conditions. Take the squadron over them in cover of the clouds or if this be impossible, owing to the mission you are on, fly at as high a speed as possible and as crooked a course as possible. If I couldn't cross the battery at above 10,000 feet I should, unless as I said before, the type of mission prevents it, fly at ground level. Below 3,000 feet small arms fire, such as 300 cal. machine guns and rifles, becomes reasonably effective - so do not wait around more than necessary and if possible, fly at ground level rather than at 3,000 feet, and as fast as possible.

From 11,000 feet to 15,000 feet is the most dangerous altitude for heavy anti-aircraft fire. However, changes in course or altitude will get you out of trouble. If it is imperative that you do not fly any straight and level course when flying between these altitudes, but I do say that the fire is ineffective if course and altitude are altered every 30 seconds or so. Above 15,000 feet one can afford to be reasonably slack. A shell takes quite a few seconds to reach this altitude so that a direct hit is most unlikely unless you have been kind enough to give them a real sitting target. Alter course continuously but one can afford to be much less violent.

The barrage system of firing does not really concern pursuit pilots because it is usually only encountered over important targets which it would never be a pursuit pilot's task to attack. However, on escort missions a pursuit pilot will get a wonderful view of this type of anti-aircraft firing in action, for as soon as the bombers near their objective this terrific gun fire will break out, but there is no need for a pursuit pilot to actually enter the zone. If enemy fighters are present, the gun fire will cease so if the bombers are attacked one will be quite immune to go into the zone, for whilst enemy fighters are in the vicinity, anti-aircraft fire ceases. In fact, the ceasing of gun fire often gives you an indication, if you have not already seen them, that enemy fighters are about. You will notice when on escort task that practically all the anti-aircraft gun fire is directed against the bombers and that almost invariably the fighters are left entirely alone.

So to sum up, one can say that

1. The most dangerous altitudes are from 1,000 feet to 10,000 feet because of quick firing light cannon. Counter this by speed and erratic flying, or preferably take cover in cloud or fly out of these altitudes.

2. Below 3,000 feet one encounters severe small arms fire, so make a difficult target by flying really low and fast.

3. About 10,000 feet and up to 15,000 feet one encounters accurate heavy anti-aircraft fire, counter by changes in course or altitude.

4. Above 15,000 feet one is reasonably safe if one changes course or altitude.

5. Sudden ceasing of anti-aircraft fire usually indicated a strong force of enemy fighters.

6. Fly at over 15,000 feet or at zero feet altitude unless mission prevents it.

On home defense it is essential that all pursuit pilots do know the abouts of the defended area so as not to embarrass anti-aircraft gunners in the defrnse of these areas. However, the control of the guns is so highly organized that this is an unimportant worry, as I consider that a pursuit pilot has more than one hundred percent chance of bringing down enemy aircraft than have the guns, and the guns come under the direct control of the same controller as the fighters so are always given the order to quit in good time. It is just as well to inform the controller by radio telephony of your intention of entering the gun zone to make doubly sure.

Finally I say that the only effective use of anti-aircraft gunnery is when it is effectively controlled and laid and fires on the barrage principle. In order to deny the essential bit of air for accurate bombing to the enemy bomber. On a small target the bombers have to fly over certain small areas to release their bombs and this area should be alive with bursting shells, making it impossible for the enemy to enter. Direct firing at enemy aircraft is in my opinion almost a waste of time.

AIR COMBAT

The subject of air combat, that is the actual fighting in the air, I have avoided purposely so far because practically everyone who has to do the actual fighting differ in their opinion as to the best methods of combating in the air. Obviously there is an aim to be achieved and no one can differ on this point; the aim is the certain destruction of the enemy aircraft in as short a time as possible without getting yourself hurt in so doing. I propose now to detail my version of how I endeavored to achieve this aim. I have listened to many discussions on the subject and I do say a great majority of fighting men agree with me and so I place these opinions on record with the idea that even if you do not accept them, you will at any rate in condemning them, perhaps discuss the merits further with your friends, and in the discussion you may learn your version of the answer. I always look on myself as a good advertisement for my method as I am still alive to tell you about it.

One of the interesting points of this war is that there are no outstanding Aces. There are however many "Ace" Squadrons and Stations. The reason is that this war is a war, not of the individual, but of teams. The Squadron being the team. The Squadrons that work well together are always successful in achieving the aim I have outlined above. Their casualties are practically non-existent, and their victories are innumerable. If a Squadron does not work as a Squadron, the results are disastrous. After quoting as above, it seems a little strange to go straight into a discussion on individual combat (this however is what this preamble is working up to) especially if I follow to say individual combats are a thing of the past. You must understand that even if you do meet an enemy on your own, you must always expect him to have his whole Squadron "just around the corner", and you must go into your combat with this in mind.

By the term individual combat, I really mean a combat by a Squadron which has broken formation and is "mixing it", and even when this occurs you are still a team and are all fighting together and must always remain in the same piece of sky, so you can always support each other and not allow yourself to be drawn away, where you are bound to be dealt with severely. If you do so, you are letting your Squadron down. The foremost thing to remember as a pursuit pilot is that your one and only task is really the destruction of ENEMY BOMBERS. Your fights against Pursuit Aircraft are really only to allow you to achieve this aim of the destruction of the bombers. Combats against pursuit should in the normal circumstances be avoided if in so doing you are allowing a free passage to enemy bombers to reach your target areas. It may be so that your Squadron be given the task of dispersing and by liquidating the enemy fighter escort of the bombers, in this case, of course the combats would be fighter against fighter. You must keep in your mind your assigned task so that if you are detailed to attack the bombers, even though they be escorted, you must attack them and if possible not become involved in a fight with the escort. If you are detailed to deal with the escort, remember that you must get at them as soon as you can because it might be that another Squadron has been detailed to attack the bombers which would be hazardous if the escort had not been dispersed. To disperse the escort is the easiest thing in the world to do, and it might be just as well if you remember when your task is escorting bombers, just how easily you drew the fighter escort from the enemy bombers and not allow yourself to be drawn away from your charges. Any sort of attack or the mere fact that you appear in the sky in the vicinity of the bombers is usually enough to get the whole lot of enemy fighters after you at once. Of course this has achieved your task, although to make a good job of it, it would be as well to be able to deal effectively with as many fighters as possible to teach them a lesson as to what to expect in the future.

This is what I mean by individual combat and it usually means that the whole Squadron becomes involved and there are no spare aircraft to act as guards. Another cause of this type of circumstances would be a surprise attack by enemy fighters while you are carrying out an offensive sweep over their country. The question of bomber escort is dealt with in my booklet so I do not propose to go into any details on that score except to again impress on the student that if he is escorting bombers, he must stay with the bombers and not be drawn away. Merely attack and disperse any immediate menace but never follow them away. So individual combat should not develop under those circumstances.

It has taken me a rather lengthy preamble to come to the point, but, I do feel a detailed explanation is required to define individual combat as I see it and the circumstances generally leading up to it. Otherwise, beginners are inclined to get the wrong impression of modern war and have dreams of making "Aces" of themselves after the style of Ball, McCudden and Bishop. These illusions are dangerous, not only from your point of view, but from the safety of your Squadron as well. So to individual combat.

Altitude and speed are the only important points in combat. Of course altitude can always be converted into speed merely by depressing the nose of your aircraft. I am convinced it is suicidal to place any importance on maneuverability. Maneuverability is only a form of defense which is not required if you have sufficient speed to get you out of the trouble. You do not require any kind of exceptional maneuverability to attack and if you have not got the speed, the enemy can always avoid combat without relying on his powers of maneuverability to do so.

Realize that circumstances for every combat are different and it is impossible to lay down any hard and fast rule what one is to do and what one is not to do in certain predicaments. It is not my intention to do so. For instance, if you have an enemy pursuit ship on your tail, you don't need any advice from me as to how to get rid of him (just one big kicking scrambling turn will take care of that and the enemy would be stupid, in my opinion, to attempt to stay behind you). However, if he were to start climbing the moment you started your "ham fisted" maneuvers, he can then open the attack whenever it pleases him, as you will be in a very much worse position when you have finished. The initiative is his and by the law of averages he must always win on these tactics. At any rate, one thing is certain, and that is, you will not. You cannot win a dog fight on maneuverability, because it is not a form of attack but merely a method of giving a momentarily respite which will only last while the maneuver is being carried out. It must eventually stop, and if you have lost a lot of altitude in your "ham fisted" flying, you will be in a very dangerous predicament. So the essence of successful dog fighting is not to sit on a man's tail indefinitely whatever the tactics or maneuvers he carries out, but to come in behind him, open fire with your sights on and just stay long enough to get a really good burst in, or until his "ham fisted" maneuverability makes firing impracticable, then break away and climb at your best climbing angle watching him and positioning yourself the whole while and as soon as he stops, renew your attack. Of course, you must take special care to see that someone else is not trying the same tactics on you. That is one of the main good points of these tactics, you always have sufficient time for thinking and careful watching. If you are attacked and some one settles on your tail, a hard steep turn with messes of rudder will always get you out of trouble. However, don't go on any longer than it is sufficient to make him break off his attack. Fight with your eyes wide open, making sure your every movement improves your tactical position. Always remain in the same piece of sky as your Squadron. Keep together. Matters are considerably simplified if you have sufficient fighters to allow about half to remain above you to keep guard; you can then allow yourself a little more latitude for "ham fisted" maneuvering and you may be more successful in "sitting" on some enemy fighter's tail until he is destroyed. Frankly, I am against even this. My method I have found really successful, which to put it simply is that if at any time your enemy does his "ham fisted" maneuvering you take advantage of it by gaining altitude, at the same time maintaining a good position aloft. When you dive to attack, you do not close your throttle, but use your extra speed to take you aloft again. Come in behind your foe, open fire at 300 yards, to any minimum range you wish, then break away zooming up so that you always maintain your tactical advantage of altitude. Fly hard, fast, and with determination. Of course, if the enemy is flying two place fighters or anything that is armed aft, you must not zoom directly up, but break away downwards until you are out of range with your engine at full power using every scrap of gained speed to carry you aloft again. If he is armed astern you do not get any closer than 150 yards.

The Squadron Commander must take great care in positioning his Squadron before he attacks the bombers. The sun, clouds and every possible aid must be used to achieve advantage in positioning and surprise.

All opening attacks should be synchronized. I shall describe in detail how I think these attacks should be carried out. In my opinion you need only three types of attacks. All these attacks can be launched from any direction. That is, from ahead, from either beam, or from astern, and if you wish (but not recommended) from above or underneath.

It is essential to leave a certain amount of initiative to the members of your Squadron because if you lay down, and practice, attacks in any rigid sequence, when the actual thing comes along, some detail is bound to be different, and if, as I said, you have laid down the law too much the attack will become chaotic.

I will go into details as to the merits of launching the attacks from the various angles later.

When the Squadron Commander has decided that the best thing is to attack with one aircraft at a time he orders a number one attack. This, of course, is a very seldom used attack as even when attacking a solitary enemy aircraft, it is still better to attack with two or three others in order to lessen the effectiveness of the fire coming from the rear of the enemy. Anyway, the point is, if the Squadron Commander decides that an attack by one aircraft in succession is the best tactics, he orders a number one attack. The direction in which it is launched does not matter. What does matter is that only one aircraft attacks at a time in succession. If a leader finds himself confronted by a formation of enemy bombers flying in a flat V, that is in almost line abreast formation and he has not sufficient fighters to engage them simultaneously. This attack can prove most useful. It is launched from the beam on the flank enemy bombers, care being taken to hide yourself from the defensive fire of the other bombers by keeping the target you have selected between you and his friends. This will mean that you only have the defensive fire of one enemy to contend with.

If the Squadron Commander decides that the attack should be carried out by two aircraft simultaneously, in succession he orders a number two attack. The circumstances leading up to this attack would be if the enemy only presented two targets by flying in sharp V formation so that it would be impossible to get at any of the other of the aircraft except the two tails of the V. This, therefore only allows two attackers at a time to get a shot. This attack may be carried out against single aircraft. Again the attack may be launched from any direction.

Lastly the No.3 Attack. The Squadron Commander decides that three or more aircraft can attack successfully at the same time. This may be against one bomber or any number. If it is against one bomber, of course, it would be impracticable to attack with more than three. However, the aim of the attack is that as many aircraft as possible attack at once. The number attacking is limited by the C.O. over the radio. There are serious snags against this attack on one bomber, the main one being that the sections have to split if you intended that attacks be delivered from both flanks.

You may however all attack from the same flank, No.1 doing a beam attack, No.2 doing a quarter attack, and No.3 doing an astern attack. No.3 is really the man that counts; it is he that is in the position to do the real accurate shooting. Nos.1 and 2 are merely there to distract the enemy's rear gun fire. These attacks have been very successful in England, but in my own mind I am not certain that if you attempt it with inexperienced pilots you are losing more than you gain by the distraction from accurate aiming due to one's attention being almost wholly occupied in avoiding collision. If you are using the four ship element, No.4 can act as a guard, getting a shot in if he possibly can. When more than three attack at the same time, the Squadron is echeloned to one side of each other so that they are flying almost in abreast formation. The leader picks out the flank enemy his side of the echelon, and goes into the attack, his No.2 taking the next target, No.3 the next and so on.

An important point is this - do not attempt to watch more than one of your friends; forget the rest of the Squadron. I mean No.2 should only watch and position himself on No.1, and No.3 should only watch and position himself on No.2 and so on. Do not attempt to watch the whole Squadron. The attacks should arrive in range as near together as possible, open fire together, and break away downwards and to the side of the leader in very quick succession; in fact as nearly together as possible. A good way to launch this attack from ahead of the bombers intending to pass some 600 yards to the flank and turn in behind and from a flank, in this the leader echelons the Squadron so that he has the longest path to make good, that is from the outside of his Squadron to the outside of the bombers; this will ensure that he has no stragglers, as all his Squadron has a shorter distance to travel than he. Of course, should the attack be launched from a flank in this manner the turn should be done in almost line astern formation, the Squadron coming into a flat echelon as the turn completes and the run on the target commences.

The Squadron Commander always informs his Squadron over the radio which ships are to attack with him by saying, "One section, number three attacks go" or "Flight number three attack go" or "Squadron: number three attack go". The ones not detailed, remain as guards. These attacks are simple and allow tremendous variations and altitude and I have found them very successful. Remember too, it is advisable to take only half your strength into the attack leaving the other half to look after you so that you can give your undivided attention on the attack and aiming instead of having to always keep such a sharp look around for surprise attacks.

In defense, I recommend the defensive circle. A great deal of practice should be given in forming this circle from the search formation in as short a time as possible. Half seconds count.

If the enemy are encountered in this circle, a section (that is a pair, or three aircraft), may be dispatched; the Squadron stands by. They enter inside of the enemy circle and turn in the opposite direction firing at each enemy as they appear in range. This invariably breaks up any enemy defensive circle then the Squadron pitches into the debris. This is possible owing to the better maneuvering qualities of American and British pursuit ships.

Not too much altitude should be lost on the breakaways because the attacks might be in need of repetition, or they may be escorted and you might place yourself badly with them. On the other hand, if a complete get-a-way is intended, you can continue to ground level. If you have ammunition left, I do not favor this.

My ideas have been to try and outline the general principles of these three attacks, and I do realize that there are so many "ifs" and "whens" that one could never discuss them in the bounds of these few notes.

I do not favor an attack in V formation because of the difficulties of breaking away.

Whatever attacks you may conceive after reading these notes, I earnestly repeat, must be simple and most easy to execute, otherwise complete chaos will result. Always unrehearsed incidents take place, so a great deal of latitude must be invested in each member of the Squadron to act as he thinks best.

SUMMARY

So to sum up the important points a pilot should remember in combat, they are:

1. That you are not an individual ace but rather a member of a team working and fighting in the organized and synchronized attacking of enemy formations. Always work and fight together.

2. That your primary aim is the destruction of enemy bombers and combat with enemy pursuit aircraft should normally be avoided unless circumstances are very much in your favor and there are definitely no enemy bombers to engaged or the enemy pursuits are actually preventing your achieving your primary aim, which is the destruction of the enemy bombers.

3. Whenever possible gain altitude. This can always be converted into speed and always allows you the initiative.

4. Maneuverability is only a form of defense and should only be reverted to when the enemy is definitely flying a faster ship than you are. If you are flying a faster ship, do not resort to maneuverability in defense. Get in, shoot, and get out.

5. When surprised, under any circumstances, always turn TOWARDS your foe. NEVER turn away. Even when surprised, still try and be the attacker. Aggressiveness is an important point.

6. Once you commence a turn to one side or the other with an enemy on your tail, you must continue to turn as steeply as you are able and not, under any circumstances whatsoever, slacken this turn or reverse it. Keep an eye on your foe and only continue this defense maneuver so long as he is actually on your tail, he will then be unable to aim sufficiently far ahead of you to hit you. Easing off the turn or better still reversing it, is exactly what he would wish you to do as this would allow him immediately to be able to lead you sufficiently to blast you out of the sky.

7. When diving to attack an enemy, whether in formation or individually, do not dive at a slight decline all the way towards him, but dive steeply to his level then flatten out, using your excessive speed gained in the dive to make a swift approach from dead astern.

8. When it becomes imperative to break off combat with enemy pursuit, do not dive away in a straight dive but dive in as crooked a course as possible. Downward rolls are ideal but make them straight down.

WHAT THE EXPERTS SAY
ADVICE ON TACTICS AND AIR FIGHTING

I am sure that Wing Commander Malan and other of our successful fighter pilots will forgive me if I enclosed in this manual his very sound advice on the subject so I have taken the liberty of enclosing some very sound notes written by them on this subject.

A FEW IMPORTANT DON'TS

DON'T dive away from a Hun in a straight dive.

DON'T alter your direction of turn in a dogfight--each time you do, you are a sitting target and your opponent can catch up on you. If you're being chased and you can't turn and face your enemy--for example, if you are limping home with a damaged engine--try kicking on rudder and doing "ham" flat turns. That puts his aim out.

DON'T do stall turns and copy-book aerobatics as evasive action. When your speed drops you are a sitter. Remember, skid and slip are good evasive tactics--but of course they ruin your own shooting, so use them properly and at the right time.

DON'T lose a little height--always try to gain height in a dogfight; unless it is "time to go home" and then lose all the height you've got and beat it.

DON'T forget to LOOK.

DON'T neglect your shooting--regular and correct practices with cine camera or with P.P. gear may easily mean--

    (a) "This pilot already has x confirmed victories and y probables--"
    (b) You get the swine who thought he could get you.

DON'T let him get away--the only decent Hun is a (confirmed) dead Hun.

DON'T LOSE YOUR HEAD.

NOTES ON TACTICS AND AIR FIGHTING

By Wing Commander A. G. Malan, D.S.O., D.F.C.

Generally speaking, tactics in air fighting are largely a matter of quick action and ordinary commonsense flying. The easiest way to sum it up in a few words is to state that, apart from keeping your eyes wide open and remaining fully alive and awake it is very largely governed by the compatibilities of your own aircraft in comparison with that flown by your opponent. For example, in the case of the Spitfire versus the ME. 109F, the former has superior maneuverability, whereas the latter has a faster rate of climb. The result is that the Spitfire can afford to "mix it" when attacking, whereas the ME. 109F, although it tends to retain the initiative because it can remain on top, cannot afford to press the attack home for long if the Spitfire goes into a turn. Obviously there are a lot of factors involved which must govern your action in combat--such as the height at which you are flying, the type of operation on which you are engaged, the size of your formation, etc.

There are however, certain golden rules which should always be observed. Some are quite obvious whereas others require amplification. Here they are:

(1) Wait till you see the "whites of his eyes" before opening fire. Fire bursts of about one to two seconds and only when your sights are definitely "on".

(2) Whilst shooting think of nothing else. Brace the whole body with feet firmly on the rudder pedals having both hands on the stick. Concentrate on your ring sight (note Rule 3).

(3) Always keep a sharp look-out even when maneuvering for and executing an attack and in particular immediately after breakaway. Many pilots are shot down during these three phases as a result of becoming too absorbed in their attack. Don't watch your "Flamer" go down except out of the corner of your eye.

(4) If you have the advantage of height you automatically have the initiative.

(5) Always turn and face an attack. If attacked from a superior height wait until your opponent is well committed to his dive and within about 1,500 yards of you. Then turn suddenly toward him.

(6) **Make** your decisions promptly. It is better to act quickly even if your tactics may not be the best.

(7) Never fly straight and level for more than 30 seconds at any time whilst in the combat area.

(8) When diving to attack always leave a proportion of your formation above to act as top guard.

(9) INITIATIVE: AGGRESSION: AIR DISCIPLINE: TEAM WORK, are words that mean something in air fighting.

(10) Get in quickly--punch hard--get out!

FORMATION FLYING.--When adopting a type of formation certain points must be borne in mind. The main point is whether you are on defensive operations, or on the offensive over enemy territory. For defensive work, formations should be maneuverable and compact. When flying on an offensive operation the formation should be stepped up and back from the given patrol height and should be divided into attacking and defensive units.

Fighter formations must maintain extreme maneuverability, while guarding the dreaded "blind spot" behind. You'll soon find that if you try to find the answer to the blind spot by simply spreading your machines over a broad front, you'll have lost the first essential, i.e. maneuverability. If you choose line astern, which is very maneuverable, you'll be blind behind.

At a very early stage of the war I discovered that the only satisfactory answer was to fly in line astern and have the leader change the course of the whole formation at regular intervals.

SQUADRON TACTICS.--At this point it would be a good thing to take you on three main types of operation.

First we'll put you into a squadron at "readiness" on a station in SE England, with bomber raids coming over. If fighters are expected it is always advisable to climb for your height outside the combat area. Your raids are reported at 20,000 ft., therefore enemy fighters may be stepped up to at least 25,000 ft. If you have no other squadrons supporting you, you should aim to intercept, if possible, from the sun--from about 23,000 ft., unless you have time to get higher. You intercept and, if there are not fighters present, you must first destroy the bombers' main method of defence, i.e., formation flying. A good maneuver would be to attack with a section of four, with the object of breaking up the formation--obviously the most effective method of achieving this is to attack from ahead. But this is generally difficult. The section should go in singly from different angles and attempt to fly through the bomber formation--with plenty of speed, and firing at the same time. With any luck the bombers should break, particularly if one or two of the leading machines get badly hit. The next thing is for the remaining eight machines to work in pairs and attack--two to one bomber. We found that formation attacks did not work in practice, for many reasons which I will not discuss here. Deflection shooting on the whole is a difficult operation, and the most effective form of attack is a diving attack approaching originally from the flank and developing into a curve which brings the attacker, with about 100 miles per hour overtaking speed, 2,000 yards behind and below. At this stage throttle back and, at about 800 yards, come up to the level position and give a short burst to put the rear defense off as you are closing in; at about 250 yards open fire, first at the fuselage and then concentrate on each engine in turn. This was found very effective with eight machine guns--the result with cannon should be quite devastating.

Should the bomber formation have fighter escort, about one-third of your formation should be detailed to engage the attention of the fighters without actually going into combat, whilst the remainder go in in two waves, with the same object as before. In the case of the squadron one section of four would maintain height and fly on the flank in such manner as to menace any enemy fighters who attempt to engage the attackers.

1. Operating from same Station during raids by bomb-carrying fighters at 23,000 ft. with escort.

If the Hun approaches from the Dover area it is best to climb well towards the flank in a southerly direction, in three sections of four in line astern on a narrow front, and climbing on a zig-zag course, keeping in a look-out, until a height of 27,000 or 28,000 ft. has been reached. Having attained your height out of harm's way, the course from now on is shaped according to the raid information. If there is any possibility of intercepting before the enemy reaches his objective every attempt should be made to meet him from the sun and with superior height of 2,000 to 4,000 ft. If, on the other hand, it is not possible to meet him on the way in it is best to curl round and attempt to meet him head-on on his way out. It is well to remember that the enemy must come home sometime and usually he has not sufficient petrol to play around. Therefore it is best to to get between him and his home with superior height because, if he dives away, as is usually the case, you can start your half-roll and dive in sufficient time to prevent the fight developing into a long, stern chase. The basic rule applies here as elsewhere, i.e., one section of four will remain up and guard against surprise attacks on the attacking eight.

(NOTE.--Had it been possible to gain height in time to await the enemy on his inward journey a good method would be to patrol about two miles up sun from his predicted course in line astern and with the sun on either one beam or the other. A useful hint when patrolling in the rarefied atmosphere at height, and when attempting to search in the direction of the sun, is to raise a wing tip until it covers the sun. It will be found that the area both sides of the wing will be quite free from glare.)

2. An offensive sweep over enemy territory:

When deciding upon a formation for offensive work the aim should be to spread the units loosely, and stepped up and back, or up and to the flanks, having the major proportion on the lower level, and smaller and looser units acting as a top guard. Owing to the clean lines and high speed of the modern fighter an engagement usually develops from an empty sky in a matter of seconds. If the enemy sights and decides to engage, the tendency will be for him to spot your lower and more obvious formations, and miss seeing your light top screen in the heat of the moment.

In most cases the patrol height is decided upon before departure. One of the important points in patrolling the other side is conservation of fuel, so climb and cruise at an economical speed with weak mixture. If the patrol height decided upon were 27,000 ft., I would climb the formation to about 31,000, and with the units stepped behind and down until crossing the lines. From then on I would proceed on a very gentle dive to 27,000 ft. and leave my rear units above and stepped up as arranged, when the lower units would be primarily for attack, whereas the upper screen would always remain up, and act purely as a defensive screen.

Rigid air discipline is essential, and idle chatter on the R/T should be almost a courtsmartial offense. It is impossible to lay down rigid rules. The two main rules, however, are that each unit must know the role it has to play--and that a whole unit should never go down to attack--always leave a top guard. If you dive, pull up again after your attack. Don't give away height.

CHARACTERISTICS OF THE HUN.--In his training the Hun fighter pilot appears to pay a great deal of attention to tactics. This is a good fault but, unfortunately for Hitler, the German fighter seems to lack initiative and "guts". His fighting is very stereotyped, and he is easily bluffed. Another factor is that his fighter aircraft in this war has been less maneuverable than ours. There are certain things which it is well to remember when fighting him.

His tactics, as I have stated before, although basically sound, are generally executed without a great deal of imagination, and he repeats the same old tricks with monotonous regularity. There was a saying in the last war: "Beware the Hun in the sun". In this war it seems to be truer than ever for three reasons:

(a) The Hun seldom attacks from any direction but from the sun.

(b) The modern machine, with its clean lines and good camouflage, is more difficult than ever to spot against the sun.

(c) With the fast speed achieved by the modern fighter little warning will be given before he gets within range and, furthermore, it is a well-known fact that the man who knocks you down in aerial combat is usually the one you did not see.

For some reason or other the Hun prefers to resort to what he considers a clever trick to catch the unwary, rather than make full use of his initial advantage and go in with a solid punch. For instance, a common trick is to detach a pair of decoys, who will dive past and in front of a British formation, hoping that someone will be fool enough to follow them, when the rest will immediately do a surprise attack from above. I am sorry to admit that some British pilots have been caught by this oft-repeated ruse. I deplore this as a tactical maneuver. The obvious, and most effective, action in this case would be for the Hun to make full use of his initial advantage in height and surprise by immediately attacking the formation below him.

NOTES

By Wing Commander A. G. Malan, D. S. O., D. F. C.

DON'T LOOK NOW!
........But I think you're being followed.

How many times have we been asked the same question—"Please sir, what do I do to get a 109 off my tail?" As if we knew. The answer really is: "Why did you let it get there, anyway?"

ATTACK.—The essence of Dogfighting is always to be the attacker—if you find yourself at the receiving end, well, we hardly like to say so, but you weren't really looking hard enough, were you? Or if you and a Hun have met suddenly, your reactions were a bit slow, perhaps. Anyhow, you're up the creek.

Well, we'll try and paddle you out of it. But remember—it's quite hard to turn defense into attack—so don't start on the defensive. First, when you are practicing dogfighting don't continue going round and round in ever decreasing circles. That's O.K. for a while—at least, if you turn hard enough. But you are unlikely to be able to get on the Hun's tail that way, so think up something more clever.

DODGE.—For example, a 109 dives on you—he's got superior speed, so you can't hope to fly away from him. Try foxing him then by closing the throttle and tightening up the turn. He's going too fast to out-turn you, so he over-shoots. Give him a moment to get by you, then—stick forward a bit, get behind him and shoot him down. That trick has worked many times.

FACE THE MUSIC.—Next, if you are about to be attacked, always turn and face your attacker once he is committed to his attack, even if you haven't any ammunition left. Look aggressive—that'll immediately cut down his self-confidence by half. As he comes up, turn in behind him. Whether you have any rounds left or not, it'll make him worried. If you have, why, go in and shoot him down. If not (say you're coming back from a sweep), choose a moment when you're pointing the right way, go straight down in a bit of a spiral, pull out, and streak for home. It'll take him probably ten seconds to realize you're no longer on his tail—then he has to turn and spot you--by which time you're well on your way. If he comes at you again, try the same trick, or pull another out of the hat...

FEINT (DON'T FAINT).--Such as doing a head-on attack and going down in a vertical spiral directly you pass him. He's fairly sure to lose you. That doesn't mean you don't have to weave though! Keep weaving till you are home--and remember, a good look out in time is worth any amount of evasive action.

CLOSE RANGE
Notes by a Polish Pilot

Firing at close range is the only way to be sure of getting your man. This has been proved by pilots of all nations in every war since flying started.

If you want confirmation, just read this:—Captain Albert Ball, V.C., D.S.O., M.C., By R.H. Kiernan.

Time and again this book states that Ball closed into extremely close range, so close in fact that even taking into account the slow aircraft of those days it leaves one gasping. On page 94 there is a paragraph:
" . . . . .Ball would then fasten on below the nearest machine, so close that other enemy aeroplanes could not shoot him off without risk of hitting their own man."

(Page 96.) "Ball was too close to miss, after five or ten shots the German toll . . . ."

(Page 104.) "Ball followed, firing another drum at twenty yards range . . . . the German crashed."

(Page 105.) "Ball closed to fifteen yards range beneath the nearest machine . . . ."

(Page 113.) "Ball had found that you must carry the flight as closely and relentlessly as possible to the enemy machines to be sure of success . . . ."

Flying Fury. James B. McCudden, V.C., D.S.O., M.C., M.M.

(Page 170.) "I closed to thirty yards on the second Hun . . . .Caught up with the Hun at the top of his zoom, opened fire, and continued doing so until I nearly crashed into his tail . . ."

Richthofan also used to stress the necessity of holding fire until extremely close range.

In this war we have Fighter Command Combat Films, Intelligence Bulletins, and the experience of pilots who have been fighting throughout the war, and one and all bear out the necessity for close-range firing, The The Air Fighting Committee Paper (A.F.C. III) states:

"The primary factors in the destruction of bombers are aim and range. It has been proved by night fighters recently that the eight-gun Hurricane, with a four-second burst, is quite capable of destroying any of the armoured German bombers, and this is probably due to the fact that the night fighter closes to a range of 100 yards or less. During daylight, it is more difficult to hold aim and to obtain close range, because of the evasive tactics adopted by the enemy. Nevertheless, the importance of closing to short range before opening fire cannot be too strongly stressed."

All the above illustrates that conclusion of different kinds of experience gained in air fighting in different times is the same: Generally speaking a short range, when shooting, is a factor of primary importance. It gives you incomparably greater chances of success than a relatively long range. Research workers who work on air firing calculations and tests say:

(a) Probability of hitting generally can be assumed as inversely proportional to the square of the range.
(That means that, for example, if you are shooting from 150 yards you will probably hit the enemy aircraft with about nine times greater number of bullets than when firing the same number of rounds from 450 yards. Remember, of course, to aim a bit high at a short range, if your guns are in the wings.

(b) The velocity of a bullet drops when range increases. Therefore, there is more certainty of piercing armour plating when the range is short.

(c) A certain Squadron during special trials was particularly asked to open fire at 300 yards, and break off at 100 yards. Believe it or not, the result (proved by camera) showed that the pilots had opened fire at distances from 800 yards to 1,200 yards.

That should have convinced you that short-range firing is the only way to get a good score sheet. Now, how to be sure you get close enough.

Firing at close range is not simply a thing that can just be done; no matter how courageous the pilot, nor how determined, he will not as a rule be able to execute close-range firing without studying it carefully and practising. The main trouble in judging distances in the air is the lack of other objects, in particular, the ground, with which to compare the objective. Speed of approach makes judgement difficult, and a subconscious fear of collision keeps telling a pilot that he is much closer than he is. General excitement is also inclined to make a pilot open fire too soon, unless he is close range conscious. At altitude the air is generally much clearer, and although the objective does not look bigger, details of it are more apparent. All this, however, can be overcome if some trouble is taken.

Here are some pointers:

COMPARISON OF THE SPAN OF AN AIRCRAFT WITH DIAMETER OF YOUR GUNSIGHT.--Try to retain general mental impressions of the attached diagram. Look through it and try to remember some easy points, as for example: If a single-engined fighter just fills the ring, the distance is of the order of 100 yards. If the same happens with a large twin-engined bomber, the distance is of the order of 250 yards. If those aircraft only half fill the ring the distances are about 200 yards and 500 yards respectively. Even quite a small bomber must appear about twice the size of the ring if you are really 100 yards from it. Try that in flight when you have an opportunity. If you know beforehand which type of aircraft is concerned in your training attacks, use the figures for that type from the diagram.

FREQUENT STUDYING OF AIRCRAFT AT KNOWN DISTANCES is essential. A good way to do this would be to put up a post at a definite distance, say 100 yards, from one aircraft dispersal point, 300 yards from another, and say 500 yards from another. By this method it would be possible to obtain a rough idea of ranges, especially if different aircraft were occasionally put in the dispersal points chosen. When doing this, an idea of detail should be established: For example, a wireless mast may be just visible at a certain distance, but not visible at any greater distance; while some colours may lose definition at certain distances. There are plenty of other such details to be found. It must be remembered, however, that generally altitude lends clearness to details.

THE CAMERA GUN is a great help in judging distances and should be more commonly used than it is. Most pilots will receive quite a shock when they realize just how far away they actually were from their target. (See Squadron results mentioned above.) Camera results are accurate and should be relied upon; they teach a lot. A general indication to know if you have really fired at close range is whether you were really impressed at the surprising closeness and size of your target. If you were not, you were probably too far off.

In conclusion, it may be said that any pilot, with practice and thought, can learn to fire at close range, and fear of collision soon goes when it has been done once or twice. The first time is the worst--but it must be close.

QUICK JUDGMENT OF RANGE BY MENTAL IMPRESSIONS OF THE WAYS IN WHICH VARIOUS TYPES APPEAR IN YOUR GUNSIGHT AT DIFFERENT DISTANCES

1. When the Aeroplanes just fill the Ring of the Gunsight they are at the following distances (to the nearest 10 yards).

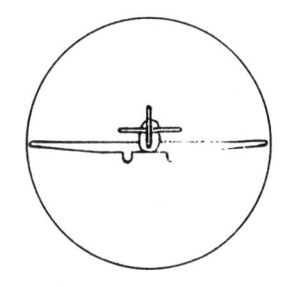

SPITFIRE
110 Yards

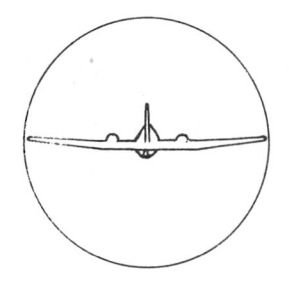

WELLINGTON
250 Yards

Corresponding Distances for other types are given below (to the nearest 10 yards).

SMALL AIRCRAFT		MEDIUM AIRCRAFT	
Distances below 150 yds. (e.g. One-Engine Fighters)		Distances between 150 & 200 yds.	
He. 113		Me. 110	150 yds.
Me. 109	90 yds.	Battle	160 yds.
Spitfire	110 yds.	Ju. 88	160, 170, or 190 yds.
Hurricane	120 yds.	Anson	160 yds.
Ju. 87	130 yds.	Blenheim	160 yds.
		Beaufort	170 yds.
		Hudson	190 yds.
LARGE AIRCRAFT		VERY LARGE AIRCRAFT	
Distances between 200 & 250 yds.		Distances over 300 yds.	
Hampden	200 yds.	Condor	310 yds.
He. III Mk V	210 yds.	Sunderland	330 yds.
Whitley IV	240 yds.	Ju. 90	330 yds.
Wellington	250 yds.		

ME 109 HE 111 JU 88

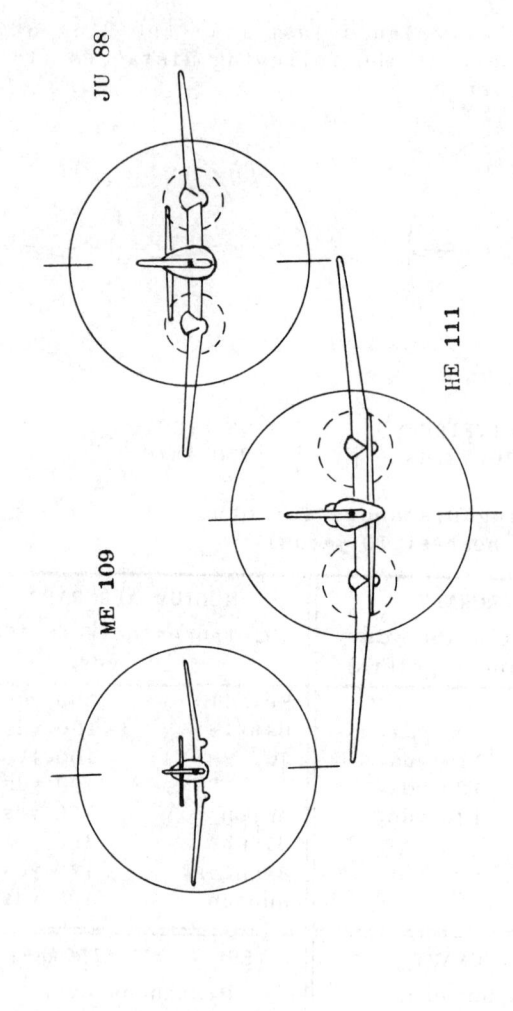

2. Your best chance of success is to Fire at Close Range. From 100 yards you get the following views in your sight

THE TIZZY ANGLE

An Interview with 'Zura' (F/O Zurakowski)

When discussing air fighting or even air firing we are always told to close to point blank range, but many pilots lament that they have been involved in a long, stern chase and have had the utmost difficulty in getting into range because when they first saw the enemy they thought they would close up quickly. The fact is that almost every pilot in his haste to get into close touch turns towards his enemy, the moment he sees him (Fig. 1).

ZURA'S PRINCIPLE.--Now we have a friend called Zura, and Zura is a practical man. He has thought this matter out and now offers a simple tip for judging correctly the distance to steer ahead in order to effect an interception at the earliest possible moment.

Zura says that if you are not steering at a point sufficiently far in front of the enemy then his aircraft will appear to move forwards in your windscreen. (Fig. 2.) If, on the other hand, you are steering too far in front of him then the aircraft will appear to move backwards (Fig. 3), and he goes on to say that only if you have allowed the correct deflection will the aircraft remain stationary, thus maintaining a constant angle (the Tizzy Angle) between the line of flight of your aircraft and his (Fig. 4). This rule is not altered by the fact that you may be climbing or diving to the attack.

We have drawn some diagrams to illustrate Zura's principle, and here are his own words describing the action he would take on sighting an aircraft to starboard, which curiously enough he wishes to intercept in the minimum time:

"Fly towards him in what you believe to be the correct direction. Fly steadily for a moment--hold your head stationary and note in which direction he appears to travel along your windscreen. If he appears to move forward steer further ahead and hold that course. Check again and continue to steer further ahead until he appears stationary.

If he appears to move backward in your windscreen then turn more towards him and repeat this process until he appears stationary. You will then be flying on the shortest route to intercept him. Check from time to time as you fly along this line for he may increase or decrease his speed".

Some of you may wonder if this tip is worth worrying about. The answer is given in Fig. 5 of our diagrams. It will be seen that the distance between the two aircraft is more than halved by keeping the angle of approach constant.

P.S.--You may say "Won't the aircraft get bigger in the windscreen as you get nearer, making it difficult to tell which way it is going?"

Zura says "this is the time to avoid a collision."

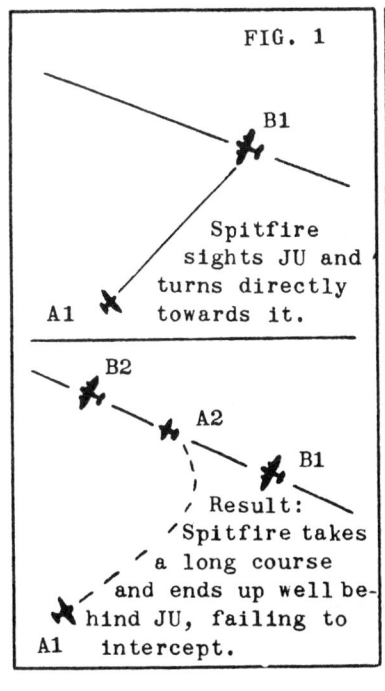

FIG. 1

Spitfire sights JU and turns directly towards it.

Result: Spitfire takes a long course and ends up well behind JU, failing to intercept.

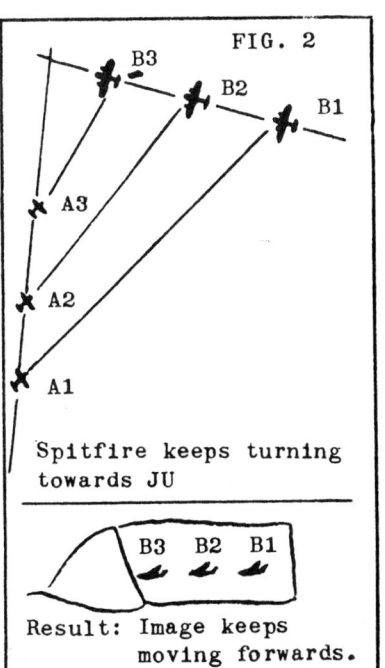

FIG. 2

Spitfire keeps turning towards JU

Result: Image keeps moving forwards.

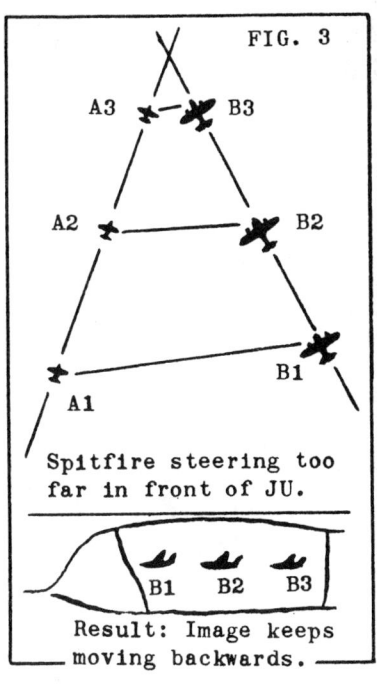

FIG. 3

Spitfire steering too far in front of JU.

Result: Image keeps moving backwards.

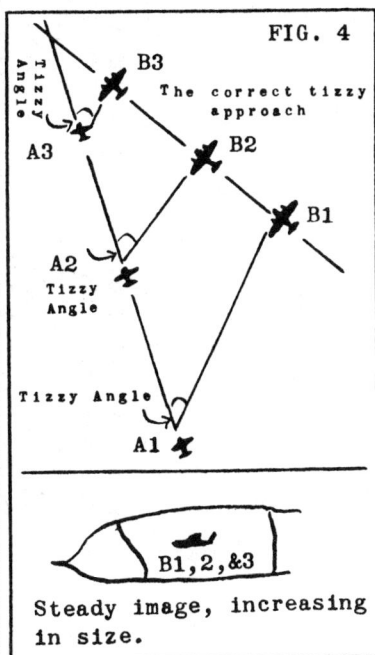

FIG. 4

The correct tizzy approach

Steady image, increasing in size.

FIGURE 5.

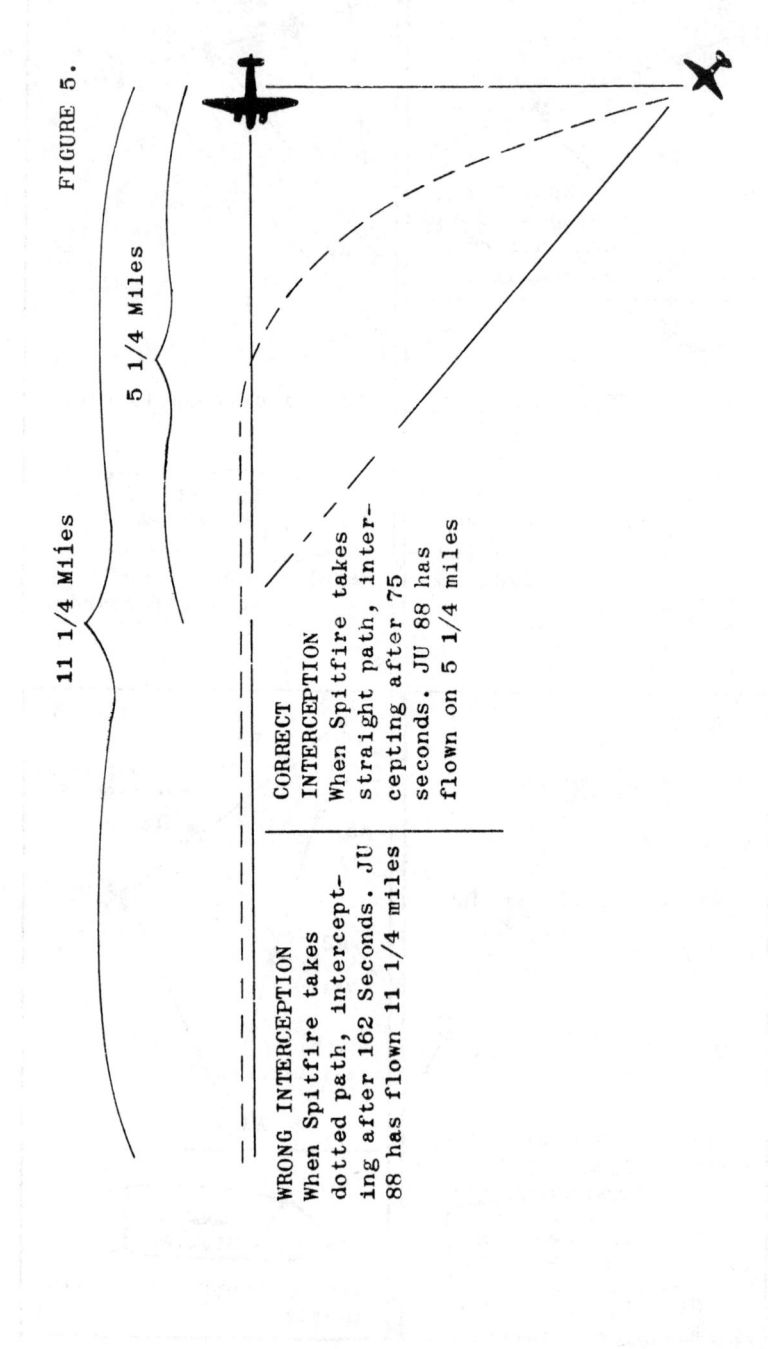

11 1/4 Miles

5 1/4 Miles

WRONG INTERCEPTION
When Spitfire takes dotted path, intercepting after 162 Seconds. JU 88 has flown 11 1/4 miles

CORRECT INTERCEPTION
When Spitfire takes straight path, intercepting after 75 seconds. JU 88 has flown on 5 1/4 miles

LECTURE OF DEVELOPMENT OF THE AIR DEFENSE OF GREAT BRITAIN AND ALSO ON AIR FIGHTING

I am going to try to describe to you tonight, very, very simply, indeed, the air defense of Great Britain. In order to do this, I go back to 1936 when this defense was practically non-existent. In 1936 we had approximately twelve squadrons of fighters defending Great Britain. These fighters were grouped around the southeast side of London, London being considered the only military target in Great Britain. The reason for this is the fact that 11,000,000 people live in greater London and in order to feed 11,000,000 people three times a day, it is necessary to have a very specialized docking system in order to get the food off the ships into the mouths of the people three times a day before it goes bad. A docking system of this nature was considered to be very vulnerable to their attacks and any sort determined bombing it was thought would disorganize the entire system. The people would then get hungry and the war would be lost. These fighters then grouped around the southeast side of London were concerned only in the defense of the Capitol. However, these few fighter squadrons were the nucleus of the tremendous defense scheme of the present day.

The equipment of these squadrons were Bristol Bulldog Aircraft. Their speed was approximately 125 m.p.h. (it is interesting to note that the slowest Italian bomber at this time did over 200 m.p.h.). The Bulldogs were armed with two vickers machine guns each. These guns were most unreliable and when they did fire, fired approximately 600 bullets a minute. When one took off in a Bulldog to carry out air firing practice, one took with one a large tool kit consisting of hammers and spanners with which to beat the guns when they stopped in the hopes that one could make them fire again. Actually, when the guns were not in use we removed them as the aircraft flew rather better without them. Fighting a war at this time certainly never entered our heads. The ground organization and control of the fighters from the ground was practically non-existent. I am not sure what the procedure would have been; I should imagine that some form of standing patrols would have been the order of the day.

In 1937 (I am speaking entirely as a person who was serving as a comparatively junior officer in the R.A.F. and was not really aware of what the powers that be had in mind) I was acting as squadron commandor of a squadron on the south coast. I was suddenly informed that one of the flights in the squadron should in the future be called No. 73 Squadron. That made things rather confusing for us as the personnel and aircraft remained the same. This was done to all the other fighter squadrons. Then some politician got up in parliament and said, "I double the air force". This state of affairs, I am glad to say, didn't last very long. Through this year and the next, we made these squadrons up to strength in personnel and aircraft. New squadrons were also formed and a new defense scheme whereby the fighters were controlled from the ground was started. I shall describe this scheme presently. In 1938 when Chamberlin went to Munich, the poor fellow didn't have much to argue with and had to accept peace at any price. The country was in a very bad state with regard to all her armaments. There were tremendous shortages in A.A. guns and such like. I had actually heard tell at the time that our main aircraft factory at Bristol was protected by four obsolete A.A. guns which had no breeches. The situation was serious everywhere. Munich gave us a shock, and it started to dawn on us the possibility of war, so we decided that something very, very drastic had to be done at once to try to put this situation right. All our factories worked in double shifts and in a year a wonderful change came about. All the squadrons were re-equipped with Hurricanes and Spitfires and dozens of new squadrons had been formed.

You can imagine now that this huge defense material needed very careful organizing to insure its best effect. The fighters were now grouped around the entire British Isles in considerable force. This, of course, meant that the command of the fighters had become too large to be handled by one headquarters, so the British Isles were divided into fighter groups, each group commanded by an Air Vice Marshal. These groups were divided into sectors commanded by group captains and in the sectors were the fighter stations and squadrons situated. Now we know the exact position, the exact number, the exact height of every enemy aircraft over or near our coast.

This information is plotted by means of small discs on operations room maps of which the headquarters fighter command, the group headquarters, the sector, commanders and the station commanders all have. All these plots appear simulteneously on all the maps throughout the country so that everybody concerned with the control of the fighters knows the position of the enemy aircraft. As each enemy raid appears on these plotting tables the Commander-in-Chief of the fighters decides which group those raiders are going to enter. He then details that group to take care of that raid, giving the raid a serial number. The Air Vice Marshal then decides which sector in this group the raid is going to enter, and details that sector commander to take care of the raid. The sector commander then orders the squadrons into the air. These squadrons come under the sector commander's direct control and are in touch with him the whole time they are in the air by R/T*. You see that as we know the exact position of the enemy raid, all we have to do is to tell the fighters where to go. We could tell them to proceed to a certain locality at a certain height, but in certain weather conditions it would be impossible for the fighter squadron commander to know when he was over the locality ordered because the ground would possibly be obscured. So we have to have a system which will work whatever the weather conditions. We accomplish this by fitting in every fighter aircraft a little device called a pip-squeak set. This set sends out a signal automatically, and this signal is picked up by Direction Finding Stations who report the exact positions of the fighters. These positions are plotted on the operations room maps throughout the country in the same way as the enemy raider plots, so that the sector commanders know the exact position of both friendly fighters and enemy bombers All he has to do is to order the fighters to steer certain courses which will bring them into contact with the enemy. The whole system is childishly simple, and is 100 percent effective, because there is nothing that can go wrong. One can see the importance we place on efficient R/T communication and I can tell you that we have developed a radio set which takes care of this important point. Of course, when the enemy is sighted by the fighters, it is up to the squadron commander to deal with them in the way he thinks fit. He takes over the control

*R/T   Radio Telegraph

and orders what attack he thinks best to suit the circumstances existing.

I should now like to just mention what sort of aircraft we are employing. It is impossible for me to go into any detail as details are secret. Suffice to say that anything that will not do over 400 m.p.h. and be able to climb to 40,000 feet is no good. I am glad to say that we have very large numbers of such aircraft. Our latest new fighter, that is not counting the latest marks of Spitfires and Hurricanes, is the Tornado and this really is a tremendous airplane. It is very heavily armed and I can tell you altogether, it is a very lethal weapon. The armament of these fighters are cannons and machine guns. Last year, of course, we only had eight Browning machine guns in each airplane. This is an interesting point to Americans because the Browning gun is an American gun; I am sure you will be proud of the fact that in my squadron alone during about five months of active warfare, we fired some 3,000,000 rounds of ammunition and you could count the number of stoppages these guns had during this time on the fingers of one hand. It really is a remarkably reliable gun. Some of you might question the effectiveness of machine gun fire against heavily armored enemy aircraft. If you do question this, I should like to tell you an incident which convinced me how effective this concentration of machine gun fire is. You must remember each gun fires 1,200 bullets a minute which makes a total of 9,600 bullets a minute coming from one airplane. This particular incident took place in France last year when we were endeavoring to back up our army which was fighting over there. I came across one German soldier and took a careful aim and pressed the trigger--I was amazed to see the man disintegrate. There is no question that the bullets just drilled him; they literally blew him apart. And so when firing against aircraft, however heavily armored, this concentration is sufficient to blow off some quite important parts to the embarrassment of the German pilots concerned. It is quite obvious that if one were to blow the tail unit off an airplane, it doesn't really matter how heavily armored he is. The cannon has tremendous power and there is no doubt as to its value in air fighting. A cannon shell can penetrate practically any thickness of armor, but of course has a slow rate of fire, and one has to be more careful in one's aim.

We picked up a German M.E. 109 fighter which had been shot by a cannon shell. This shell had penetrated through the rudder, stern post, through various members of the fuselage, the wireless set, two thicknesses of armor plate, both sides of the gas tank, the back of the pilot's seat, through the pilot's chest removing various ribs and passed out through the dashboard and out the front of the airplane. This was a most effective demonstration of the power of penetration of the cannon shell.

The Americans, I think, are of the opinion that the English are rather slow, but I should like to say that in most of the important points, we have led the Germans. For instance, all British aircraft were heavily armored before the outbreak of war. The value of this has been demonstrated to us a thousand times in the saving of pilot's lives. No German aircraft at the outbreak of war were armored, and it was an easy thing to destroy them with a very small burst of fire. After the fall of France the Germans decided that they would have to armor heavily their aircraft for that reason. All our fighters were so armored fore and aft including the fitting of bullet proof windshields. The German fighters were not so armored until a year later. The German bomber had no protective armament except one machine gun which we ignored as the rear gunner stood in the slipstream of the propellers and couldn't really aim carefully. Compare this with our heavily armored bombers with carefully protected power operated turrets.

I should like to discuss next in very simple language some of the difficulties a fighter pilot has in air firing. I should like to do this because most of you think that all one has to do is to point at the German and press the trigger and down goes the German, but it is not like this. In order to hit a German aircraft traveling at 240 m.p.h. at a range of 400 yards, one has to aim 180 feet ahead of that aircraft in order to hit it. Mind you, 240 m.p.h. is a very slow speed for modern fighting as I have said before. Modern fighters now go at more than 400 m.p.h. so these distances are considerably increased. In other words, one has to anticipate the position your target will be in a fraction of a second later. This is the point you must aim at because the bullets take a certain length of time to travel 400 yards. Unfortunately, it is not even as easy as this because by application of rudder and holding off bank, one can make an airplane go along like a crab--that is, it doesn't travel in the direction that it is pointing. The difficulty is, of course, to tell what direction it is actually traveling in order to be able to aim the required amount ahead. Another difficult problem is that the fighter pilot is inclined to to bring his sights to bear by pulling the nose of his aircraft around by use of the rudder only; this, although actually bringing his sights to bear, causes the fighter to skid sideways thereby imparting a sideways velocity to the bullets which is enough to take them quite clear of what he is aiming at.

Now the next important thing in air fighting is the identification of the enemy aircraft. It is obviously no good if you are going up to fight the enemy if you cannot at once recognize an aircraft to be friend or foe. I should like to tell you two incidences in which this mistaken identity proved an important point. The first concerns a sergeant pilot in my squadron who one day became detached during an offensive patrol over enemy territory. These offense patrols last year were very hazardous, indeed, and unless a squadron stuck rigidly together it was liable to get into very serious trouble from attack by overwhelming numbers of enemy fighters. So to become detached was an unforgivable sin. This pilot became detached during a maneuver we were carrying out after some member of the squadron had shouted the alarm on the radio. After this maneuver we straightered up and continued our patrol and it was then that I noticed that I only had eleven airplanes instead of twelve. I thought the poor chap had been picked off during this maneuver. We returned to England and were refueling when this sergeant pilot arrived back. Of course, I was livid with him for breaking formation and demanded an explanation, informing him that if it were not a good explanation, I should have him courts martialed. His explanation was that after straightening up from the maneuver in question, he had continued on at the back end of the squadron until he became seriously worried regarding the amount of gas he had left. He then looked ahead at the aircraft that he had been following some twenty yards astern of and noticed that it had bracing struts from the tailplane to the fuselage. He said he then opened his cockpit hood and looked behind at his own tail unit; to his horror he saw that he had no struts. He then moved out slightly to one side and saw black crosses painted all over this airplane he had been following. He said he he thought the German squadron commander would be just I was patrolling the beaches and had notification that didn't know what to do as he was following a squadron of twelve M.E. 109's. He eventually got fed up with following and took a careful aim at the last M.E. 109 and pressed the trigger. This M.E. blew up so he rolled on to his back and dived to ground level. As he was beating this hasty retreat, he looked back and saw that the enemy squadron were continuing their patrol. The other incident occurred when we were defending Dunkirk. I was patrolling the beaches and had notification that some British bombers would be returning through my area and would I keep a friendly eye on them. After a while seven Bristol Blenhiems appeared out of the smoke of Dunkirk. To my horror, I noticed they were closely followed by seven twin-engine German fighters, M.E. 110's. So I detailed seven of my fighters to accompany me and we went in behind the M.E.'s. I was about to open fire on the leading M.E. when the rear gunner started to wave at me. I immediately thought that the M.E.'s were in fact British Hampdens bombers which are quite similar in appearance having the double rudders which the M.E. has. I ordered my squadron to break away at once without firing and we were in the process of reforming when the M.E. decided that we were enemy. A terrific fight ensued in which we only were able to shoot down three of them--this was a disappointment to us as we should have got the lot. Now you see what had happened. The M.E.'s had obviously got orders to escort seven of their Junkers 88 which were to bomb the shipping off the coast and had by accident formed up on our Bristol Blenheims (which are not dissimilar in appearance) and were actually escorting their enemy. When we arrived they must have mistaken us for M.E. 109's which had probably been detailed to escort them. So there were the Blenheims being escorted by M.E.'s who were being escorted by Hurricanes, so you can see that these mistakes in identity do happen and are a very serious point.

I should like now to discuss the German and the British fighter pilots. If an English fighter pilot comes across half a dozen M.E. fighters and runs away, he is considered by Englishmen to, perhaps, have a cowardly streak in him. The German fighter that runs away from any English fighter is considered by the Germans to be a shrewd person, and not a coward in any sense of the word. One time I can remember having to escort thirty-three Blenheim bombers on a raid to France to try and disperse tank concentrations. Before we reached the coast, I noticed smoke pouring from one of his engines and I expected him to immediately turn for home. However, he appeared to ignore it and after a little while the engine stopped solid. Although he couldn't maintain height, he still continued on his course. It then became difficult for me owing to the fact that he was getting so far behind, to effectively look after both him and the other Blenheims. I decided that he was too good a man to lose and that I should look after him myself and told my No. 2 to carry on the close escort of the other thirty-two Blenheims. This man was unable to maintain altitude and passed over the gun positions on the enemy coast at a very dangerous altitude and at times was almost invisible from the bursts of the A.A. shells; but still he continued. He reached the first concentration of tanks, shut off his good engine, dived down and dropped two perfect bombs which blew a tank well into the air. He then went to the next target and did the same thing again. I knew that he only carried four such bombs and expected him to make for home now. But he didn't. He went down to ground level flying like a huge crab on one engine whilst his rear gunner machine gunned German infantry which were moving up in support of their tanks. He appeared in no hurry to start for home and it was not until he had completely finished all his ammunition that he eventually started across the seventy miles of water back to England. Now the important part of this story lies here. On arriving home I got in contact with this pilot's squadron commander intending to have him commended on his very brave action. I was almost disappointed when talking to the C.O. to find that he thought nothing of the incident at all; he thought the pilot had done his job and that was merely what was expected of him. I found that act a tremendous inspiration and I certainly never have seen a German pilot do anything but make for home on the very slightest pretext of engine failure. Another incident occurred when my squadron was ordered up to dispose of some 250 enemy fighters over a south coast port. We had been in a lot of action around about that time and were reduced to eight airplanes. We had a ninth, but unfortunately because of damage by enemy bullets, I didn't consider it safe to fly. So I proceeded to this port with the eight serviceable airplanes. We arrived at the port at about eight thousand feet and we could see the Germans, masses of them, from about thirteen thousand feet right out of sight. We started to climb to engage them which appeared to me to be almost a forlorn task. However, after climbing for a while, I saw that we were not gaining on the Germans--they were climbing too. I cannot understand why they did this. At this moment, two M.E. 109's with yellow noses broke formation and started to come down. I thought that this was the beginning of the lot, but I was glad to see that only two came. I then noticed that those two M.E. 109's were not coming down on me at all but to a point about three miles astern of us. Looking carefully, I saw that they were diving on the ninth Hurricane that I had forbidden to come. I shouted a warning over the radio which he purposely ignored. The leading M.E. went in behind him and opened fire. This he appeared to ignore, merely dodging very slightly from one side to the other. He kept the M.E. this way engrossed and I was able to settle in behind the M.E. and shoot it down. My No. 2 got the other M.E. which was a beautiful flamer and exploded after burning for a short while. I thought that would start the fight as I anticipated the Germans would be very cross to see two of their number dealt with in this fashion, but on looking back I saw that they were all returning home. They had obviously been recalled by their home base, but I cannot imagine any English squadron allowing eight enemy aircraft to get away with such cold-blooded murder. The other point in that story is the typical spirit which prompted this English pilot to take a bullet-riddled airplane into combat knowing that he was to fight 250 of the enemy when he had a perfectly good excuse to stay on the ground. I am sure you will admit that this spirit is unbeatable--especially as these incidences I have related are every day occurrences. Compare this to the way I saw some German fighters, flying M.E. 109's, amusing themselves. These pilots were diving on milk cows and firing at them with their cannon. One cow I saw had a hind hoof blown off and was rushing around making the most awful noises in agony. The German pilots didn't fire any more, but merely dived on the cow to make it run on its three legs. I must say I cannot see any point in this brutality at all. Another incident I had the misfortune of witnessing occured in France when a number of women and children were walking along the roads from a town with all their belongings on some old carts, etc. A German pilot in a Henchle 126 (a slow airplane used for army cooperation purposes) descended to within about twenty feet of them and opened fire on them with his rear gun. He went up and down the road a number of times until not a living thing appeared to remain. I saw a little child sitting on a woman's chest trying to bring the woman back to life. After awhile this little child discovered the bullet holes which had completely pierced the woman's bosom, and he was sitting there sticking its little fingers into the bullet holes. I am sure that these things should not be.

Now everybody the world over knows that the Germans are the most wonderful organizers. They work out the most complicated schemes to the minutest details, yet often one small, but very important, detail is overlooked, consequently spoiling all their carefully laid scheme. There are many instances of this, but two come to my memory now. The first one concerns the placing of hospital buoys which are moored some ten miles off their coast. These buoys were placed in these positions all around the coast with the object that aircraft which was severely damaged and would obviously not be able to reach the shore would be able to land in the water beside one of these buoys and the crew could swim to the buoy where they would find everything with which to make themselves comfortable. The buoys were visited by a patrol boat sometime during the night to pick off any visitors. They have the most luxurious equipment, four comfortable beds, a special heater for drying clothes, another for heating water, first-aid outfits, brandy, whiskey, beer, and some choice wines, cigars, cigarettes, pipe tobacco and pipes are all provided. Yet, perhaps the most important item, seeing that to get any heat from their heating aparatus or to light any of these cigars, cigarettes and pipe tobacco would be the provision of matches or some such thing with which to light them. The importance of matches is accentuated when one bears in mind that to reach the buoys from the aircraft one has to swim through some distance of sea water. The second instance is rather of a different nature, but I think serves to illustrate how this cleverness on the part of the

Germans is a fallacy. When Germany was building her immense aircraft manufacturing organization, their experts traveled around the country selecting suitable sites to build the factories. Camouflage was the order of the day. Sites in one instance were selected in fir tree forests, and special railways were constructed for transportation purposes and the factory buildings were built to a special design so that they exactly reached the top of the trees and were suitably screened and were literally invisible from the air. Should, however, enemy air forces manage to locate one of those factories, which would have been an almost impossible task, the buildings were so situated in the forest that one bomb could not possibly damage more than one building, the factory being divided into the smallest working parts. On the face of it, one would despair of attempting any successful air action against such a layout. Yet if one remembers last autumn when these fir trees oozed their most inflammable resin the Royal Air Forces flew over these forests, dropping tons and tons of incendiary material and getting the forests well and truly on fire. The factories were burned with the forest. If one considers it in this light one realizes that perhaps the worst place in the world to construct a factory would be in such a highly inflammable position. Everyone knows that the most complete destroyer of material of any description is fire.

Other instances of Germany's so called cleverness comes most apparent in their propaganda broadcasting service. I don't suppose the person who talks on the radio from Germany almost hourly is so well known to you Americans as he is to us in England. We call this person Lord Haw Haw. He takes his task incredibly seriously and pours out the news in the most serious tone. He is English and the subjects he talks about are very cleverly thought out. To the uninformed they would be liable to make a very grave impression, making this propaganda service a very serious potential weapon. So you would think that the Germans would take a certain amount of trouble, not necessarily to speak the truth, but to tell clever lies, ones that would not readily be found out. However, they have completely spoiled any value this service could have by failing in this very point. For instance, Lord Haw Haw one night regretted in a most regretful tone of voice that he had to announce that H. M. S. KESTREL had been sunk. He even went into a fairly lengthy description of the sinking, presumably to lend his information more weight. It was a pity that H. M. S. KESTREL is in fact the Royal Air Force post at Worthy Down near Winchester, more than a hundred miles from the nearest sea. So you might say that through these trifling, though important, mistakes Germany has nullified any military value their radio propaganda service might have had. Of course it was obvious that in the instance I have described, Lord Haw Haw had gleaned the information regarding H. M. S. KESTREL from the Admiralty list published before the war, the navy calling all their shore bases a ship.

One doesn't have to look very far to discover other blunders that the Germans have made. For the first nine months of war the average Englishman hardly knew there was a war on. I suppose an Englishman with his placid nature might be termed lazy, seeming just to do enough work to keep things going. Perhaps even, there were some signs of discontent, people were getting bored with their neighbors' company, there being little else to talk about except a war which wasn't even being fought. From the English point of view something very drastic was required to be done to bind these neighbors together and to bring home to the English the seriousness of the war. The Germans have done both these most successfully for us. They have bound the nation together by their ruthless bombings of our oldest towns as it has never been bound together before. Everyone is now working their hardest with only one object in view and that is revenge. The Germans don't seem to understand that when one has a dear relative killed or maimed for life, one doesn't throw in the sponge and give in, but does everything in his power to get even. This would be obvious psychology to anyone except the Germans. Another blunder in my opinion and I think a serious blunder, was the attempted bombing of Buckingham palace, the home of our King in London, by a Nazi airplane in broad daylight. This attempted bombing did not make the nation cringe and cower as it was supposed to have done, but had the exactly opposite effect. It brought home to us English all the love and affection that an Englishman has for his King and Queen, in that here was a man whom all were extremely fond of, who is an idol to us all, in serious danger sharing with us all the perils of the war. It showed at once that our King had no more special protection or was any more exempt from the perils of war than the ordinary man on the street. This little incident did our country a world of good.

1943
Bag the Hun!
(estimation of range & angle off)

CHAPTER I
ESTIMATION OF RANGE

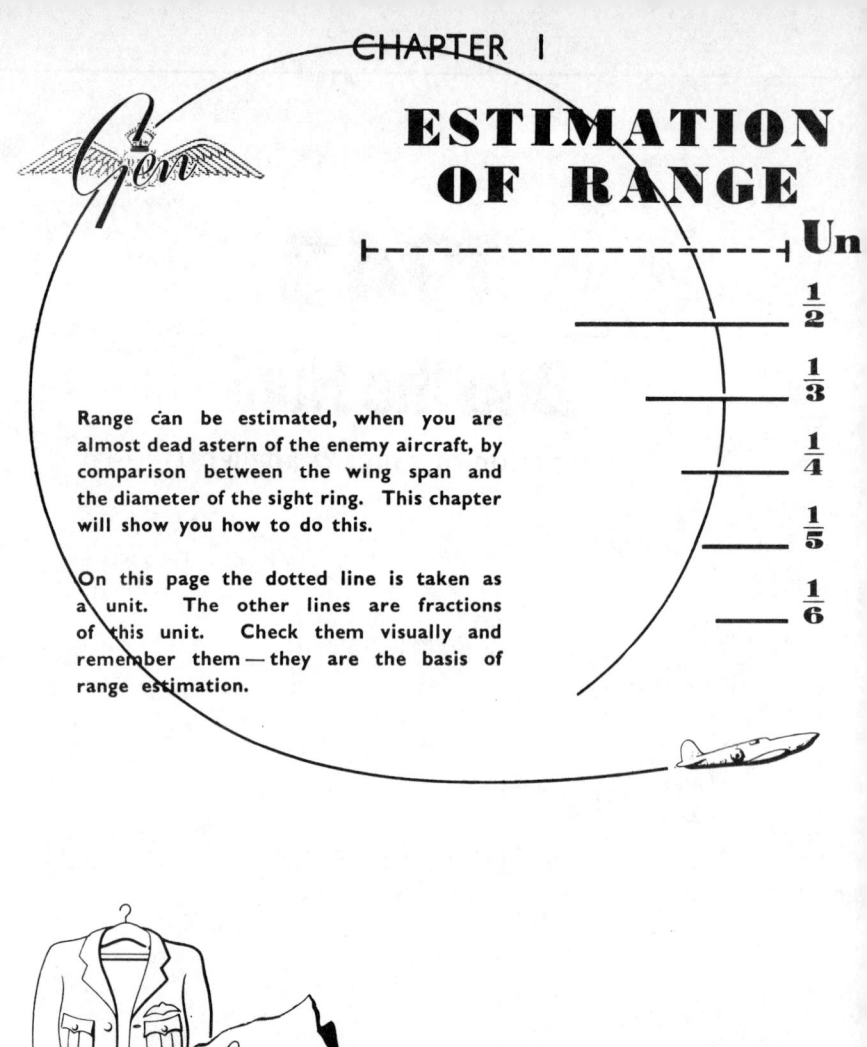

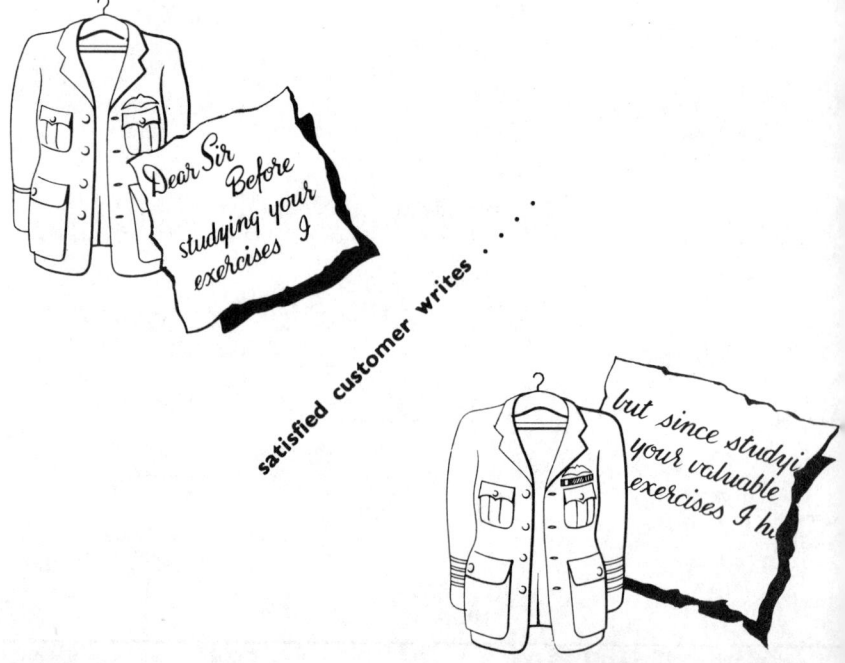

Un
$\frac{1}{2}$
$\frac{1}{3}$
$\frac{1}{4}$
$\frac{1}{5}$
$\frac{1}{6}$

Range can be estimated, when you are almost dead astern of the enemy aircraft, by comparison between the wing span and the diameter of the sight ring. This chapter will show you how to do this.

On this page the dotted line is taken as a unit. The other lines are fractions of this unit. Check them visually and remember them — they are the basis of range estimation.

Dear Sir, Before studying your exercises I

satisfied customer writes ....

but since studying your valuable exercises I h...

The dotted line is the unit. What fraction of this unit are the lines marked A, B, C, D, and E?

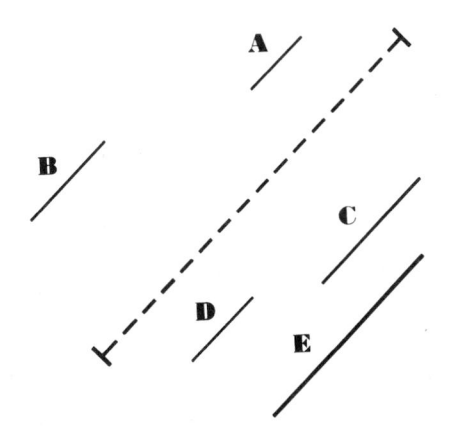

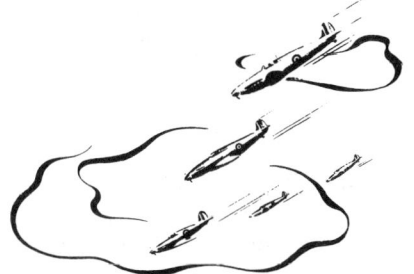

Solution

$$A = \tfrac{1}{6} \qquad B = \tfrac{1}{4}$$
$$C = \tfrac{1}{3} \qquad D = \tfrac{1}{5}$$
$$E = \tfrac{1}{2}$$

Tally-Ho——

The dotted line has now become the diameter of the red circle. What fractions of the diameter of the circle are the lines A, B, C, D, E, and F?

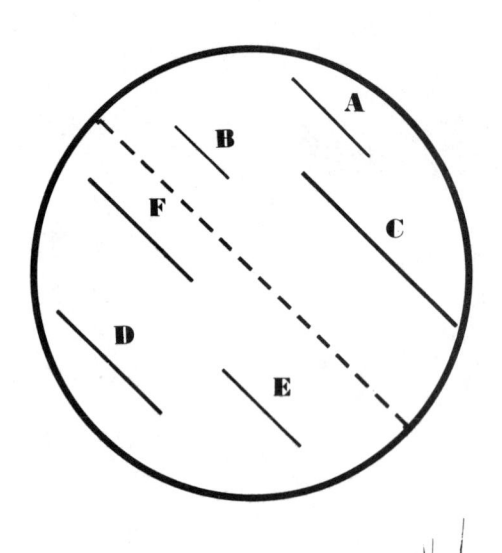

Solution

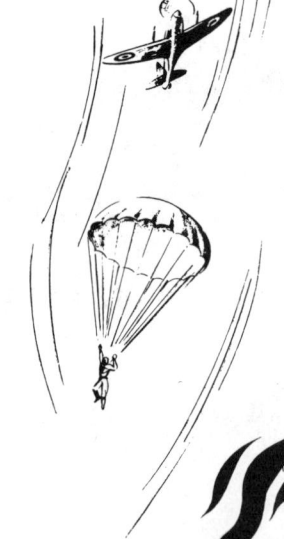

$$A = \tfrac{1}{4} \qquad B = \tfrac{1}{6}$$
$$C = \tfrac{1}{2} \qquad D = \tfrac{1}{3}$$
$$E = \tfrac{1}{4} \qquad F = \tfrac{1}{3}$$

—and funnily enough, it worked . . . .

From this point onwards the dotted line, which was drawn in as the diameter of the ring, is omitted and can appear only in your imagination.

Now state what fractions of this diameter are represented by the lines A, B, C, D, and E.

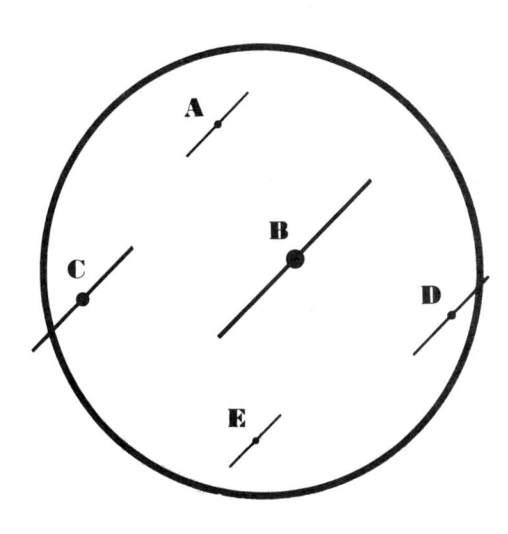

Solution

$A = \frac{1}{5}$ $B = \frac{1}{2}$

$C = \frac{1}{3}$ $D = \frac{1}{4}$

$E = \frac{1}{6}$

that's when I let him have it . . . .

The ring has now become the sight ring. The lines will shortly appear as Fw 190's. The span of a Fw 190 (and Me 109, too) is such that it appears equal to a diameter of a ring when it is 100 yds. away, half a diameter when it is 200 yds. away, and so on.

In future, then, instead of 1/2 state 200 yds.
                                1/3   300 yds.
                                1/4   400 yds.
                                1/5   500 yds.
                                1/6   600 yds.

You will then be giving the range of the Fw 190.

This method is definitely dated . . . .

Now the Hun has appeared. You ought to know what to do to estimate his range. Jot down your answers.

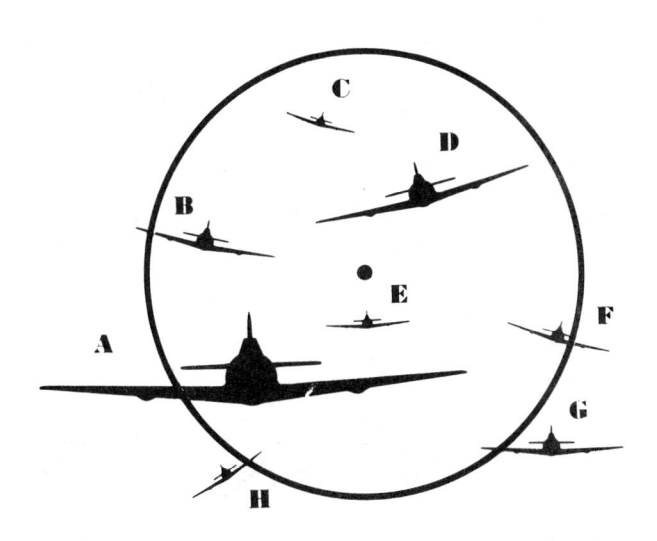

Solution

A = 100 yds.   B = 300 yds.   C = 600 yds.

D = 200 yds.   E = 500 yds.   F = 400 yds.

G = 300 yds.   H = 500 yds.

The Hun knew <u>his</u> range

Try these too

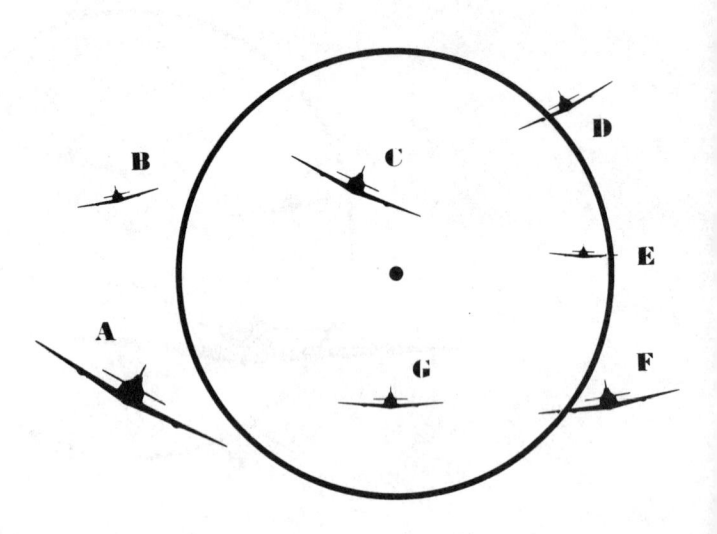

Solution

A=200 yds.   B=500 yds.
C=300 yds.   D=400 yds.
E=600 yds.   F=300 yds.
G=400 yds.

The chapter ends

CHAPTER 2
ESTIMATION of DEFLECTION

Deflection depends chiefly on the angle off and on the speed of the Hun.

The angle off is the angle between your sighting line and the Hun's line of flight. This diagram will make it clearer.

The picture of the Hun presented to the eye can differ even when the angle off remains the same.

For example, whether you are at A, B, C, or D, the angle off is the same. The pictures of the Hun, however, are different, as shown in the diagrams corresponding to A, B, C, and D.

This makes it difficult to estimate angle off without a great deal of practice.

Stern — View

ANGLE OFF

5°

10°

20°

30°

Make yourself familiar with these pictures

A

B

K

J

I

L

Jot down what you think are

C   D

E

G   F

H

the angles off for these planes

Solution

A _____ 20°
B _____ 5°
C _____ 5°
D _____ 5°
E _____ 20°
F _____ 20°
G _____ 30°
H _____ 5°
I _____ 30°
J _____ 10°
K _____ 10°
L _____ 30°

R.I.P.
VON MUCK

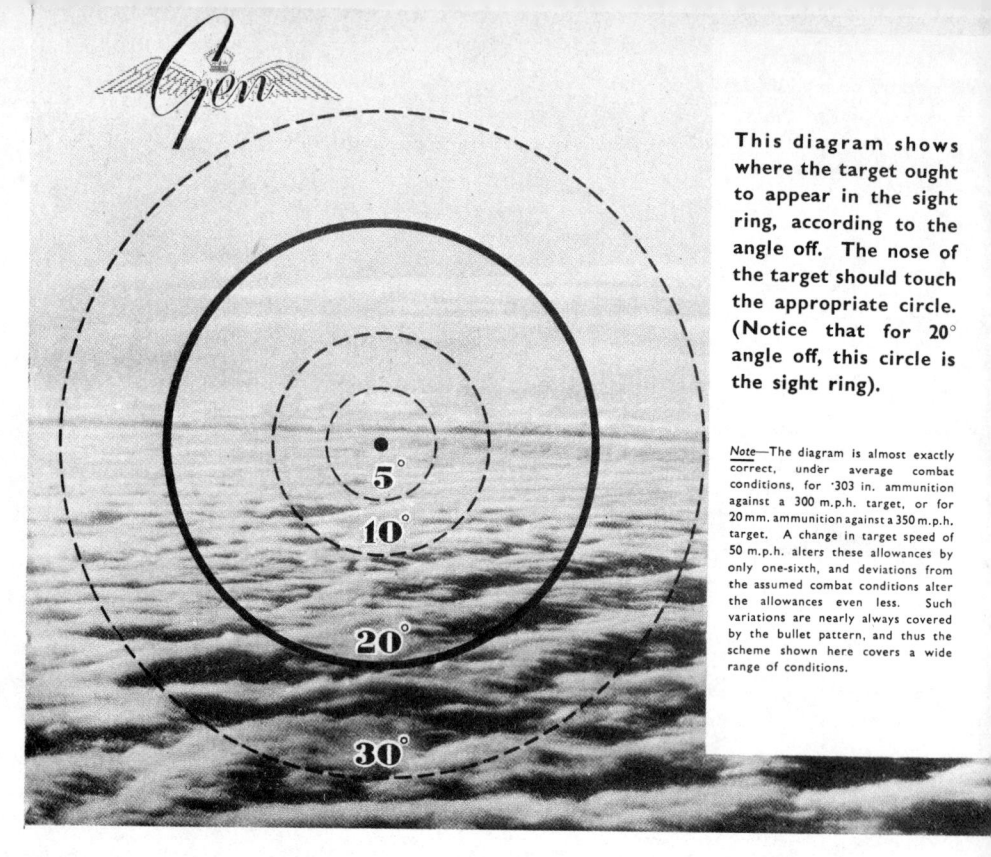

This diagram shows where the target ought to appear in the sight ring, according to the angle off. The nose of the target should touch the appropriate circle. (Notice that for 20° angle off, this circle is the sight ring).

Note—The diagram is almost exactly correct, under average combat conditions, for ·303 in. ammunition against a 300 m.p.h. target, or for 20 mm. ammunition against a 350 m.p.h. target. A change in target speed of 50 m.p.h. alters these allowances by only one-sixth, and deviations from the assumed combat conditions alter the allowances even less. Such variations are nearly always covered by the bullet pattern, and thus the scheme shown here covers a wide range of conditions.

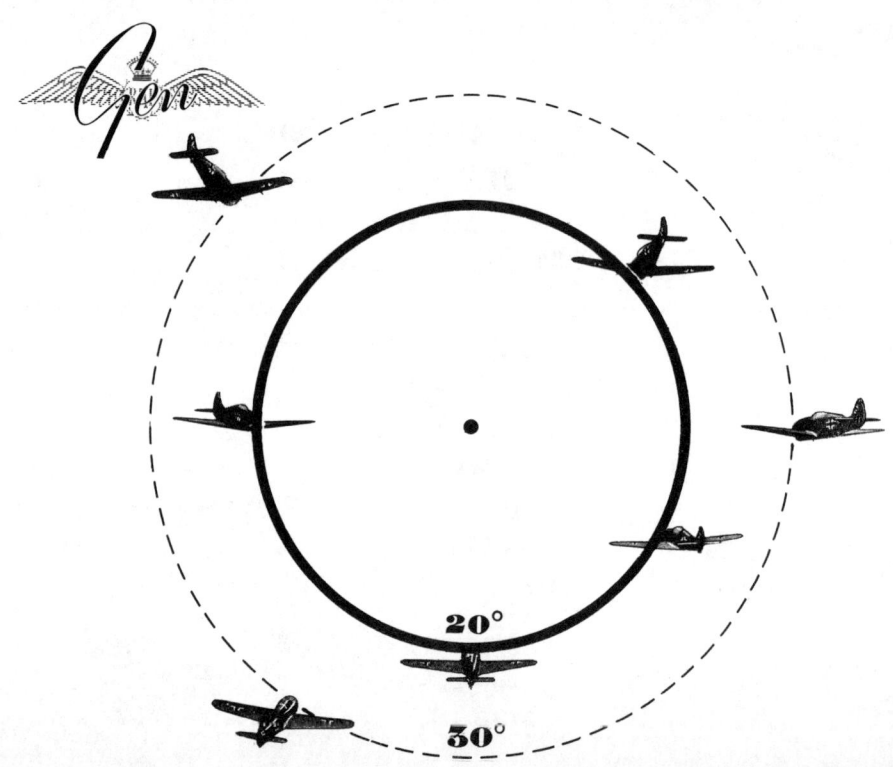

Diagrams on pp. 28, 29 and 30 show the Hun at various angles off, and with various appearances for the same angle off, positioned correctly. Study these carefully.

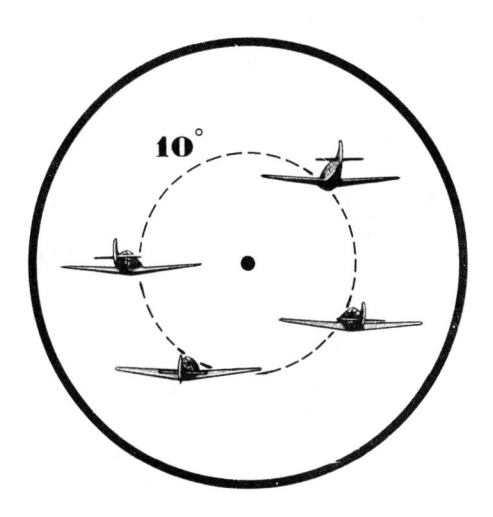

Combat films show that very often only half the correct allowance is made !

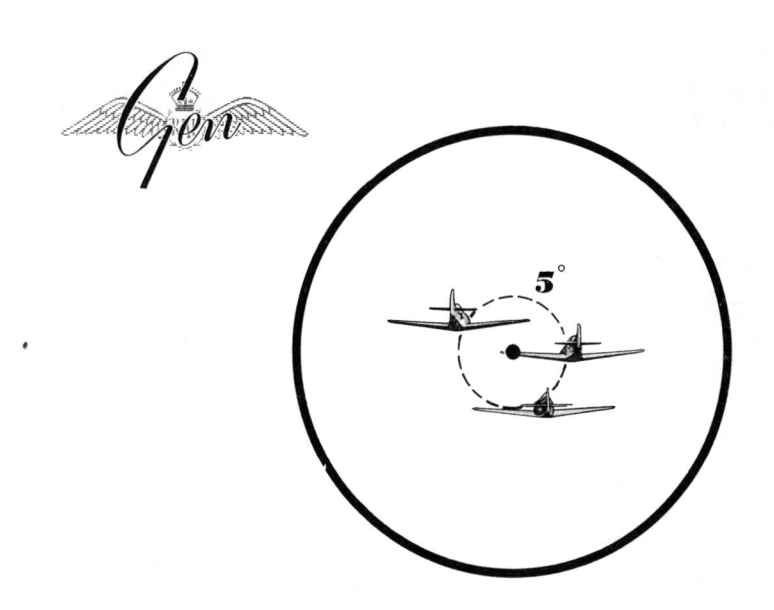

Study and remember

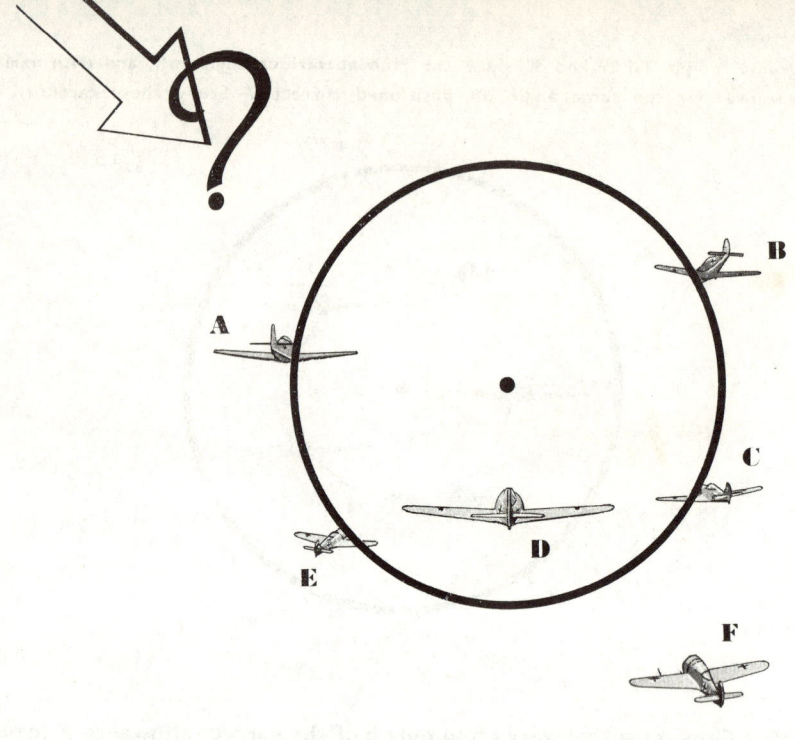

Some of these aircraft are positioned correctly: some are not. For each aircraft, estimate the angle off. Is correct deflection being made? If not, is it too great or too small?

Solution

	ANGLE OFF	DEFLECTION
A	10°	TOO GREAT
B	20°	O.K.
C	20°	O.K.
D	10°	O.K.
E	30°	TOO SMALL
F	30°	O.K.

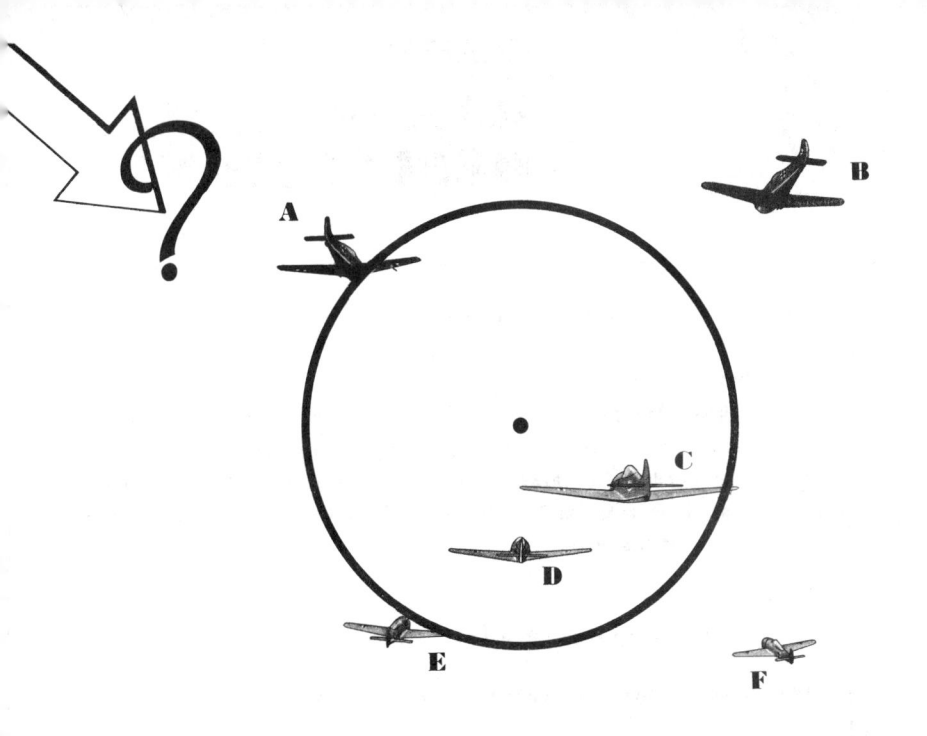

Try these exercises as well—you can't have too much practice!

	ANGLE OFF	DEFLECTION
A	20°	O.K.
B	30°	O.K.
C	10°	O.K.
D	10°	O.K.
E	20°	O.K.
F	30°	O.K.

CHAPTER 3
RANGE AND DEFLECTION

We now combine the work of the first two chapters.

1. Range

   Estimate the number of times the span of the Fw 190 goes into the diameter of the sight ring. The range is that number of hundreds of yards. This method holds even when the angle off is as large as 30°. Remember always to concentrate on the span of the aircraft.

2. Deflection.

   Estimate the angle off and position the enemy aircraft accordingly.

With practice these two operations should become one.

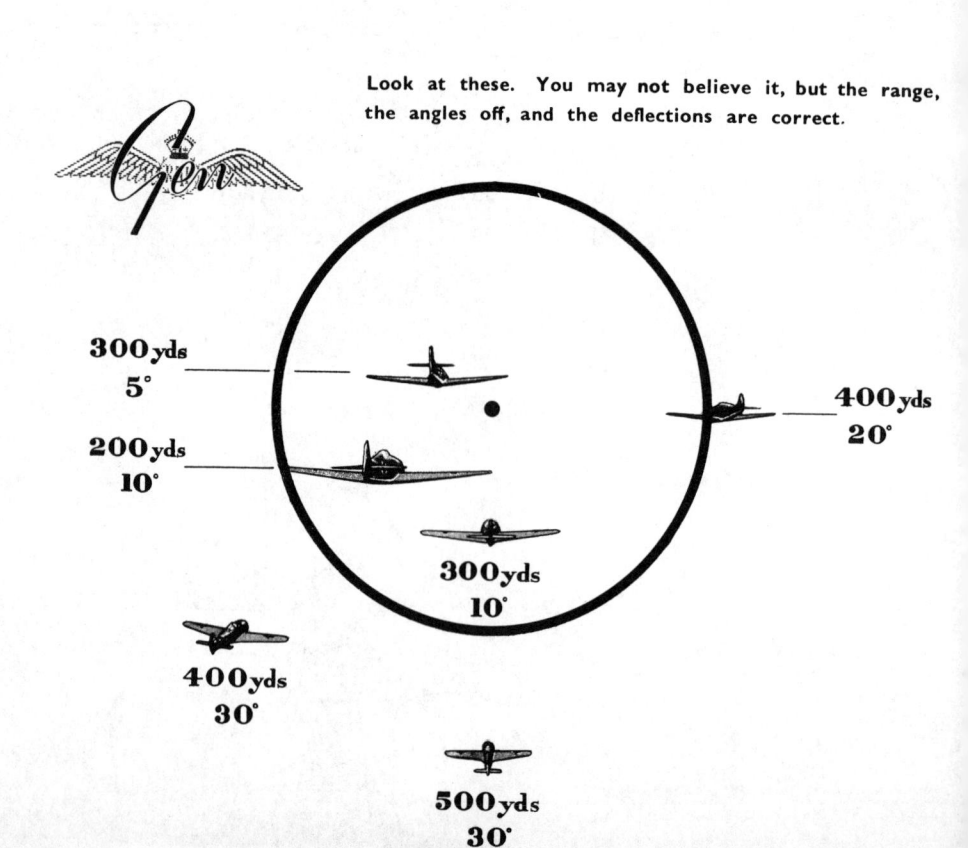

Look at these. You may not believe it, but the range, the angles off, and the deflections are correct.

300 yds
5°

200 yds
10°

400 yds
20°

300 yds
10°

400 yds
30°

500 yds
30°

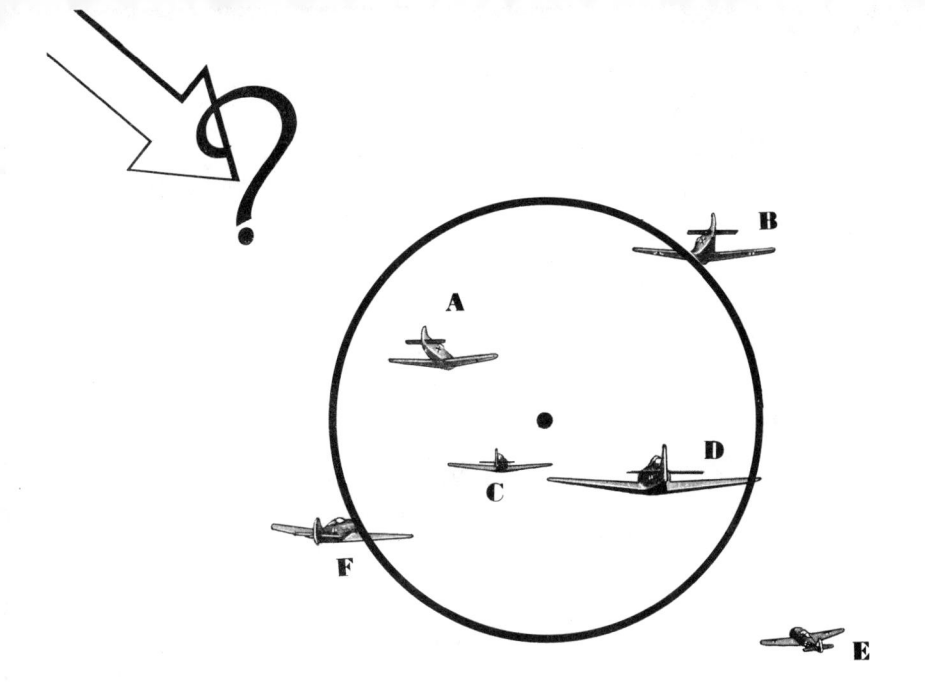

1. Estimate the ranges of the aircraft shown on pp. 31 and 33.
2. Try your hand now at estimating the ranges and the angles off in this diagram. Is the deflection correct, too great, or too small?

Solution

	RANGE	ANGLE OFF	DEFLECTION
A	400 yds.	20°	TOO SMALL
B	300 yds.	10°	TOO GREAT
C	400 yds.	5°	O.K.
D	200 yds.	5°	TOO GREAT
E	500 yds.	30°	O.K.
F	300 yds.	20°	O.K.

PAGE 31

A	300 yds.
B	400 yds.
C	400 yds.
D	200 yds.
E	500 yds.
F	300 yds.

PAGE 33

A	300 yds.
B	300 yds.
C	200 yds.
D	300 yds.
E	400 yds.
F	500 yds.

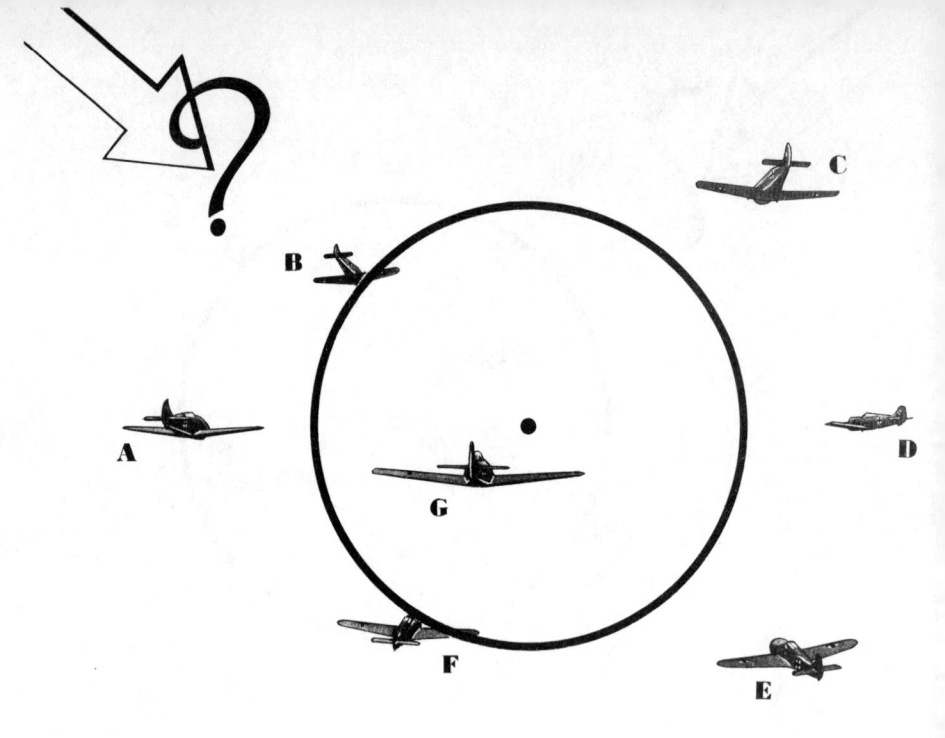

Now try these

Solution

	RANGE	ANGLE OFF	DEFLECTION
A	300 yds.	20°	TOO GREAT
B	500 yds.	30°	TOO SMALL
C	300 yds.	20°	TOO GREAT
D	500 yds.	45°	TOO SMALL
E	300 yds.	30°	O.K.
F	300 yds.	20°	O.K.
G	200 yds.	5°	O.K.

CHAPTER 4
SPEED TESTS

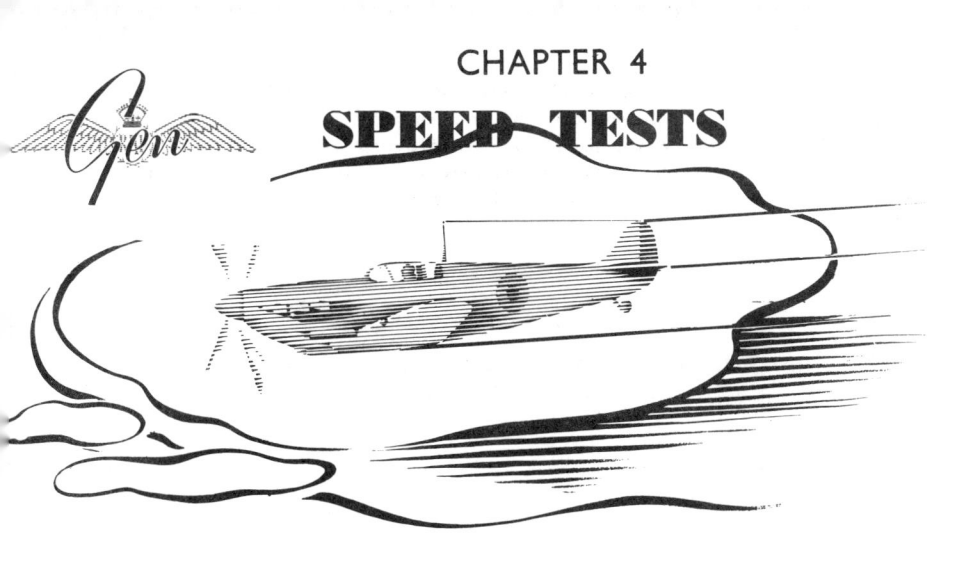

To do these exercises correctly is not enough; they must be done speedily.

Make up your mind to answer the following tests as quickly as possible. Get someone to time you—you can have your own back by timing him! Each test after the first has a time estimate given. See if you can beat it.

From now on use the celluloid ring which you will find in the pocket at the end of the book. Estimate the range of the aircraft shown, and the correct point of aim.

In the table below, fill in the range, and the number corresponding to what you think is the correct point of aim for each of the aircraft on the page opposite. Although no time limit is set in this instance, bear in mind that, in the subsequent tests, you are fighting against time as well as the Hun.

Aircraft	A	B	C	D	E	F
Range						
Point of aim						

Solution

	RANGE	POINT OF AIM
A	200 yds.	5
B	300 yds.	7
C	300 yds.	8
D	100 yds.	12
E	200 yds.	3
F	400 yds.	2

First speed test. Complete the table as in previous exercise, but remember that you are being timed.

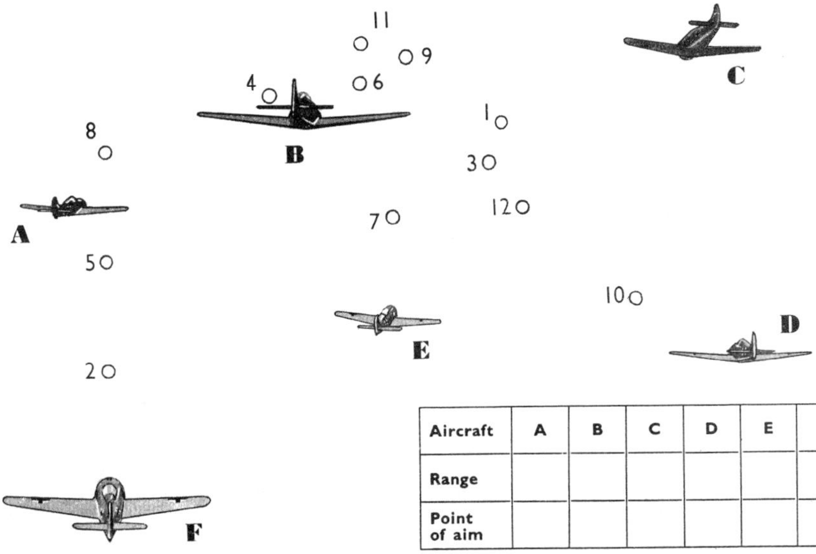

Aircraft	A	B	C	D	E	F
Range						
Point of aim						

Solution

	RANGE	POINT OF AIM
A	400 yds.	4
B	200 yds.	6
C	300 yds.	3
D	300 yds.	10
E	400 yds.	1
F	200 yds.	5

<u>IF</u> (a) you have less than 10 items correct, or
(b) you took more than 45 seconds, your performance is unsatisfactory.

<u>More practice is indicated.</u>

Beware the 'Waistammo' gremlins

303

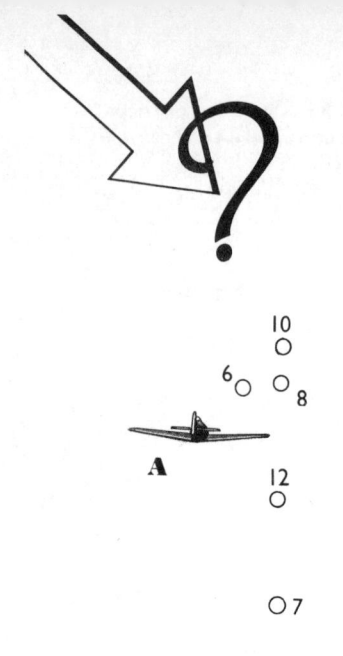

Second speed test

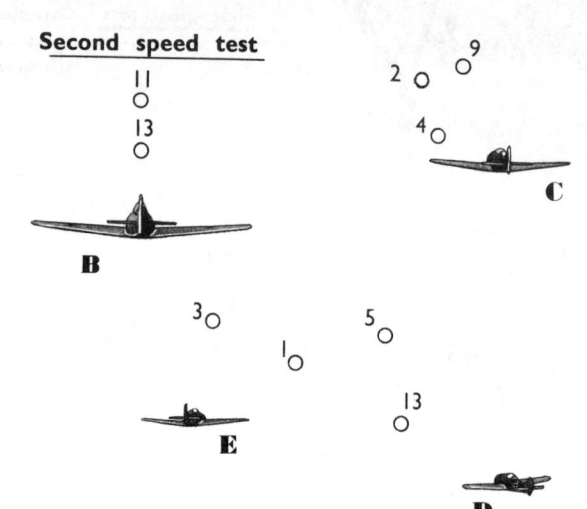

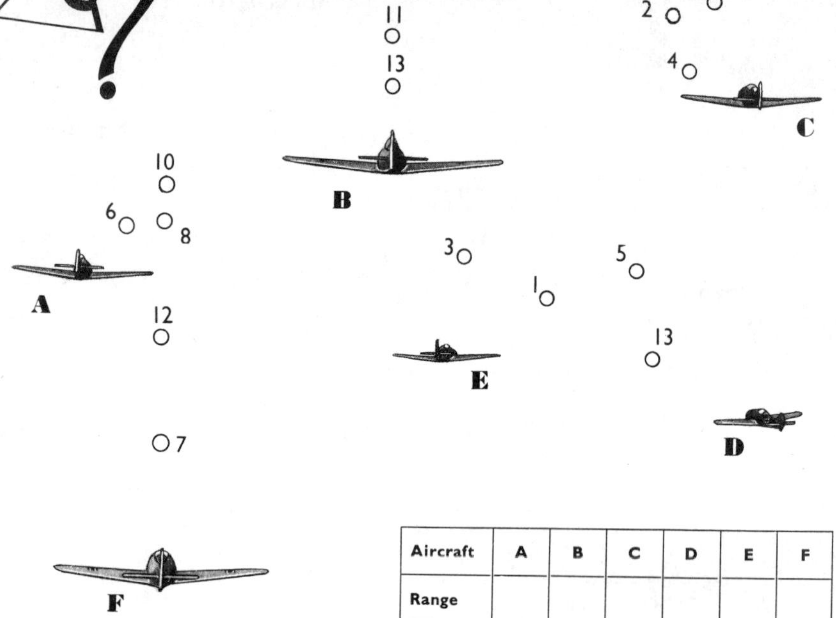

Aircraft	A	B	C	D	E	F
Range						
Point of aim						

Solution

	RANGE	POINT OF AIM
A	300 yds.	6
B	200 yds.	13
C	300 yds.	2
D	500 yds.	3
E	400 yds.	1
F	200 yds.	7

TIME 45 secs.

Fighter Pilots should—

BE MODEST   **BE TOUGH**   **FLY LIKE ANGELS**   **AND SHOOT LIKE W/Cdr. W. TELL**

1943

Central Gunnery School (diagram excerpted from *Pilot Gunnery Instructors Course*)

FRONT GUN QUARTER ATTACK
a) FIRE BETWEEN 60° AND 20° ANGLE OFF
b) RED FIRES ON RED PORT ATTACK, GREEN GREEN STARBOARD ATTACK.

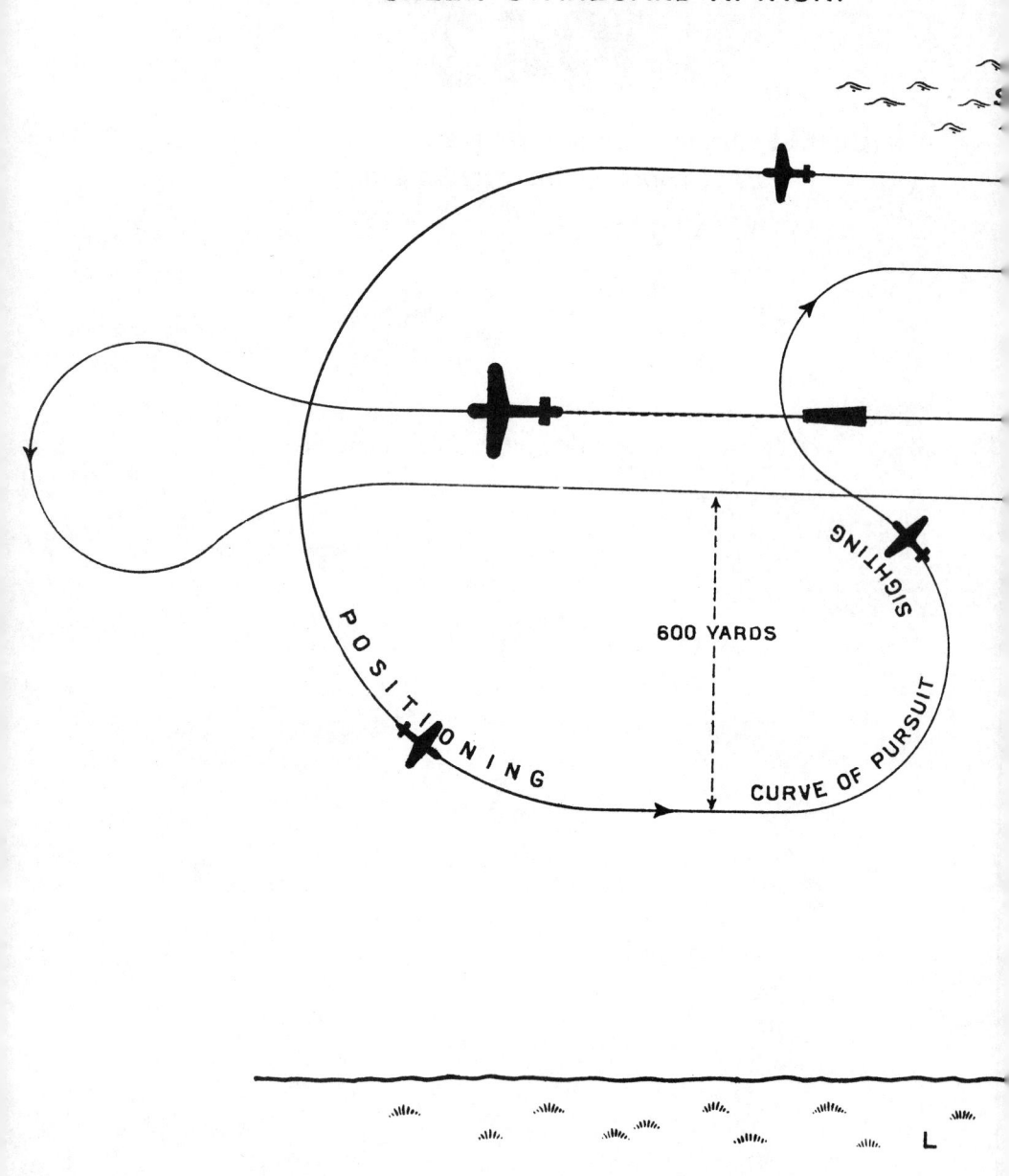

600 YARDS

POSITIONING

CURVE OF PURSUIT

SIGHTING

NOT TO SCALE

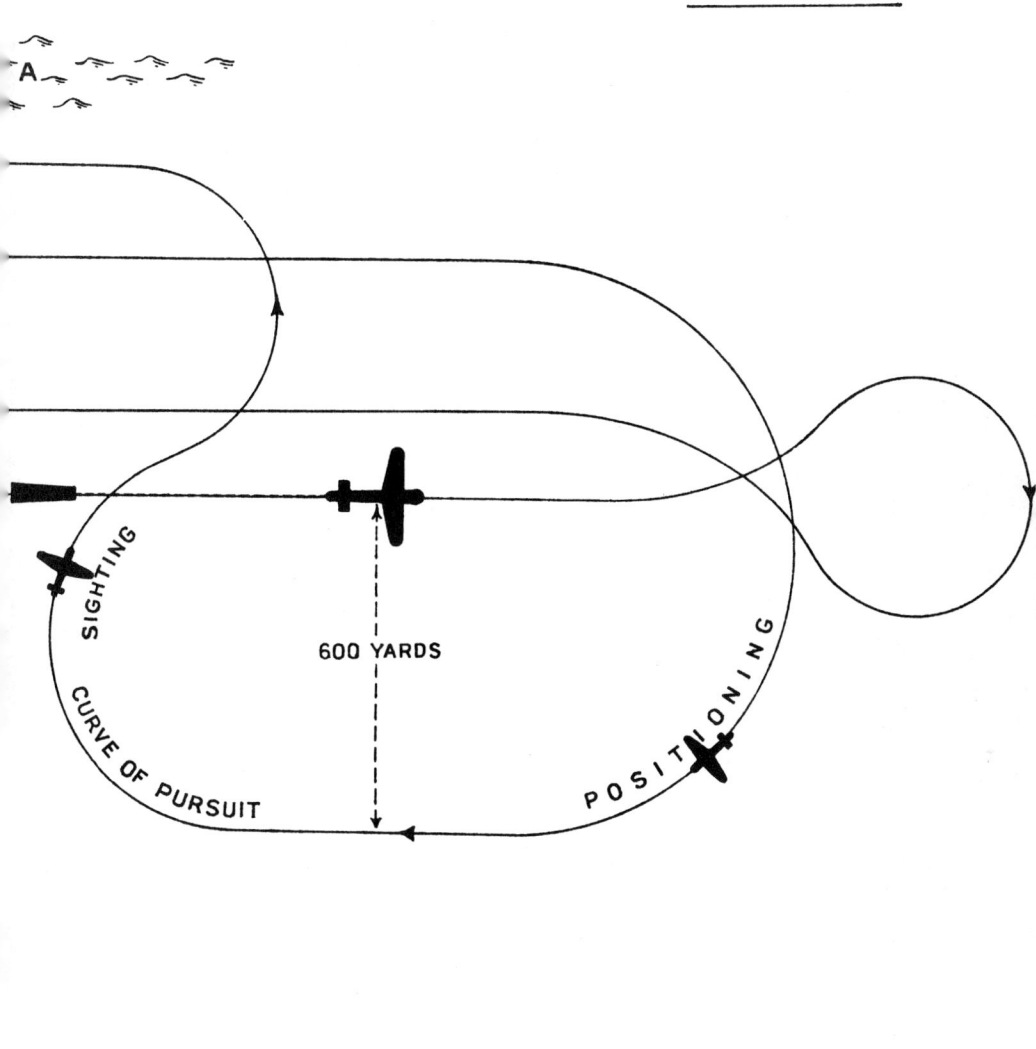

A

SIGHTING

CURVE OF PURSUIT

600 YARDS

POSITIONING

D